A MORAL THEORY OF POLITICAL RECONCILIATION

Following extended periods of conflict or repression, political reconciliation is indispensable to the establishment or restoration of democratic relationships and critical to the pursuit of peacemaking globally. In this important new book, Colleen Murphy offers an innovative analysis of the moral problems plaguing political relationships under the strain of civil conflict and repression. Focusing on the unique moral damage that attends the deterioration of political relationships, Murphy identifies the precise kinds of repair and transformation that processes of political reconciliation ought to promote. Building on this analysis, she proposes a normative model of political relationships. *A Moral Theory of Political Reconciliation* delivers an original account of the failure and restoration of political relationships, which will be of interest to philosophers, social scientists, legal scholars, policy analysts, and all those who are interested in transitional justice, global politics, and democracy.

COLLEEN MURPHY is an associate professor of philosophy at Texas A&M University. She has published widely on topics pertaining to political philosophy, philosophy of law, and risk analysis.

A MORAL THEORY OF POLITICAL RECONCILIATION

COLLEEN MURPHY

Texas A&M University

CAMBRIDGE
UNIVERSITY PRESS

CAMBRIDGE UNIVERSITY PRESS
Cambridge, New York, Melbourne, Madrid, Cape Town, Singapore,
São Paulo, Delhi, Dubai, Tokyo

Cambridge University Press
The Edinburgh Building, Cambridge CB2 8RU, UK

Published in the United States of America by Cambridge University Press, New York

www.cambridge.org
Information on this title: www.cambridge.org/9780521193924

First published 2010

Printed in the United Kingdom at the University Press, Cambridge

A catalog record for this publication is available from the British Library

Library of Congress Cataloging-in-Publication Data
Murphy, Colleen, 1974–
A moral theory of political reconciliation / Colleen Murphy.
p.   cm.
ISBN 978-0-521-19392-4 (hardback)
1. Reconciliation–Political aspects.   2. Reconciliation–Moral and ethical aspects.
3. Rule of law.   4. Truth commissions.   5. War crimes trials.   I. Title.
JC580.M87 2010
172–dc22

2010028678

ISBN 978-0-521-19392-4 Hardback

Contents

Acknowledgements   *page* vi

Introduction   I

PART I   CONCEPTUAL FRAMEWORKS   39

1   The rule of law   41

2   Political trust   71

3   Capabilities   94

PART II   PROMOTING POLITICAL RECONCILIATION   121

4   Evaluating processes of political reconciliation   123

5   Truth commissions   144

6   International criminal trials   167

Conclusion   187

Bibliography   200
Index   209

Acknowledgements

Fifteen years ago, while an undergraduate student at the University of Notre Dame, I spent a semester studying abroad in London and took a course on the conflict in Northern Ireland taught by Brendan O'Duffy. This course was of special interest given my Irish-American ethnic background and a childhood spent primarily among the large Irish-American community in Chicago. Going into this course I considered the solution to resolving the conflict in Northern Ireland in a just manner quite simple and straightforward: reunify Ireland. This course showed me how profoundly misguided I was to think that the resolution of the conflict was either simple or straightforward. Ongoing discussions with Alasdair MacIntyre over the years, beginning during my time at Notre Dame, have further deepened and enriched my grasp of different aspects of the situation in Northern Ireland. Because of that class, these discussions, and extensive examination of other conflicts around the world, I developed an enduring interest in understanding how it becomes possible for human beings, who live in the same society and who have suffered and inflicted suffering on one another in a systematic and widespread manner, to live peacefully and justly with each other again. This book represents my attempt to answer this question.

My efforts to develop a theory of political reconciliation began while a graduate student at the University of North Carolina – Chapel Hill. My dissertation, and subsequently this book, would not have been possible without the support of my advisor and mentor Gerald J. Postema. When I began my dissertation, political reconciliation was not a subject of philosophical reflection. Philosophers had begun to consider the moral justifiability of truth commissions, but were not concerned with the meaning of political reconciliation itself. I am deeply indebted to Jerry for his confidence in my ability to tackle new intellectual terrain, for maintaining that confidence as my dissertation progressed, and for continually pushing me to further refine and better articulate my ideas.

Although this book bears little resemblance in content to my dissertation, it bears the mark of the intellectual guidance that Jerry provided.

During my graduate study at the University of North Carolina – Chapel Hill, I developed a wonderful cohort of dear friends that I would like to thank for their intellectual engagement with and moral support of my project. Yaacov Ben-Shemesh, Katya Hosking, and Susanne Sreedhar spent countless hours discussing my project with me and reading drafts of my dissertation. Susanne deserves special recognition in this regard. Not only did she engage with my project during graduate school, she has remained intimately involved with the progression of my work on this book during my time at Texas A&M University. Susanne has read and extensively commented on almost every chapter that follows; my book is significantly improved because of her feedback.

The Department of Philosophy at Texas A&M University provided the ideal environment for transforming the ideas that I explored in my dissertation into a book. I thank all of my colleagues for their ongoing support for and interest in my project. Within the department I want to recognize in particular Theodore George, Ben McMyler, and Linda Radzik. Conversations with Ted forced me to rethink my analysis of the impact of truth commissions, and those with Ben have been particularly valuable in writing the introductory chapter. Linda has read every page of this manuscript, often multiple times. She has been the ideal interlocutor and sounding board. The mark of her invaluable feedback and constructive criticism permeates the final manuscript.

There is a long list of individuals who have influenced particular arguments I advance and a number of venues where I presented different chapters of my book and received valuable feedback. Each chapter begins by acknowledging the specific places where I presented the ideas from the chapter as well as the particular individuals whose criticisms and suggestions informed the argument I make and to whom I remain grateful. A much earlier version of Chapter 1 first appeared in "Lon Fuller and the Moral Value of the Rule of Law," *Law and Philosophy*, 24(3) (2005), 239–262. Chapter 6 is a revised version of "Political Reconciliation and International Criminal Trials," which appeared in Larry May and Zach Hoskins (eds.), *International Criminal Law and Philosophy* (Cambridge University Press, 2010), pp. 224–44.

I would like to thank the National Endowment for the Humanities, as well as the Office of the Vice-President for Research, the College of Liberal Arts, and the Melbern G. Glasscock Center for Humanities Research at Texas A&M University for funding this project. The Department of

Philosophy and the Melbern G. Glasscock Center for Humanities Research at Texas A&M University each supported a sabbatical period that allowed me to complete substantial portions of this book during the fall 2007 and spring 2008 semesters, respectively.

Hilary Gaskin at Cambridge University Press has been a superb editor. I would like to express my gratitude to her for guiding me throughout the publication process and ensuring that reviews from readers were completed in a very timely fashion. Two anonymous readers provided insightful, detailed, and constructive comments and criticism in their reports. I thank them for their thorough evaluation of my manuscript, which is substantially improved as a result of their comments. Finally, I thank Cyndy Brown for her editorial and indexing services.

I come from an extremely close family that is an enduring source of love and support. I want to recognize and thank my parents, Robert and Kathleen Murphy; my brothers and sister, Jack, Kevin, and Mary Beth Murphy; my sister-in-law, Amanda Murphy; and my grandmother, Marion Morris, for their ongoing enthusiasm for my project and willingness to engage in countless conversations about political reconciliation during family gatherings for many years. My parents deserve special recognition. My mother read and edited multiple versions of every page of this manuscript, while my father continuously reminded me (and others) of how proud he was that I was working on this project. I also thank the new family I gained during the course of writing this book. My father-in-law and mother-in-law, Giulio and Anna Gardoni, and brother-in-law and sister-in-law, Alberto Gardoni and Silvia Pasolini, warmly welcomed me into the family and became keen supporters of my project. My nieces and nephew, Abigail and Connor Murphy, and Giulia Gardoni, are too young to talk with me about political reconciliation, but they serve as continual reminders of the kind of bright future I hope all children might have and motivate me to continue to work to understand how such a future might become possible.

My greatest debt of gratitude is to my husband, Paolo Gardoni, to whom this book is dedicated. I could not imagine a more perfect partner to have in life. I thank Paolo for his unconditional love; for his deep and steadfast support, both intellectual and emotional, as I wrote this book; and for being a continual source of joy, laughter, and inspiration in my life.

Introduction

"I cry over what has happened, even though I cannot change anything. Then I look inside myself to understand how it is possible that no one knew, how it is possible that so few did something about it, how it is possible that often I also just looked on. Then I wonder how it is possible to live with this inner guilt and shame."[1]

"What kind of man . . . uses a method like this one with the wet bag to people . . . to other human beings . . . repeatedly . . . and listening to those moans and cries and groans . . . and taking each of those people very near to their deaths . . . what kind of man are you, what kind of man is that, that can do . . . what kind of human being can do that."[2]

This book focuses on political reconciliation, the process of rebuilding damaged political relationships. Political reconciliation is widely recognized to be one of the most important challenges for societies attempting to democratize following periods of repressive rule or civil conflict characterized by widespread and systematic human rights abuses. Indeed, the consensus among politicians, academics, and human rights activists is that political reconciliation is a condition for successful democratization and a critical component of peacemaking globally. The well-being of current and future generations in transitional societies is considered to be dependent on the success of efforts at political reconciliation.

Politicians, academics, and human rights activists have called for reconciliation in dozens of transitional societies including Iraq and

I am grateful to Daniel Conway, Paolo Gardoni, Theodore George, David Lefkowitz, Ben McMyler, Kathleen Murphy, Gerald J. Postema, Linda Radzik, and Susanne Sreedhar for their comments on earlier drafts of this chapter.

[1] From an anonymous letter written in Afrikaans to the South African Truth and Reconciliation Commission cited in Antjie Krog, *Country of My Skull: Guilt, Sorrow, and the Limits of Forgiveness in the New South Africa* (New York: Three Rivers Press, 1998), p. 62.

[2] Tony Yengeni questioning his former torturer Jeffrey Benzien during an amnesty hearing of the South African Truth and Reconciliation Commission in Cape Town. Cited in Krog, *Country of My Skull*, p. 93.

Afghanistan today, and South Africa, Northern Ireland, and Sierra Leone in the recent past. Appeals to political reconciliation are now ubiquitous in discussions about policy and politics in transitional societies. In Iraq, Prime Minister Nouri al-Maliki and non-governmental organizations like the United States Institute of Peace have developed a comprehensive reconciliation plan, while the Iraqi Ministry for National Dialogue has organized a national reconciliation conference.[3] Reconciliation also plays a prominent role within the literature in moral and political philosophy that analyzes the nature and justifiability of responses to wrongdoing, and in the burgeoning multidisciplinary literature on transitional justice. Scholarship in the latter category considers how societies in transition from repressive rule to democracy should respond to a legacy of human rights abuses. Reflecting this consensus about its importance, political reconciliation now holds a powerful rhetorical and political force; the failure to pursue reconciliation is often taken to be sufficient grounds for criticism.[4] In his resignation address following the threat of impeachment in August 2008, the then President of Pakistan, Pervez Musharraf, accused his opponents of "opt[ing] for the politics of confrontation over reconciliation."[5]

Civil conflict and repressive rule have historically been and continue to be global phenomena, inflicting enormous suffering, causing intense upheaval, and leaving in their aftermath an overwhelming catalog of issues for transitional societies to address. Despite the fact that conflict and repression are not new, the distinctive emphasis on political reconciliation within transitional societies is. What explains the intense and unprecedented global interest in political reconciliation? To a significant extent, the answer is South Africa. During its historic transition from apartheid to democracy, South Africa made the pursuit of reconciliation a central focal point of concern and, as a result, placed the issue of reconciliation firmly at the center of the global peacemaking agenda. To understand the questions and concerns that this book sets out to address and answer, then, it is instructive to begin with South Africa.

[3] James Phillips, "What is Needed for Reconciliation in Iraq," June 28, 2006, www.heritage.org/research/iraq/wm1139.cfm; David A. Steele, "Reconciliation Strategies in Iraq," *United States Institute of Peace Special Report*, 213 (October 2008), www.usip.org/pubs/specialreports/sr213.pdf.

[4] For a discussion of the rhetorical dimensions of reconciliation see Erik Doxtader, "Reconciliation – A Rhetorical Conception," *Quarterly Journal of Speech*, 89 (2003), 267–92.

[5] Candace Rondeaux, "Musharraf Exits, but Uncertainty Remains," *Washington Post*, August 19, 2008, www.washingtonpost.com/wp-dyn/content/article/2008/08/18/AR2008081800418.html. Accessed August 20, 2008.

In 1994, after more than forty years of apartheid, South Africa held its first democratic elections. During apartheid, the South African minority white government had institutionalized racism, racially segregating every dimension of South African society by law and systematically oppressing the black South African population.[6] Such oppression depended on intense repression at the hands of an extensive security force. The anti-apartheid opposition movement, initially non-violent, soon turned to violent tactics to overthrow the apartheid regime. Negotiations to end the ensuing civil conflict occurred from the late 1980s through the early 1990s, led by Nelson Mandela of the African National Congress (ANC), who was freed from prison in 1990 after twenty-seven years, and the then South African President F. W. de Klerk. The negotiations eventually resulted in the crafting of an interim constitution and paved the way for democratic elections. On May 10, 1994, Nelson Mandela became President of South Africa.

Enormous uncertainty surrounded the negotiations and the official transfer of power. Many within South Africa and around the world anticipated and feared an all-out bloodbath. Yet, to the astonishment of many, widespread conflict never materialized. Historian Leonard Thompson captures the amazement over the South African transition in his description:

Between 1989 and 1994, South Africans surprised the world. Although the country was wracked by unprecedented violence and teetered on the brink of civil war, black and white politicians put an end to more than three hundred years of white domination and fashioned a nonracial constitution, which effectively transferred political power from the white minority to the black majority. May 10, 1994, the day the presidency of South Africa passed from an Afrikaner who led the party of white supremacy to the leader of an African nationalist movement, was the culmination of one of the finest achievements of the twentieth century.[7]

One primary issue facing the new South African government was how to deal with the human rights abuses committed during apartheid. A product of the negotiations to end apartheid was the inclusion in the Interim Constitution of 1993 of a commitment that the institution established to confront the legacy of human rights abuses during apartheid

---

[6] Black South Africans, the overwhelming majority of the South African population, were stripped of their political rights, forcibly removed from their homes, and subjected to social, legal, political, educational, and economic discrimination.

[7] Leonard Thompson, *A History of South Africa* (New Haven, CT: Yale University Press, 2000), p. 241.

would contain an amnesty provision for parties responsible for offenses committed for political reasons during the prior conflict.[8] This would ensure that the past was confronted in a manner that fostered reconciliation. Following the emerging model of previous transitional societies, the South African Parliament passed the Promotion of National Unity and Reconciliation Act, No. 34 of 1995, establishing the Truth and Reconciliation Commission (TRC). The mandate of the TRC was to "investigat[e] and document gross human rights violations committed within or outside South Africa in the period 1960–1994."[9] The specific violations under investigation were killing, abduction, torture, and severe ill-treatment. The amnesty provision stipulated that a perpetrator of such abuses could be granted amnesty if he made a full disclosure of the acts for which he was responsible and showed that such acts were carried out for political reasons.[10]

Although South Africa was not the first country to establish a truth commission to investigate and document systematic and widespread human rights abuses, the proceedings of the TRC were in many respects unprecedented. For example, the level of participation in and publicity surrounding the work of the TRC was unparalleled. The testimony of over 20,000 individuals was collected and over 7,000 individuals applied for amnesty.[11] Most importantly for my purposes, the TRC made the pursuit of reconciliation a primary aim of its work. According to the Final Report of the TRC, "the overarching task assigned to the Commission by Parliament was the promotion of national unity and reconciliation."[12] The task of the TRC was "to uncover as much as possible of the truth about past gross violations of human rights – a difficult and often very unpleasant task. The Commission was founded, however, in the belief

---

[8] David Dyzenhaus, "Survey Article: The South African TRC," *Journal of Political Philosophy*, 8(4) (2000), 470–96, at 475.

[9] Truth and Reconciliation Commission of South Africa, *Truth and Reconciliation Commission of South Africa Report*, 5 vols. (London: Macmillan Publishers, 1999), vol. 1, ch. 2, p. 24.

[10] Those granted amnesty were immune from both civil and criminal prosecution. The TRC was divided into three committees, one of which focused on human rights violations, another on amnesty, and a third on reparations to victims. Dyzenhaus, "The South African TRC," 477.

[11] In addition, by individualizing amnesty, the TRC allowed for a measure of accountability for human rights abuses that contrasted with previous commissions that had been preceded by a blanket amnesty allowing general immunity for human rights abuses. The TRC also held institutional hearings to determine the role of the media, law, health sector, business, and religious communities during apartheid; these were designed to understand how apartheid was sustained. Public hearings of the Human Rights Violations Committee and the Amnesty Committee of the TRC were extensively covered by the media on radio, in newspapers, and on television. Dyzenhaus, "The South African TRC," 479.

[12] TRC, *Truth and Reconciliation Commission of South Africa Report*, vol. 1, ch. 5, p. 106.

that this task was necessary for the promotion of reconciliation and national unity."[13] This commitment was embodied in the work of the TRC commissioners throughout the hearings. Most famously, the chairman of the TRC, Archbishop Desmond Tutu, publicly encouraged reconciliation and forgiveness between perpetrators and victims, praising those who did forgive as models for the new South Africa.

The work of the TRC captured the world's attention, sparking theoretical and political debates both within and well beyond the boundaries of South Africa. One debate centered on the exportability of the South African model of transitional justice and reconciliation. The question was whether a TRC established in different transitional contexts could be as successful as the TRC in South Africa. Skepticism about this possibility focused on the factors unique to South Africa that contributed to the achievements of the TRC. For example, both Mandela and Tutu played critical roles in promoting the TRC and reconciliation; indeed, Archbishop Tutu believes that Nelson Mandela will be remembered primarily as "the icon of reconciliation and forgiveness, of holding together a country that everybody kept predicting 'give them six months, and this country will be down the tubes.'"[14] Analogous figures may not be present in other transitional contexts. Further, South Africa had distinctive cultural resources that facilitated the pursuit of reconciliation; the African notion of *ubuntu*, which emphasizes the humanity and interconnectedness of all South Africans and was appealed to by Archbishop Tutu, laid the foundation for the possibility of reconciliation.

A different debate concerned whether South Africa *should* serve as a model for other transitional societies to emulate. The TRC was the subject of numerous critiques that called into question its justifiability. A number of criticisms focused on the underlying rationale of the truth commission, which was to investigate and document the truth about past atrocities in order to facilitate reconciliation. Some questioned whether the pursuit of the truth would indeed facilitate reconciliation if punitive justice was then denied; from this perspective, when punishment is denied it leads to resentment and vigilantism. Others opposed the emphasis of the TRC on reconciliation. Critics charged that the TRC failed to

---

[13] Ibid., vol. 1, ch. 4, p. 49.

[14] B. J. de Klerk, "Nelson Mandela and Desmond Tutu: Living Icons of Reconciliation," *The Ecumenical Review* (October 2003), http://findarticles.com/p/articles/mi_m2065/is_4_55/ai_111979985/pg_3?tag=artBody;col1. Accessed October 22, 2008.

sufficiently respect the dignity of victims, and indeed wronged victims a second time, when it encouraged them to forgive and reconcile with past wrongdoers.[15] Others argued that the pursuit of reconciliation by the state was fundamentally illiberal, insofar as it hoped to inculcate a single attitude of forgiveness throughout the population and establish a single authoritative account of the past in its Final Report. For many, pursuing reconciliation through the TRC was a morally second-best strategy, necessary because of the negotiated compromise that required an amnesty provision and because punishment and retribution were not viable options given the scale of atrocities committed and the state of the judicial system. As South African lawyer Paul van Zyl writes, "Transitional societies are often left with a legacy in which thousands (sometimes hundreds of thousands) of people are victims of gross violations of human rights. Criminal justice systems are designed to maintain order in societies where violation of law is the exception. These systems simply cannot cope when, either as a result of state-sanctioned human rights abuses or internal conflict or war, violations become the rule."[16]

The fundamental questions about political reconciliation raised in the debates over the South African TRC have not been resolved. Indeed, South Africa remains the point of departure for many academic and policy discussions and debates about reconciliation and transitional justice. An underlying source of the ongoing controversies surrounding political reconciliation is disagreement about the nature of reconciliation itself: Is political reconciliation fundamentally illiberal? Does it require citizens to adopt a unitary account of the past? Must the interests of individual victims be subordinated to the interests of the community? Are reconciliation and retribution incompatible? Is the pursuit of reconciliation merely a second-best option in transitional contexts? Is political reconciliation necessary for successful democratization and the prevention of future conflict and repression?

---

[15] For a detailed review of these various critiques, and responses to the critiques, see Robert I. Rotberg and Dennis Thompson (eds.), *Truth v. Justice: The Morality of Truth Commissions* (Princeton University Press, 2000) and Dyzenhaus, "The South African TRC."

[16] Paul van Zyl, "Justice Without Punishment: Guaranteeing Human Rights in Transitional Societies," in Charles Villa-Vicencio and Wilhelm Verwoerd (eds.), *Looking Back, Reaching Forward: Reflections on the Truth and Reconciliation Commission of South Africa* (University of Cape Town Press, 2000), p. 46. One additional objection to the framework of the TRC focuses on its emphasis on gross human rights violations, which, the objection claimed, relegated the crime against humanity that consisted of the practices of apartheid itself to the background context. The TRC consequently failed to acknowledge the millions of individuals who were victims of practices like forced removals. For this criticism see Mahmood Mamdani, cited in Priscilla Hayner, *Unspeakable Truths: Confronting State Terror and Atrocity* (New York: Routledge, 2001), p. 74.

The central objective of this book is to develop an analysis of what political reconciliation involves, one that answers the fundamental questions raised by the South African TRC. Before beginning my analysis, however, it is important to explain why a new examination of political reconciliation is needed. Despite the emerging consensus about the importance of political reconciliation for transitional contexts and its prominence in debates about transitional justice, until recently political reconciliation was not the subject of sustained theoretical attention. Although political reconciliation is now becoming the subject of theoretical interest, there is no consensus about what political reconciliation is. In the words of the International Center for Transitional Justice (ICTJ), "The word 'reconciliation' continues to figure prominently both in the literature and the practice of transitional justice, despite a lack of consensus about what the term exactly means, what activities it encompasses, or what achieving such a condition would require."[17] In addition, within the little literature that now exists on political reconciliation there is no robust debate about the nature of political reconciliation. Typically, a conception of reconciliation is developed without citing alternative conceptions or subjecting such conceptions to a sustained critique.

In the next section I develop a set of desiderata that an adequate view should meet by considering the limitations of the available understandings of reconciliation found in the literature. I then describe the methodology that I employ to develop a conception of political reconciliation that fulfills these criteria. Finally, I conclude with a general overview of the conception of political reconciliation I defend in the chapters that follow, which captures the complex set of problems pertaining to political relationships in transitional contexts that processes of reconciliation must repair, without losing sight of individuals and respect for their agency.

---

[17] The International Center for Transitional Justice (ICTJ) was established in 2001 and advises countries on whether to confront the legacy of human rights abuses through criminal trials and/or truth commissions and the appropriate relationship to establish between different programs (i.e., the truth and reconciliation commission and special court in Sierra Leone); trains and assists prosecution efforts in both domestic and hybrid tribunals; files *amicus curiae* briefs in domestic tribunals; monitors domestic criminal justice proceedings; publishes studies on the use of hybrid tribunals; and holds conferences on domestic prosecutions with international representatives involved in such efforts to create a network of advisors and offer a forum for exchanging investigation strategies. It currently works in such capacities in over twenty-five countries around the world. See ICTJ, www.ictj.org/en/tj/784.html. Accessed September 1, 2008.

CONCEPTIONS OF POLITICAL RECONCILIATION

As noted above, political reconciliation broadly refers to the process of rebuilding political relationships.[18] Given this basic idea, a conception of political reconciliation will clarify what this process entails. In particular, it will provide a diagnosis of why political relationships must be rebuilt, which will in turn clarify how relationships have gone wrong or been damaged. It will spell out what transformed and rebuilt decent relationships are like. It will also clarify what a process must do if it is to be effective, namely, rebuild political relationships in the requisite ways.

The discussion in the previous section suggested that to articulate the basic idea of political reconciliation in an adequate manner, a conception should provide the theoretical resources for resolving the controversies about political reconciliation. That is, an adequate theory of political reconciliation should respond to the urgent and pressing practical need for a normative theory of political reconciliation.[19] A theory should be normative in the sense of being action- and policy-guiding, providing the theoretical resources for understanding what should count as success for the purposes of evaluating public policies designed to foster political reconciliation. It should also be normative in the sense that it clarifies what is at stake, morally speaking, in the success or failure of the process of rebuilding political relationships in the aftermath of conflict and repression. In particular, it should shed light on the moral value and justifiability of its pursuit and the kinds of processes that foster reconciliation. We should also look to it to confirm and explain why reconciliation is vital for successful democratization.

In this section I critically evaluate four different conceptions of reconciliation articulated in the literature: reconciliation as forgiveness; reconciliation as the creation and stabilization of normative expectations and trust; reconciliation as a political value; and reconciliation as the

---

[18] This core idea can be found in John Roth, "Useless Experience: Its Significance for Reconciliation after Auschwitz," in David Patterson and John K. Roth (eds.), *After-Words: Post Holocaust Struggles with Forgiveness, Reconciliation, Justice* (Seattle: University of Washington Press, 2004), pp. 85–99, at p. 86; Daniel Philpott, "Introduction," in Daniel Philpott (ed.), *The Politics of Past Evil: Religion, Reconciliation, and the Dilemmas of Transitional Justice* (Notre Dame, IN: University of Notre Dame Press, 2006), p. 14; Trudy Govier and Wilhelm Verwoerd, "Trust and the Problem of National Reconciliation," *Philosophy of the Social Sciences*, 32(2) (2002), 178–205. This is the second sense of reconciliation that Paul M. Hughes identifies in his "Moral Atrocity and Political Reconciliation: A Preliminary Analysis," *International Journal of Applied Philosophy*, 15(1) (2001), 123–35.

[19] I take this phrase from Allen Buchanan, who develops his theory of secession in response to a distinct practical need. See Allen Buchanan, *Secession: The Morality of Political Divorce from Fort Sumter to Lithuania to Quebec* (Boulder: Westview Press, 1991), p. 2.

constituting of a political community. Although each conception is useful and captures important insights, it is ultimately inadequate because it is incomplete. My discussion highlights two general limitations of prevailing understandings. The first is that available conceptions offer a simplistic diagnosis of what the rebuilding of political relationships involves because they focus on certain problems (e.g., attitudinal or interpersonal) regarding political relationships in transitional contexts, while ignoring others (e.g., institutional). As a result, available conceptions fail to capture the complex changes that rebuilding political relationships requires. I suggest that an additional constraint on an adequate conception of reconciliation is that it provides a multifaceted characterization of how political relationships go wrong during conflict and repression.

The second limitation of available conceptions is a product of the methodology used to analyze political reconciliation. We can speak of the reconciliation between a husband and wife, parent and child, close personal friends, individual perpetrator of wrongdoing and individual victim, or societal reconciliation. A common strategy in the literature is to develop a general theory of moral reconciliation that is applicable for these various relationships.[20] I do not want to deny the value of more abstract analyses, nor am I suggesting that various kinds of reconciliation are not related. Indeed, it would be surprising if personal relationships remained unaffected in contexts where general political relationships are deeply flawed. Rather, I challenge the usefulness of such analyses for the pressing moral and policy questions about reconciliation that arise in transitional contexts. In particular, abstract analyses provide little guidance for effective and justifiable policy formulation and few resources for understanding why political reconciliation is critical for successful democratization. This suggests that a conception of political reconciliation must capture what is distinctive about the repair of political, as opposed to more personal, relationships.

Reconciliation as forgiveness

One prominent way of understanding political reconciliation is in terms of forgiveness. Forgiveness involves the overcoming of negative emotions,

---

[20] For a general examination of reconciliation see Margaret Urban Walker, *Moral Repair: Reconstructing Moral Relations After Wrongdoing* (Cambridge University Press, 2006). She describes her project as trying to "understand how responses to wrong and harm, in personal and political cases, can be ways to repair and sustain the grip of morality as a force in our shared lives" (p. 6). Linda Radzik also offers a general moral theory of making amends that has as its goal achieving reconciliation in her *Making Amends: Atonement in Morality, Law and Politics* (Oxford University Press, 2009).

such as anger, hatred, resentment, and indignation, which are natural responses to wrongdoing.[21] In this view, then, a primary source of the damage to and problems with political relationships is attitudinal in nature, and concerns the presence of pervasive and widespread negative reactive attitudes. Political relationships are rebuilt when such negative reactive attitudes are overcome.[22] Processes of political reconciliation are effective if they foster and encourage the desired kinds of changes in citizens' attitudes.

This view seems attractive because it focuses on what many regard as necessary for the long-term maintenance of personal relationships: forgiveness. Given the fallibility of human beings, it is inevitable that individuals will wrong those they care about at some point. If an individual who is wronged retains the resentment and hatred felt in response to being wronged, interaction can become stifled, clouded, and can ultimately cease. The maintenance of long-term personal relationships thus depends on a willingness to overcome resentment and hurt, and a willingness to trust that the wrong done does not represent the core of the other individual. In other words, the maintenance of relationships depends on a capacity and willingness to forgive.

Despite its initial appeal, however, forgiveness provides an inappropriate starting point for understanding political reconciliation. The fittingness of forgiveness as a response to wrongdoing is most plausible in the context of normal personal relationships. In such relationships, wrongdoing is the exception or aberration, not the rule. This makes the claim that an individual who was wronged should overcome his or her resentment through forgiveness reasonable and appropriate. Through forgiveness a valuable relationship can be restored. However, in transitional contexts the conception of a prior normal, acceptable political relationship that has been ruptured by

---

[21] This idea of forgiveness draws on the basic understanding articulated by Bishop Butler and developed in various ways by theorists including Norman Richards, "Forgiveness," *Ethics*, 99(1) (1988), 77–97; Paul M. Hughes, "What Is Involved in Forgiving?" *Philosophia*, 25 (1997), 33–49; Pamela Hieronymi, "Articulating an Uncompromising Forgiveness," *Philosophy and Phenomenological Research*, 62(3) (2001), 529–55. Authors disagree on precisely which negative emotions need to be overcome in forgiveness. For an example of two different views, see Jeffrie Murphy and Jean Hampton, *Forgiveness and Mercy* (Cambridge University Press, 1998).

[22] For authors who define reconciliation in terms of forgiveness, see Rajeev Bhargava, "Restoring Decency to Barbaric Societies," pp. 45–68; Elizabeth Kiss, "Moral Ambition Within and Beyond Political Constraints: Reflections on Restorative Justice," pp. 68–98; David Crocker, "Truth Commissions, Transitional Justice, and Civil Society," pp. 99–121 – all in Rotberg and Thompson, *Truth v. Justice*.

wrongdoing does not pertain.[23] Rather than being reasonable and appropriate, urging forgiveness and the overcoming of resentment in contexts where wrongdoing is systematic and ongoing seems at best naïve and at worst a form of complicity in the maintenance of oppression and injustice.

Relatedly, placing the primary focus of political reconciliation in the aftermath of systematic wrongdoing on the internal changes victims should undergo is misguided. For one thing, it may reflect an ongoing, insufficient appreciation and recognition of the wrongs that victims suffered. Given the horrific character of the violence so many endure during civil conflict and repressive rule, for example, it is not surprising that resentment is widespread; resentment is a reactive attitude that communicates the belief that one has been wronged. Indeed, the absence of resentment on the part of victims toward a wrongdoer can signal an insufficient sense of self-respect or self-worth. To take the overcoming of resentment as the primary goal of policies of political reconciliation problematically implies that the primary change to relationships should occur among the innocent. There is a certain passivity in forgiving attitudes, and policies that promote forgiveness among victims may be implicitly encouraging precisely the kind of capitulation that violence was trying to achieve in the first place.

Moreover, the emphasis on internal changes in attitude overlooks the external change that is imperative in the aftermath of civil conflict and repressive rule characterized by systematic wrongdoing and oppression.[24] A primary concern of policies of political reconciliation should be ending injustice and oppression, and addressing the conditions that facilitate and support injustice and oppression. Consider violence, an obviously important source of the damage to political relationships caused during civil conflict and repression. Widespread and frequently systematic abuses of human rights are characteristic of conflict and repression. Violence has

---

[23] There may also be personal relationships where the idea of a prior normal, acceptable relationship does not hold as well. Abusive relationships seem to be a paradigm case. However, such relationships seem the exception and are not typically treated as constituting the cases that should serve as the starting point for theoretical reflection upon how it is appropriate to respond in the aftermath of wrongdoing. Instead, we are inclined to judge that forgiveness, while normally appropriate, is not appropriate in such cases. I thank Linda Radzik for pressing this point and helping me to articulate my concerns with conceptualizing reconciliation as forgiveness.

[24] Proponents of forgiveness do often acknowledge the need for external change as a condition for the justifiability of forgiveness. However, such external changes are of derivative, not primary, interest. They are of interest insofar as they relate to the primary concern, which is the internal change in attitude among victims constitutive of forgiveness. In the context of political reconciliation, such external changes should be of central interest.

taken many forms in recent decades, including execution, rape, kidnapping and disappearing of individuals, the amputation of limbs, physical and psychological torture, and enslavement. For the year 2000, the estimate of direct deaths due to conflict worldwide was 310,000.[25] Such violence serves many functions: to terrorize a population into submission, to ethnically cleanse an area, or to demoralize an antagonistic community or organization and thereby secure its defeat. Violence is an important tool for displacing populations and, in general, achieving political goals in the contexts of civil conflict and repressive rule. In 2007 government armed forces, militias supported by governments, rebels, non-state armed groups, and hostile communities in situations of civil conflict all were responsible for the displacement of civilians.[26] Internally displaced individuals are frequently vulnerable to a range of human rights abuses and subsist with inadequate access to food, water, health care including maternal health care, and shelter. Women and girls are especially vulnerable to sexual violence and abuse.[27] Violence is a form of injustice and facilitates the pursuit of broader oppression and injustice. Given its pervasive and damaging impact on individuals and political relationships, it is clear that a primary emphasis of political reconciliation should be on ending violence and addressing the institutional and social conditions that make violence possible. However, because reconciliation as forgiveness places principal emphasis on internal changes among victims, these imperatives are its primary concern.

---

[25] C. J. L. Murray, G. King, D. Lopez, N. Tomijima, and E. G. Krug, "Armed Conflict as a Public Health Problem," *British Journal of Medicine*, 324 (2002), 346–9.

[26] Despite their obligations under international humanitarian law and international human rights law, governments again were among the primary perpetrators of forced displacement in 2007. In twenty-one of the twenty-eight countries where there was new internal displacement in 2007, governments were responsible for forcibly displacing people, either directly through their own security forces (as was the case in CAR and DRC), indirectly through allied irregular armed groups (in countries such as Sudan, Colombia, and India), or through implementing policies that directly entailed forced displacement (such as the governments of Myanmar/Burma or of Israel in the Occupied Palestinian Territory). Rebel groups were responsible for forcible displacements in eighteen countries in 2007. During 2007, 16 million individuals were refugees. See United Nations High Commissioner for Refugees, "2007 Global Trends: Refugees, Asylum-seekers, Returnees, Internally Displaced and Stateless Persons" (June 2008), www.unhcr.org/statistics/STATISTICS/4852366f2.pdf. Accessed November 5, 2008. An additional 26 million individuals were internally displaced due to armed civil conflict. Of that number, 11.3 million subsisted without any form of humanitarian aid from their governments, and 9.3 million faced either indifference or active hostility from their government. See Internal Displacement Monitoring Centre, *Internal Displacement: Global Overview of Trends and Developments in 2007*, www.unhcr.org/refworld/publisher,IDMC,THEMREPORT,48074b842,0.html, at p. 6. Accessed November 4, 2008.

[27] See Internal Displacement Monitoring Centre, *Internal Displacement*.

Finally, conceptualizing reconciliation as forgiveness makes it difficult to satisfactorily answer the theoretical questions outlined above. Consider the question of whether and in what way political reconciliation is necessary for successful democratization and the prevention of future conflict. While the long-term maintenance of personal relationships can plausibly be said to depend on a willingness to forgive, political relationships frequently persist despite a history of wrongdoing and the presence of resentment. Similarly, victims could forgive yet continue to be oppressed, so that relationships are continuously damaged anew. Thus the overcoming of resentment among individual perpetrators and victims does not seem to be what is critical for successful democratization and peacekeeping globally. Negative reactive attitudes signal that there are problems in political relationships. However, such attitudes are not in themselves the problems that need to be addressed if political relationships are to be rebuilt in a way that prevents future conflict and repressive rule.

In addition, the moral justifiability of pursuing political reconciliation is harder to establish when reconciliation is conceptualized as forgiveness. The justifiability of forgiveness requires more than showing that it is reasonable for a particular individual to forgive. It requires establishing the more complicated claim that it is justifiable for a state to exercise its power by encouraging individuals to forgive in the name of promoting a societal good like reconciliation. Citizens reasonably disagree about the justifiability of forgiving both in general and especially in transitional contexts. State policies designed to encourage victims to forgive fail to acknowledge such disagreement. Instead of grounding the shared conviction that reconciliation is vitally important and justifiable to achieve in transitional contexts, reconciliation as forgiveness calls into question the presumed importance and justifiability of its pursuit in transitional contexts.

Reconciliation as the creation and stabilization of normative expectations and trust

The second conception found in the literature defines reconciliation as the process of codifying and reinforcing the normative expectations that structure moral relationships predicated on trust.[28] In the words of

---

[28] See Walker, *Moral Repair*. Other theorists who emphasize trust include Govier and Verwoerd in "Trust and the Problem of National Reconciliation" and the ICTJ.

Margaret Urban Walker, moral relationships are "trust-based relations anchored on our expectations of one another ... we rely on each other to be responsive to expectations and to understand that accounting is owed when we do not behave in the ways upon which others rely."[29] According to Walker, all moral relationships are defined by normative expectations. The maintenance of such relationships and expectations depends on confidence in the shared standards for behavior that inform the expectations we make of others; such confidence reflects a belief that the standards for interaction are good, shared by others, and recognized as shared by others. Moral relations are also predicated on trust that others will respect such standards. According to this conception, then, political relationships are damaged when shared normative expectations are violated and trust is undermined. The task of processes of reconciliation is to develop and reinforce the normative expectations constitutive of moral relationships, and to cultivate trust.[30]

Conceptualizing reconciliation in terms of the creation or stabilization of normative expectations and trust-based relations overcomes some of the limitations of reconciliation as forgiveness. Unlike reconciliation as forgiveness, this conception does not focus primarily on the change demanded of victims. It also has theoretical resources for identifying the sources of damage to relationships and of resentment, and the corresponding requirements for repair, that seem relevant and appropriate to consider in transitional contexts. Resentment arises when normative expectations and trust are unjustifiably violated. Framing wrongdoing in terms of the violation of normative expectations and trust also provides resources for explaining the necessity and moral value of pursuing reconciliation. Normative expectations define the contours of any moral relation including political relationships, and so any plausible conception of reconciliation should consider the expectations that citizens and officials should have of one another and how to respond when such expectations are violated. Similarly, this conception takes seriously the moral psychology of both stable and disrupted relationships, highlighting what is lost in disrupted relationships and present in stable relationships, including, importantly, trust. The attitudes that citizens and officials hold of each other in contexts of repressive rule and civil conflict are often a significant source of moral concern. Indeed, the absence of trust is frequently cited as a primary reason for the faltering success of self-rule in Northern Ireland since the Good Friday/Belfast Agreement in 1998.

[29] Walker, *Moral Repair*, p. 23.   [30] Ibid., p. 38.

However, despite its strengths, reconciliation as the creation and stabilization of normative expectations and trust has significant limitations. This conception offers a general theory of the process of repairing and transforming relationships, encompassing both personal and political cases of reconciliation.[31] The limitations of this conception are a product of its generality. Because it does not consider what is distinctive about political relationships and political reconciliation, reconciliation as the creation and stabilization of normative expectations and trust offers an insufficiently complex characterization of how political relationships go wrong and overlooks central justificatory questions that the pursuit of political reconciliation raises.

Consider first this conception's diagnosis of how relationships go wrong and are damaged during periods of repressive rule and civil conflict. It focuses on the importance of the creation, stabilization, and reinforcement of normative expectations and of trust. However, this description is so abstract that it does not provide concrete guidance for transitional societies. There is no pretheoretical reason to think that the reconciliation of Hutus and Tutsis in Rwanda following the genocide in 1994 will have much in common with the reconciliation of husband and wife after adultery. The expectations that citizens should have of officials are importantly different from those that spouses have of one another. If governments are going to develop effective strategies for facilitating political reconciliation, they need to know more than simply the abstract structure of general moral relationships or general characteristics of processes of moral repair. They need to understand the *specific* characteristics of normatively defensible forms of political interaction, and the conditions that undermine or contribute to a breakdown in such relationships. However, this conception does not provide sufficient theoretical resources for identifying which particular normative standards and expectations are violated during civil conflict and need to be developed by processes of political reconciliation.

More fundamentally, the diagnosis of how political relationships go wrong is incomplete. Certainly the creation, stabilization, and reinforcement of normative expectations and shared standards are critical features of rebuilt political relationships. Psychological attitudes like trust arguably play a critical role in supporting such expectations. However, the maintenance of normative expectations in political relationships depends on more than psychological attitudes. In particular, institutions

---

[31] Ibid., p. 6.

(e.g., legal, political, economic) play a critical role in defining and maintaining the shared standards of behavior and normative expectations constitutive of political relationships. Thus, by focusing exclusively on psychological attitudes and normative expectations, this perspective over-looks both how institutions in general, as well as the breakdown of a shared system of rules regulating the conduct of citizens in particular, also damage relationships and the corresponding institutional dimen-sions of the rebuilding of political relationships.

Indeed, institutional factors help to explain *why* the atmosphere within societies during civil conflict and repressive rule is often one of fear and distrust: of government officials, the judicial system, the media, and fellow citizens. Such fear and distrust are the natural product of an environment in which there are rumors of state-sponsored abuse coupled with official denial of wrongdoing, the absence of an effective independent judicial system to check allegations of abuse, the absence of an independent media to bring public attention to allegations of abuse, and the presence of a desire among citizens unaffected by abuse to deny its existence. Repressive governments often intimidate human rights lawyers, motivating those who know about specific abuses or want to protect human rights to remain silent. Hugo Fruhling describes the purpose and methods of repression used as General Augusto Pinochet came to power after leading a coup d'état and then consolidating power in Chile:

The repression that began on 11 September 1973 cannot be understood without reference to the Allende government's experiment in socialism from 1970 to 1973. Especially during the first stage, repression was aimed at destroying the social and political organizations that had supported Allende in an attempt to prevent another socialist regime in the future ... The aim became one of building a market economy in an authoritarian state, and a change in the political values of the society was needed. To implement this, large doses of coercion were required. It was necessary to modify democratic values at every level of society in such a way that the past would be forgotten and the individual would turn back to the sphere of his private relationships ... The methods of repression, which included courts-martial, ordinary trials, repressive laws, and various illegal disappearances and killings, changed in response to the political needs of the moment, long-term political necessities and pressures from hostile international public opinion.[32]

As this description makes clear, conflict and repressive rule undermine political and legal institutions, which in turn disrupt political life and

---

[32] Hugo Fruhling, "Stages of Repression and Legal Strategy for the Defense of Human Rights in Chile: 1973–1980," trans. Frederick Woodbridge, Jr., *Human Rights Quarterly*, 5(4) (1983), 510–33.

relationships. In particular, the undermining of legal and political institutions can erode trust in political relationships by rendering the political sphere uncertain and motivating individuals to opt out of participating in politics and civil society. Similarly, the erosion of institutions can undermine the normative expectations that citizens and officials in moral relationships should make of each other. By defining the tasks of repair in terms of the cultivation of normative expectations sustained by attitudes like trust, the second conception overlooks the institutional dimensions of political reconciliation.

The generality of reconciliation as the creation and stabilization of normative expectations and trust also results in silence about the distinct justificatory questions that the pursuit of political reconciliation triggers, which do not arise when considering reconciliation in personal cases. As we saw when considering reconciliation as forgiveness, the kinds of practices that it is justifiable for a state to pursue in the name of reconciliation are not identical to those that it is permissible for an individual to pursue. The justifiability of reconciliation in personal cases need only take into account what reasons would make it permissible or obligatory to reinforce normative expectations when violated or view another in a trusting manner. It is more complicated, however, to establish that it is justifiable for a state to encourage individuals to change their attitudes in the name of promoting a societal good like reconciliation. Furthermore, there are restrictions on the permissible ways for states to create and stabilize normative expectations among citizens and officials. By abstracting away from the differences that define personal and political relationships, reconciliation as the creation and stabilization of normative expectations maintained by trust fails to address some of the central issues that the pursuit of political reconciliation raises.

Reconciliation as a political value

A third conception specifies reconciliation as a political value.[33] In this view, reconciliation exists when "former strangers view and treat each other as equal citizens" after prior conflict and injustice.[34] According to the philosopher Darrel Moellendorf, reconciliation has both attitudinal and institutional requirements. Reconciliation is achieved when all

---

[33] See Darrell Moellendorf, "Reconciliation as a Political Value," *Journal of Social Philosophy*, 38(2) (2007), 205–21.
[34] Ibid., 206.

individuals within a political community come to be seen and recognized as fellow citizens, not as strangers or as enemies to be suppressed. Citizens must also come to comparatively endorse the institutional order, or shared public rules regulating contestation among citizens.[35] To distinguish reconciliation from mass resignation, the endorsement must be based on good reasons, and the institutional order must meet minimal moral requirements. In particular, institutions must ensure a "minimal basis for politics based upon democratic equality" and "a measure of equality in relations" by protecting the "formal equality of rights, liberties, and protections under the law," an equal opportunity to participate in the political process, a "constitutional democratic legal framework," and "juridical equality."[36]

This conception of reconciliation overcomes the limitations of reconciliation as the creation and stabilization of normative expectations and trust. It explicitly restricts its focus to political reconciliation and, as a result, emphasizes the role of institutions in structuring political relationships. It also specifies the demands of reconciliation at a level of concreteness that makes it useful for the purposes of public policy formulation. In addition, the concentration on political relationships leads this conception to address the distinct justificatory questions surrounding the pursuit of political reconciliation by the state. Moellendorf argues that the value of political reconciliation does not stem from an appeal to any comprehensive conception of the good with which citizens might reasonably disagree. According to Moellendorf, refraining from justifying principles on the basis of a comprehensive conception respects citizens' freedom of conscience.[37] Rather, the requirements of political reconciliation are specified by appeal to an ideal of free and equal citizenship.

While it avoids the limitations that result from conceptualizing reconciliation too broadly, reconciliation as a political value does not maintain the strengths of reconciliation as the creation and stabilization of normative expectations and trust. The description of the requirements of political reconciliation advanced by Moellendorf outlines what institutions should be like so that they reflect a commitment to and encourage respectful interaction among equals. However, the predominant emphasis on institutions obscures the important interpersonal, relational aspects of

---

[35] Moellendorf distinguishes complete and comparative endorsement. An individual completely endorses an institutional order if and only if she would choose them over all conceivable alternatives. An individual comparatively endorses an institutional order if she sees it as better than some alternatives: 207.

[36] Ibid., 208.   [37] Ibid., 217.

political interaction among citizens and officials that were included in Walker's account. Consequently, this conception overlooks important sources of damage to political relationships during civil conflict and repressive rule, stemming from the ways that damaged political relationships impact the lives of individuals who participate in such relationships.

To illustrate the human costs and impact of violence, consider the story of Susan, a 16-year-old girl abducted by the Lord's Resistance Army in Uganda and forced to partake in killing another abductee, whom she knew from her village. Susan describes the killing and its enduring impact on her in these words:[38]

> One boy tried to escape, but he was caught. They made him eat a mouthful of red pepper, and five people were beating him. His hands were tied, and then they made us, the other new captives, kill him with a stick. I felt sick. I knew this boy from before. We were from the same village. I refused to kill him and they told me they would shoot me. They pointed a gun at me, so I had to do it. The boy was asking me, "Why are you doing this?" I said I had no choice. After we killed him, they made us smear his blood on our arms. I felt dizzy. There was another dead body nearby, and I could smell the body. I felt so sick. They said we had to do this so we would not fear death and so we would not try to escape. I feel so bad about the things that I did ... It disturbs me so much – that I inflicted death on other people ... I still dream about the boy from my village who I killed. I see him in my dreams, and he is talking to me and saying I killed him for nothing, and I am crying.

As Susan's story makes clear, the effects of the damage that stems from violence are profound and exist long after the violence ceases. A conception of reconciliation that focuses on institutions may capture the conditions that make violence like that described by Susan possible, and so draw attention to the institutional reform needed to repair political relationships. However, an institutional conception cannot adequately capture the attitudes and emotions, trauma, ostracism, terror, guilt, and shame that are the products of interaction during civil conflict and repressive rule, nor can it account for the role that tradition and social norms play in structuring political interaction and making wrongdoing possible. Thus the focus of reconciliation as a political value on the structure of the institutional political and legal order, and the recognition that citizens must come to endorse the reform of such institutions for

---

[38] Human Rights Watch, "Coercion and Intimidation of Child Soldiers to Participate in Violence" (April 2008), http://hrw.org/backgrounder/2008/crd0408/8.htm. Accessed November 6, 2008.

political reconciliation to be successful fail to provide an accurate picture of the devastation inflicted by interaction that goes wrong and the requisite comprehensive diagnosis of the ways in which political relationships must be rebuilt.

Reconciliation as the constituting of a political community

The fourth and final conception of reconciliation provides a stark contrast to the three conceptions of reconciliation articulated above. According to the philosopher Andrew Schaap, appealing, as the first three conceptions do, to a normative ideal of political relationships to understand what processes should promote is inappropriate in transitional contexts. The concern with such normative ideals is twofold: they undermine the political relevance of reconciliation, and they risk legitimizing relationships of oppression in the future. According to Schaap, for an understanding of political reconciliation to be relevant and normatively effective in transitional contexts, it must be endorsed by citizens.[39] There is likely to be disagreement about what rebuilt relationships entail in transitional contexts, which supports skepticism about the actual relevance and normative effectiveness that any normative theory of political reconciliation will have in particular transitional contexts. Further, given the expected disagreement about the contours political relationships should take, the pursuit and enforcement of a particular normative conception of relationships will require the coercive imposition of that ideal by the state on those who reasonably disagree with that normative ideal. This is fundamentally illiberal and oppressive. The adoption of any ideal of how relationships should be risks the pursuit of illegitimate political action, insofar as citizens are forced to enter into relationships with which they might substantively disagree. In Schaap's words, "There is good reason to be suspicious of an ideal of community as it is in the name of this ideal that oppression is legitimised."[40]

More fundamentally, Schaap questions the basic idea of reconciliation guiding the formulation of the conceptions above. In his view, conceptualizing political reconciliation as the rebuilding of political relationships presupposes precisely what processes of reconciliation must promote, namely, a political community. Conceptions of reconciliation as the righting of political relationships are thus irrelevant for transitional contexts. They fail to recognize and acknowledge the fragility of political

---

[39] Andrew Schaap, *Political Reconciliation* (New York: Routledge, 2005).   [40] Ibid., p. 85.

relationships in transitional contexts and the fact that the continued existence of a political community is not a given, but must be something a transitional society strives to achieve.

In light of these concerns, Schaap suggests that we think of reconciliation not as the repairing or rebuilding of political relationships, but as the founding of a political community.[41] The starting point for an adequate analysis should be the recognition of the fragility of political relationships in transitional contexts and of the relationships of enmity that exist. The goal of processes of reconciliation should be to cultivate civic friendship and a sense of a community. The actual definition of this community should be the subject of political discussion. Leaving the process of defining the shared principles that organize and structure political relationships to political processes in transitional contexts ensures that such principles will be relevant because they are actually adopted.

Reconciliation as the constituting of a political community has the virtue of taking seriously the specific transitional context within which the pursuit of political reconciliation occurs. Consequently, it draws attention to important dimensions of the rebuilding of political relationships in such transitional contexts that may be overlooked in more general conceptions of reconciliation. Specifically, this conception highlights the fragility of political relationships in transitional contexts. Members of transitional societies face the challenge of living with the same individuals who directly or indirectly suffered from, were perpetrators of, condoned, or were beneficiaries of human rights abuses. Lingering anger, resentment, hatred, and a sense of humiliation are widespread products of the human rights abuses and wrongdoing of the past. Yet so many people are wrongdoers, in one way or another, that members of transitional societies often cannot choose to live away from them. At the same time, the legacy of conflict and repressive rule is so immediate that many people wonder if it is possible to interact more peacefully with other members of society and, indeed, whether they will remain part of the same society. Ambivalence and skepticism about the transition itself, stemming in part from fear, resentment over anticipated loss of power and potential reprisals for past actions, and uncertainty as to whether a transition is permanent or fleeting shape the attitudes of populations in transition. Because it is premised on the fragility of political relationships in transitional contexts, this view powerfully captures the lack of inevitability of a successful transition. Relatedly, this conception draws attention to the fact that

---

[41] Ibid., p. 78.

shared standards and expectations need to be defined and cultivated. Unlike many personal cases of reconciliation, political reconciliation in transitional contexts is not simply about reinforcing standards that have been violated, but is rather about defining what the shared standards should be.

Despite these significant strengths, however, the fourth conception has important limitations, which stem from its central metaphor that characterizes the basic idea of political reconciliation. Conceptualizing political reconciliation as the constituting of a community offers a misleading description of the task of political reconciliation. Societies in transition do not simply constitute communities, but rather try to confront and, ideally, rebuild and transform ongoing relationships. Reconciliation implies a past of conflict and discord, as well as a pivotal moment in which there is a break with the past and the beginning of a movement toward a better future with regard to political interaction. Framing the project of reconciliation as the constituting of a political community conceptually obscures the history that informs relationships and influences the success of attempts to transform interaction.

More significantly, the rejection of the appropriateness and relevance of an ideal of political relationships undermines the ability of this conception of reconciliation to resolve the moral and policy debates surrounding the pursuit of political reconciliation. The failure to clarify and articulate a specific understanding of how relationships are in need of righting and how political relationships should be structured simply perpetuates and exacerbates the already prominent ambiguity and implicit disagreement about the concept of reconciliation. As a result, advocates of political reconciliation and transitional justice continue to talk past one another, failing to resolve underlying theoretical or practical disagreements. To evaluate whether policies can be expected to facilitate the desired change in political relationships, it is necessary to first have some sense of what such change looks like. Absent such an understanding, attempts at reconciliation risk becoming ineffective and possibly counterproductive.

Schaap is correct that there is always the risk that a normative conception may be manipulated for the purpose of consolidating power. It is important to consider how to mitigate such risks. However, there are also important risks in *failing* to put forth a normative conception of political relationships. Ambiguity about the meaning of reconciliation creates a space and incentive for political manipulation of the term. Absent a conception of the kinds of relationships we should strive to cultivate and an explanation of why such relationships are important, the task of demonstrating and challenging the political manipulation of the term becomes much more difficult. There is reason to think there is *greater* risk for oppression in the name of reconciliation by failing to articulate a normative understanding of political relationships than in offering such a conception. Such an understanding can help us identify the conditions under which a morally defensible kind of political engagement and interaction can occur.

Finally, while this conception takes seriously the need to offer an understanding of political reconciliation that is politically and morally relevant for transitional contexts, its response to this need is misguided. The test of the relevance and appropriateness of an understanding of political reconciliation should not be that it is actually adopted, but rather that it can and should be adopted in transitional contexts. Simply looking at what understanding of political change is adopted does not demonstrate that it is appropriate to pursue and that the change it embodies should be endorsed, nor is a conception necessarily irrelevant if it is not endorsed. A conception of political reconciliation is relevant politically if it provides insight into which aspects of interaction should be of moral concern. Through a philosophical analysis, we can elucidate what is at stake morally in attempting to change relationships. A normative conception clarifies why efforts to see a conception endorsed in practice in particular transitional contexts is significant and worth pursuing.

Desiderata of an adequate theory

The previous discussion of the limitations of available conceptions of political reconciliation puts us in a position to understand the general desiderata that a conception should meet if it is to respond adequately to the practical need for a normative theory of political reconciliation. Given the basic idea of political reconciliation, the task of a philosophical analysis of political reconciliation is threefold. First, an analysis should diagnose how relationships have gone wrong and been damaged. That is, the first central task of a philosophical analysis is to diagnose *why* characteristic patterns of interaction during civil conflict and repressive rule are appropriately regarded as damaging to political relationships and *why* such damage is of moral concern. A conception of political reconciliation must offer an illuminating normative analysis of the descriptive characteristic patterns of interaction found during conflict and repression. Second, an analysis should specify the end to be achieved, or the characteristics of rebuilt political relationships. Any diagnosis of how relationships are damaged will also be prescriptive, suggesting how political relationships should change or be rebuilt. These implied prescriptions provide the basis for the specification of the end or goal of processes of reconciliation. Third, an analysis outlines the means to the end. That is, an analysis should provide theoretical resources for understanding how political relationships can be effectively and justifiably rebuilt, that is, the kind(s) of processes that will rebuild political relationships in an effective and justifiable manner.

To overcome the limitations of prevailing conceptions, the diagnosis of why political relationships are in need of being rebuilt must have three features. First, it must account for the various distinct problems from which relationships may suffer, which may be attitudinal, institutional, and/or political in nature. An adequate conception, for example, should articulate what expectations citizens and officials should have of each other, what attitudes they should have with respect to each other, and how institutions should be if they are to structure political relationships in a just manner. Available conceptions, as argued above, offer a simplistic conception of what the rebuilding of political relationships entails because they diagnose the damage to relationships solely as a product of one kind of failure – attitudinal, interpersonal, institutional, or political.

Second, when explaining how political relationships have gone wrong and the ways in which they should be rebuilt, a conception must not be based on a general, abstract description of relationships. Rather, it must focus specifically on the distinctive character of political relationships, capturing both their institutional dimensions and the interpersonal character of political interaction. In the previous section I challenged the usefulness of general analyses for the pressing policy and practical questions of reconciliation and transitional justice that arise in transitional contexts. Restricting the focus to the rebuilding of political relationships ensures that the diagnosis of where relationships have gone wrong and the ways in which they need to be rebuilt is specific and concrete enough to provide guidance for public policy making. Keeping political relationships and transitional contexts in mind also ensures that the characterization of the issues facing political relationships is relevant in the sense that it reflects actual matters of concern in transitional contexts, such as the fragility of political relationships. This in turn will strengthen the resources that a conception has for providing a rationale for the importance of pursuing reconciliation in transitional contexts.

Third, in order to provide theoretical resources for resolving the debates about political reconciliation sparked by the TRC in South

Africa, the diagnosis of the damage to political relationships during civil conflict and repressive rule should emphasize the moral concern with patterns of interaction, and clarify the moral significance of rebuilding such relationships. In so doing, a conception will clarify the moral value of the pursuit of political reconciliation.

RECONCILIATION AS RECIPROCAL AGENCY[42]

Before developing my conception of reconciliation in detail in the chapters that follow, I want to conclude this chapter by discussing the methodology I use, summarizing the main features of my proposed conception, and providing an overview of the chapters that follow.

Methodology

As with the first three conceptions considered in the previous section, the starting point of my analysis is that political reconciliation is the process of rebuilding political relationships. To acknowledge the fragility of political relationships in transitional contexts, I understand the meaning of the term "relationships" minimally, to simply imply an extended prior history of interactions among citizens and officials. "Political" relationships refer to the general interactions among individuals in their roles as citizens or officials that are structured and regulated by the state.[43] Such interactions can be delimited in terms of claims, which will be backed up by the coercive power of the state, that people living within the borders of a state can make on others.

In the aftermath of systematic and egregious wrongdoing there are many different political relationships that may need to be rebuilt, including the relationships among individual perpetrators and victims. I restrict my focus to broader, society-wide political reconciliation. Society-wide reconciliation refers to the rebuilding of the relationships among individuals in their general interactions and relationships with ordinary citizens or officials within a particular state. I am thus not primarily concerned with the reconciliation of a particular perpetrator and victim. I focus on society-wide political reconciliation because this is the type of political reconciliation considered critical for the successful consolidation of new democracies and for peace-keeping generally.

---

[42] I owe the title of this section to Linda Radzik.

[43] My use of "citizen" is to be understood broadly, to refer to all permanent residents of a political community who share ongoing political relationships. I use this broad understanding in part because who counts as a citizen is precisely one of the questions at issue in processes of reconciliation.

A central assumption underpinning my analysis is that an adequate analysis of reconciliation must be informed by a careful and accurate understanding of the dynamics of conflict and repression. That is, the patterns of interaction during repressive regimes or civil conflict should provide the subject matter and starting point for a philosophical analysis. A conception of political reconciliation should develop out of an analysis of political relationships in transitional contexts. Anchoring an analysis in the circumstances of conflict and repression ensures that a conception speaks to the actual problems with political relationships in transitional contexts and addresses what political communities have been through during conflict and repression, acknowledging the depth and complexity of the damage done to political relationships.

My understanding of the proper methodology to use when analyzing political reconciliation implies that political reconciliation should not be treated as a question of applied philosophy. In other words, it is a mistake, in my view, to analyze political reconciliation by first articulating an abstract characterization of ideal or just relationships and then applying that characterization to the particular case of political reconciliation. Instead, the moral demands of political reconciliation must be organically related to conflict and repression itself. A conception of political reconciliation should be argued for and understood historically, with reference to the actual general challenges facing political relationships in transitional contexts. Failure to ground an analysis in this way leads precisely to the limitations illustrated and discussed above: an insufficient recognition of the legacy of conflict and repression that theorizing about political reconciliation should confront, reflected in an underestimation of the damage to political relationships during conflict and repression, and a corresponding failure to capture the distinctive and complex ways in which political relationships must be rebuilt. By contrast, a general account of political reconciliation constructed from the bottom up, starting from the general dynamics and characteristics of conflict and repression, is positioned to accurately describe the damage done to political relationships during conflict and repression and the complex ways in which political relationships must be rebuilt.[44]

---

[44] One may wonder whether it is necessary to have a prior notion of good or just political relationships to identify what counts as morally problematic and damaging for political relationships. However, this is mistaken. We need not have a fully worked-out conception of ideal political relationships in order to know that indefinite detention without trial or rape as a method of interrogation constitute morally problematic political relationships between those in power and their victims.

In keeping with the conception of the proper methodology for developing a conception of political reconciliation, in the chapters that follow I draw on three normative frameworks – the rule of law, political trust, and capabilities – that provide useful theoretical resources for diagnosing in an illuminating manner particular ways in which political relationships are damaged during conflict and repression.[45] My selection of normative ideals is based on their relevance and value for my purpose. That is, frameworks are chosen in the service of understanding the moral significance of patterns of interaction during repressive rule and conflict. In addition to helping us understand where relationships have gone wrong, the discussed normative frameworks provide resources for conceptualizing what the goal of processes of political reconciliation should be. They also clarify and codify what the aim of public policies designed to rebuild political relationships should be.

Analyzing political reconciliation in the way I suggest above does not map neatly onto standard understandings of ideal and non-ideal theory, but rather captures dimensions of both.[46] Like ideal theory, in articulating the goal of processes of political reconciliation, a conception specifies important dimensions of just political relationships. However, its emphasis is restricted to the salient dimensions of just political relationships for political reconciliation.

Unlike ideal theory, the primary objective is not to develop an ideal for political relationships for its own sake. Rather, it is to articulate an ideal in the service of conceptualizing why and how political relationships must be rebuilt in the aftermath of conflict and repressive rule. Further, the conception of the goal of processes of political reconciliation is not developed in the context of idealizing assumptions about strict compliance, the absence of massive historical injustice, or the feasibility of realizing the ideal given current historical and economic

---

[45] This normative conception need not have been obtained or been realized in the historical past; however, it provides a framework in terms of which we can understand how relationships have gone wrong. It also provides a normative sense of rebuilding, namely, the rebuilding of a kind of community from which a political society has become, or always has been, alienated.

[46] The definition of ideal and non-ideal theory that I am appealing to follows that articulated by John Rawls in *A Theory of Justice* (Cambridge, MA: Harvard University Press, 1971).

conditions.[47] Instead, it is developed within the context of societies characterized by the systematic flouting of normative regulations, the presence of a recent (and often long-standing) period of massive injustice, and economic and political conditions that challenge the practical feasibility of any normative ideal. The consideration of such circumstances is one way in which theorizing about political reconciliation is non-ideal. The primary question political reconciliation raises is: how should societies respond in the face of the systematic and pervasive failure to realize decent political relationships? The question of political reconciliation is fundamentally a question about how to transition toward the realization of normatively desirable political relationships.

Broad outlines of the developed view

My central thesis in the chapters that follow is that civil conflict and repressive rule systematically undermine the conditions in which political relationships can express reciprocity and respect for moral agency, or reciprocal agency. At its most general level, the goal of processes of political reconciliation is to cultivate political relationships premised on these values. To specify this basic idea and so provide concrete guidance for public policy purposes, I argue that the ideals of the rule of law, political trust, and support of individual capabilities provide us with rich, theoretical resources for understanding what the rebuilding of political relationships specifically involves. The rule of law captures important institutional dimensions of political relationships, specifically how legal institutions structure political interaction and define the expectations citizens and officials have of one another. Political trust reflects the attitudinal component of political interaction and highlights the view that citizens and officials should ideally take of each other. Capabilities refer to the genuine opportunities of individuals to achieve valuable doings and beings, such as being adequately nourished or being respected. What capabilities an individual enjoys are dependent on both what a person has (e.g., resources) and what she can do with what she has (e.g., given the social and material environment). Capabilities focus our attention on how conceptions of group identity and social norms, as well as political and economic institutions,

---

[47] These are two of the assumptions Christine M. Korsgaard considers in her discussion of ideal theory in *Creating the Kingdom of Ends* (Cambridge University Press, 1996), pp. 147–8.

affect political relationships and the genuine opportunities political relationships make (or fail to make) possible.

The rule of law, political trust, and capabilities represent distinct ways in which political relationships can respect moral agency and reciprocity. Thus these ideals help us understand how and why the erosion of the rule of law, political trust, and relational capabilities damage political relationships by undermining respect for moral agency and for reciprocity in political relationships. These ideals in turn suggest that the rebuilding of political relationships in transitional contexts is a complex, multifaceted process involving the cultivation of mutual respect for the rule of law, reasonable political trust and trust-responsiveness, and three central relational as well as basic capabilities. By drawing on these three theoretical frameworks, my analysis draws attention to the complex, multifaceted (official and unofficial) changes that the rebuilding of political relationships entails. Because it conceptualizes how political relationships go wrong along multiple dimensions and demonstrates the underlying practical and theoretical connections among these dimensions, my account overcomes the limitations of current analyses.

To preview the outline of the main argument, consider first the rule of law.[48] Very often the governance of conduct by law, or on the basis of declared rules, breaks down during civil conflict and repressive rule. Citizens' disregard of legal rules may become common. More often, official restraint dictated by the requirements of the rule of law erodes. Actions such as torture that are officially proscribed become part of the practice of law enforcement officials. Alternatively, declared rules are framed in a way that provides maximal flexibility for government officials and minimal practical guidance for citizens; for example, statutes outlawing certain forms of conduct may be phrased so vaguely that they enable officials to appeal to them as a justification for targeting political dissidents.

The result of the erosion or absence of the rule of law is the creation of an environment conducive to injustice and inhospitable to the exercise of agency and respect for reciprocity. When functioning properly, the rule of law ensures a certain kind of transparency of official (and unofficial) action. Citizens and officials can look to legal rules to know what practices and actions are occurring (or not occurring). However, that transparency is diminished when official conduct does not reflect declared rules. The absence of transparency removes an important check on the pursuit of

---

[48] My conception of the rule of law is based on the work of Lon Fuller.

injustice, which is the desire of individuals to maintain their sense of self and of their community as fundamentally good. The rule of law forces us to confront and be held responsible for our actions, and in the process can constrain what we are willing to do.

The erosion of the rule of law frustrates individual agency because it prevents the self-directed action and interaction that law makes possible. When law governs conduct, citizens are treated as responsible agents, judged and responded to by officials on the basis of a standard of conduct that citizens have a real opportunity to follow. It is the decisions and actions of individuals and not the whims of officials that determine the legal treatment they receive. Departures from the principles of the rule of law disrespect this agency; it is the choices and actions of officials, not the decisions of citizens, that determine their legal treatment. Further, the framework of law enables citizens to pursue their goals and plans by allowing individuals to formulate reliable and stable mutual expectations of how others will behave and respond to their actions, and, in turn, base their decisions about how to act so as to achieve their goals on these expectations. By contrast, the erosion of the rule of law creates an environment of uncertainty and destabilizes our expectations.

The framework of law depends on reciprocity, and thus the breakdown of the rule of law reflects an erosion of reciprocity. The expectations that we form of fellow citizens and officials, stemming from law, and that are formed with respect to us constitute the basis of the duties that others have toward us and that we have toward others. However, very often in contexts of repression and civil conflict the official expectation of obedience on the part of citizens is maintained while the corresponding obligations of officials are flouted.

One impact of violations of the rule of law is enhanced distrust. Indeed, transitional contexts are often characterized by pervasive and deep distrust toward, for example, members of certain ethnic groups or government officials. I argue that such distrust is a reflection of the widespread disrespectful, non-reciprocal character of interaction and general moral corruption during conflict and repression. Trust reflects an attitude of optimism about the competence and lack of ill will of fellow citizens and officials, coupled with an expectation of trust-responsiveness.[49] The reasonableness of trust as a default depends on the reasonableness of assuming that others are capable of fulfilling the responsibilities associated with

---

[49] This understanding of trust is based on that first proposed by Karen Jones, "Trust as an Affective Attitude," *Ethics*, 107 (1996), 4–25.

the roles of citizens and officials, are basically decent (and so willing to abide by norms structuring interaction and to refrain from harming others), and care about one's good opinion (and so will be moved to prove reliable when trusted by others so as to maintain the good opinion that being trusted expresses). Because trust is neither reasonable nor present during periods of civil conflict and repressive rule, none of these assumptions is prudent to make. Consequently, the respect that can be shown toward others through presumptions of competence and decency, and the reciprocity that can be expressed by a willingness to view and respond to the expectations of others in ways that we would like them to view and respond to us cannot be realized in political relationships.

The capability framework helps us understand the character of the general moral corruption during conflict and repression by drawing attention to the broader ramifications for political relationships of violence, economic oppression, and certain formulations of group identity that lead to the exclusion or ostracization of individuals from membership in the political community. I trace the ways in which these forms of injustice systematically diminish four important capabilities: being respected by others; participating in the social, economic, and political life of a community; being recognized as a member of a political community; and surviving and escaping poverty. The first three capabilities are fundamentally relational; they implicate doings and beings that are necessarily achieved in relationships. The fourth capability captures a necessary condition for having an opportunity to achieve relational capabilities. The forms of injustice I consider reduce the capabilities of some or all citizens because of their impact on the personal and external resources of individuals, as well as on the general social and institutional structure within which individuals act.

The reduction of capabilities is of concern because capabilities are a form of positive freedom; to diminish capabilities, then, is to diminish the extent to which individuals are free to shape their lives and the terms of their interaction with others. In other words, it reduces the opportunity of individuals to exercise their agency. The diminishment of capabilities is additionally of concern because it constitutes a violation of the demands of justice and undermines relationships of equality within political communities. To be ostracized or not recognized as a member of a political community is, by definition, to be precluded from relating as an equal member of a political community. To be disrespected, humiliated, or degraded signals one's lack of standing within a political community. Exclusion from the economic, political, or social domain indicates that one has an inferior status relative to other members of society. To have no genuine opportunity to achieve basic functionings is in practice to often have no genuine opportunity to participate in the life of one's community or be respected within it.

The goal of processes of reconciliation such as criminal trials and truth commissions is to contribute to the rebuilding of political relationships. The general task of processes of reconciliation, I argue, is to cultivate the rule of law, reasonable default trust, and trust-responsiveness, and the capability to be respected and recognized as a member of one's political community, which includes the capability to participate in the economic, political, and social life of a community and to achieve basic functionings. Processes of reconciliation may contribute to this transformation either directly or indirectly. Such processes directly transform political relationships insofar as they directly increase respect for the rule of law, trust, or capabilities. For example, reconciliation processes may increase the personal or external resources of individuals, or the social and material structure, in ways that enhance their freedom to participate in the social, political, or economic arena or to be respected. Reconciliation processes indirectly repair political relationships by promoting the conditions on which the possibility of successfully cultivating the rule of law, trust, and capabilities depends. Hope, an end to violence, and recognition that wrongdoing occurred in the past are examples of some of these conditions.

Before summarizing the overall plan for the book I want to address two initial objections that may be raised to my analysis: it sets the bar for achieving political reconciliation too high and omits important moral frameworks for understanding how moral relationships are damaged. According to the first objection, the standards for political relations that I claim processes of reconciliation should aim to cultivate are rarely realized even in stable democratic contexts. Within transitional contexts this is even more radically the case: legal systems are characteristically corrupt and ill-functioning, distrust is deep and pervasive, and basic capabilities are often not enjoyed. My discussion of the rule of law, reasonable trust, and robust relational capabilities may seem vulnerable to precisely the objection I raised against available conceptions, namely, that it has little relevance for transitional contexts where the achievement of these ideals remains a remote practical possibility. By articulating a robust ideal of political reconciliation, I overlook the basic repair that should be the central focus of processes of reconciliation and undermine the ability of my analysis to respond effectively to the practical needs that underwrite the need for a theory of political reconciliation.

In response, I want to defend the relevance and importance of a robust conception of political reconciliation. Far from being irrelevant, the robust conception of political reconciliation I develop provides ongoing, concrete guidance for dealing with the pressing moral and policy questions surrounding political reconciliation in transitional contexts. Each ideal provides important theoretical resources for understanding the social and political conditions that must be in place for relationships premised on respect for moral agency and reciprocity to become possible. The rule of law, for example, depends on a certain faith in law and decency on the part of legal officials. Thus, even when the achievement of an ideal may be remote, such as the establishment of a functioning system of law, the ideal of the rule of law provides guidance on the social conditions that need to be fostered so that the ideal becomes more practically feasible in the future. Equally significant, one virtue of the three normative ideals I consider is that each can be realized to varying degrees. There are degrees of respect for the rule of law, the reasonableness and robustness of trust, and the enjoyment of relational capabilities about which we may speak. Given this, it is natural to talk about the progression (or lack of progress) of societies in realizing these ideals. Though transitional societies may lack anything close to a robust legal system, we can still use the framework of the rule of law to assess a society's progress in restoring law.

Developing a robust conception of political reconciliation is important for two reasons. First, such a conception focuses attention on the long-term work required in transitional contexts if more decent political relationships are to be achieved and the long-term consolidation of democracy is to be successful. Thus a robust conception offers a continual reminder that the work of promoting and advancing political reconciliation is not over once minimal conditions for more peaceful coexistence have been achieved. It provides a framework whereby we can label policies and actions for what they are, and not delude ourselves into thinking that minimal efforts to advance political reconciliation, pursued initially in transitional contexts out of expediency, are sufficient. Rather, it highlights what is at stake in the achievement or failure to achieve certain kinds of institutional reform.

Furthermore, the significance of the pursuit of political reconciliation, as well as the relationship between political reconciliation and democratization, also become clearer with a more robust conception. Political reconciliation, as I understand it, reflects many of the aspects of democratic political relationships; political reconciliation is necessary for democratization because such reconciliation is partly constitutive of such democratization. The rebuilding of political relationships through processes of reconciliation cultivates forms of interaction premised on the equal respect for individuals and their agency; a commitment to the reciprocal sharing of the benefits and burdens of social cooperation; and an institutional structure that is based on the rule of law and on political, economic, and social institutions in which all individuals have a genuine opportunity to participate.

The robustness of my account may lead some to conclude that I am actually offering a full-blown theory of just or decent political relationships, as realized in a good or decent society. However, this would be inaccurate. Though robust, the conception of reconciliation I articulate and defend is not intended to constitute a complete ideal of a just or decent political relationship and my analysis is not committed to the claim that it does. Rather, the ideals I discuss in the chapters that follow are intended to capture the dimensions of just or decent relationships that are especially salient for processes of political reconciliation to seek to cultivate. My conception of rebuilt political relationships may thus constitute a component of any fully worked out comprehensive ideal, and also specify some of the necessary conditions for the realization of such an ideal.

I have argued that the ideals I have selected capture salient features of relationships for processes of reconciliation to cultivate in transitional contexts. It is precisely this claim that the second objection challenges. According to this objection, my analysis omits normative frameworks that are necessary for describing central sources of damage to political relationships in transitional contexts. In particular, my account does not consider the importance of recognition, especially recognition of social identities, and does not discuss social justice.[50] An appeal to the frameworks of recognition and of social justice seems intuitively compelling, given the prevalence of entrenched ethno-national conflicts around the globe and the deep patterns of social injustice that often characterize societies in conflict and under repressive rule.

In response to this objection, I first want to briefly explain why I did not use the frameworks of recognition and social justice. I then discuss in greater detail the basis on which normative frameworks for conceptualizing political reconciliation should be selected, since the objection draws attention to the grounds for demonstrating that the three normative frameworks I discuss are sufficient for understanding how political relationships are damaged during conflict and repression.

---

[50] I am grateful to an anonymous reader from Cambridge University Press for pressing this point.

Turning first to the idea of recognition, it is certainly important to acknowledge the powerful impact that the recognition or denial of social identities, especially ethnic or national identities, can have on the well-being of individuals. As many theorists have pointed out, social identities play a significant role in shaping the horizon of practical possibilities for individuals, provide a framework for the meaning of activities and goals, and affect the degree to which individuals view themselves or are seen by others as equal or full members of a political community.[51] For these reasons an appeal to the idea of recognition seems promising in the context of thinking about political reconciliation.

Despite its appeal, however, there are two main reasons why I did not rely on the framework of recognition. First, social identities are not always a salient feature of civil conflict or repressive rule. That is, the grounds for conflict and the individuals who benefit from or are targeted by repressive regimes are not always demarcated on the basis of a given ethnic, racial, religious, or linguistic identity. Thus an appeal to recognition might misleadingly suggest that questions of identity are always at the root of conflict or motivate repression. Second, the framework of recognition does not provide the most informative resources for understanding how the construction of identities damages relationships during conflict and repression, and the subsequent ways that political relationships must be rebuilt through processes of reconciliation. Societal exclusion or discrimination on the basis of a social identity is of fundamental concern because of how such exclusion or discrimination restricts what individuals are free to do or become in their relations with others. That is, the fundamental normative concern in the context of reconciliation is not with misrecognition or the absence of recognition itself; rather, it is with the ramifications of such exclusion or misrecognition. Recognition is of importance because of the way that the recognition of a given identity, or the absence of recognition, affects the relational freedom of individuals. The absence of recognition is significant because of the way it prevents individuals from being able to be seen as members of the political community and participate in the economic and social life of a community. Such relational freedom is precisely what is focused on by the capability framework. Concentrating on recognition instead of the source

---

[51] On this point see Yael Tamir, *Liberal Nationalism* (Princeton University Press, 1993); Will Kymlicka (ed.), *The Rights of Minority Cultures* (Oxford University Press, 1995); Will Kymlicka, *Multicultural Citizenship* (Oxford University Press 1995); Amy Gutmann (ed.), *Multiculturalism* (Princeton University Press, 1994).

of fundamental normative concern, namely relational freedom, may prevent us from seeing other ways in which relational freedom can be restricted during conflict and repression. By contrast, the capability framework offers resources for understanding *when* the construction of social identities is of normative concern. As I demonstrate in Chapter 3, the framework of capability can account for the problems associated with the absence of appropriate recognition of ethnic identities, while not suggesting that identity is always an issue in conflict and drawing attention to other, non-identity-based ways in which relational freedom can be restricted.

There are similar limitations with appealing to the normative framework of social justice. In contemporary philosophical discussions, social justice is often equated with distributive justice.[52] Given this association, appealing to a framework of justice suggests the need to consider how goods are distributed within a given community. What the information from social justice does not tell us, however, is how a given distribution of goods or a specific kind of distributional inequality damages political relationships. A concern with distribution for its own sake draws attention away from what is of primary normative concern in the context of political reconciliation, namely the character of political relations, not the pattern of a given distribution of goods. In practice, the way and degree to which distributional inequality damages political relationships may vary. For example, distributional inequality may impact the freedom of individuals to participate in the political life of their community if having certain goods is taken to be a prerequisite for such participation. However, this may not always be the case. On the other hand, the capability framework concentrates on what is of fundamental normative concern when questions of social justice are raised. It provides a way of conceptualizing dimensions of justice that are fundamentally relational in nature. Justice is conceptualized not in terms of a given distribution of goods, but in terms of the genuine opportunity that individuals have to achieve important relational doings and beings.

To this point, I have responded to the concern about the exclusion of the normative frameworks of recognition and social justice by suggesting that the capability framework can account for the normative concerns

[52] See, for example, Rawls, *A Theory of Justice*; Richard Arneson, "Liberalism, Distributive Subjectivism, and Equal Opportunity for Welfare," *Philosophy and Public Affairs*, 19 (1990), 158–94; John E. Roemer, *Theories of Distributive Justice* (Cambridge, MA: Harvard University Press, 1996); G. A. Cohen, "Where the Action Is: On the Site of Distributive Justice," *Philosophy and Public Affairs*, 26 (1997), 3–30.

underpinning an appeal to the frameworks of recognition and social justice. The full demonstration of my claims will be borne out in the analysis presented in Chapter 3. However, I also want to highlight more general reasons for conceptualizing political reconciliation on the basis of the frameworks of the rule of law, trust, and capability, which suggest additional desiderata of an adequate conception of political reconciliation. One virtue of the analysis I develop is that it provides a unified picture of the ways in which political relationships are damaged during civil conflict and repression, as well as of the corresponding aspects of political relationships to be rebuilt. The theory developed in the following chapters is not simply a collection of disparate moral concerns that are combined in an ad hoc manner whereby they have "no coherent rationale for the principles they have combined – apart from the fact that they have been explicitly manufactured to yield results more attuned to our settled moral convictions."[53] Rather, my analysis of political reconciliation is unified in two important senses. First, the three frameworks I select are interrelated and mutually reinforcing in practice. They thus enrich our understanding of the relationship among diverse kinds of damage and the broader ramifications or implications of each kind of damage considered in isolation. For example, the institutional damage that is constitutive of the breakdown of the rule of law has consequences for the attitudes of citizens and, importantly, for the reasonableness of trust. I consider the connections in detail in Chapter 4. The second sense in which my analysis of political reconciliation is unified is moral in nature; all the frameworks I consider are premised on a core moral value and concern: reciprocal agency. Each framework represents a different way in which reciprocal agency can be undermined during conflict and repression. Thus, while capturing distinct dimensions of concern, the frameworks offer a unified picture of what the concern with conflict and repression should be and of the goal of processes of political reconciliation.

Plan of the book

In Part I, I analyze the character and extent of the damage done to political relationships during repressive rule and civil conflict. Each chapter considers one of three distinct normative frameworks: the rule of law, political trust, and capabilities. The question that guides my discussion in

---

[53] This is taken from a discussion of mixed theories of punishment. John Tasioulas, "Punishment and Repentance," *Philosophy*, 81 (2006), 279–322.

Part II is: how should political relationships be rebuilt? My interest in this part is normative and conceptual. The overall objective is to provide the conceptual tools for explaining the success or failure of processes like amnesty, truth commissions, and criminal trials in promoting reconciliation.[54] To achieve this objective, I develop criteria that clarify how we should conceptualize what should count as success in public policy, based on the analysis from Part I. Part II thus addresses the preconditions for social scientific empirical research about reconciliation, and is intended to serve as a guideline for public policy formulation. The developed criteria offer more robust and systematic guidelines than other philosophical analyses to date because they do not focus on justifying one particular kind of public policy, such as a truth commission, while failing to make explicit the general principles guiding the justification of truth commissions that could direct the formulation, justification, and critique of alternative policies.[55] The guidelines I develop also take seriously the distinct justificatory questions raised by the pursuit of reconciliation by the state. In particular, I articulate constraints on the ways that it is permissible for governments to pursue the repair and transformation of political relationships. As a way of demonstrating the practical usefulness and relevance in answering the complex policy questions that the pursuit of political reconciliation raises, I apply the criteria for success to the particular processes of truth commissions and international criminal trials. In the conclusion I return to the central debates about political reconciliation that a theory of political reconciliation should provide resources for answering, and show the answer my analysis would provide to these questions.

---

[54] The application of these criteria to particular processes of reconciliation depends on detailed knowledge of the particular context in question. While numerous societies emerging from periods of conflict or repressive rule face the challenge of reconciliation, the particular character of this challenge differs, for example, the damage done to political relationships by repressive regimes or during civil conflict varies. Sometimes certain groups of citizens are targeted and treated unfairly; in other cases all citizens are treated badly. The particular history and character of relations in specific transitional contexts will determine the specific needs that a process of reconciliation must address. Thus, in making the argument in Part II, I do not propose to determine the actual effectiveness of historical or potential effectiveness of proposed processes of reconciliation in specific contexts.

[55] Rotberg and Thompson, *Truth v. Justice*; Philpott, *Politics of Past Evil*; Villa-Vicencio and Verwoerd, *Looking Back, Reaching Forward.*

PART I

Conceptual Frameworks

CHAPTER I

The rule of law

INTRODUCTION

A philosophical analysis of political reconciliation should diagnose how relations are damaged during civil conflict and repressive rule, and should specify how political relationships should be rebuilt. My discussion in this chapter sheds light on some of the institutional dimensions of political reconciliation. I argue that one important source of damage to political relationships stems from the absence or erosion of the rule of law. A primary task of processes of political reconciliation, I claim, is to cultivate mutual respect for the rule of law.

The rule of law specifies a set of requirements that lawmakers must respect if they are to govern legally. As such, the rule of law restricts the illegal or extralegal use of power. When a society rules by law there are clear rules articulating the behavior appropriate for citizens and officials. The rule of law structures political relationships insofar as legal rules determine their particular contours. When the requirements of the rule of law are respected, the political relationships structured by the legal system constitutively express the moral values of reciprocity and respect for moral agency. The rule of law is instrumentally valuable, I argue, because in practice it limits the kinds of injustice that governments could pursue. Thus the erosion of the rule of law is morally concerning and damaging to political relations, insofar as it entails an erosion of important conditions for relationships to express reciprocity and respect for agency, and creates an environment conducive to injustice.

The first section of this chapter outlines Lon Fuller's conception of the rule of law and his explanation of its moral value. The second section discusses how a Fullerian analysis draws attention to the detrimental

I am grateful to Macalester Bell, Yaacov Ben-Shemesh, Lorraine Besser-Jones, Thomas Hill, Jr., Katya Hosking, Nancy Lawrence, Larry May, Kathleen Murphy, Ram Neta, Gerald J. Postema, Matthew Noah Smith, and Susanne Sreedhar for their very helpful comments on earlier drafts of this chapter.

impact that state-sanctioned atrocities can have on the institutional functioning of the legal system, and thus their damaging impact on the relationships between officials and citizens that are structured by that institution. The third section considers the objection that my analysis exaggerates the moral value of political relationships structured by law. Against my assertion that the rule of law has significant non-instrumental value, this objection argues that the rule of law is a negative virtue. The rule of law merely prevents certain affronts to individual agency that law itself makes possible and is compatible with the pursuit of gross injustice. This suggests that respect for the rule of law is not always damaging to political relationships; indeed, political relationships structured by law can become a source of moral concern when law is used to pursue immoral ends and respect for law facilitates the efficient achievement of such ends. The fourth and final section considers a second objection to my analysis. This objection grants that the rule of law has non-instrumental moral value, and therefore supports the claim that there is something non-instrumentally valuable about structuring political relationships by law. However, it claims that my account of the requirements of the rule of law is incomplete; the moral values of reciprocity and respect for agency imply substantive requirements of the rule of law. According to the objection, since my analysis of the rule of law is silent on its substantive dimensions, my account of how the rule of law is eroded during civil conflict and repressive rule and of what must change if citizens and officials are to respect the rule of law is fundamentally incomplete.

FULLER ON THE RULE OF LAW

It is generally agreed that Lon Fuller's eight principles of legality capture the essence of the rule of law. Some argue that Fuller's criteria for the rule of law are incomplete, but few dispute the basic criteria he identifies. Therefore, to develop a working understanding of the rule of law, his account is a natural starting point. In *The Morality of Law,* he identifies eight requirements of the rule of law.[1] Laws must be *general (#1),*

---

[1] Lon Fuller, *Morality of Law,* rev. ed. (New Haven, CT: Yale University Press, 1969), p. 39. Fuller has an extended discussion of each criterion on pp. 46–90. My summary of Fuller is based on *Morality of Law* as well as on Jeremy Waldron, "Why Law – Efficacy, Freedom or Fidelity?" *Law and Philosophy,* 13 (1994), 259–84; David Luban, "Natural Law as Professional Ethics: A Reading of Fuller," *Social Philosophy and Policy,* 18(1) (2001), 176–205; and Gerald J. Postema, "Implicit Law," *Law and Philosophy,* 13 (1994), 361–87.

specifying *rules* prohibiting or permitting behavior of certain kinds.[2] Laws must also be widely *promulgated (#2)*, or publicly accessible. Publicity of laws ensures citizens know what the law requires. Laws should be *prospective (#3)*, specifying how individuals ought to behave in the future rather than prohibiting behavior that occurred in the past. Laws must be *clear (#4)*. Citizens should be able to identify what the laws prohibit, permit, or require. Laws must be *non-contradictory (#5)*. One law cannot prohibit what another law permits. Laws must *not ask the impossible (#6)*. Nor should laws change frequently; the demands laws make on citizens should remain relatively *constant (#7)*. Finally, there should be *congruence between what the written statute declares and how officials enforce those statutes (#8)*. So, for example, congruence requires legislatures to pass only laws that will be enforced, and requires officials to enforce no more than is required by the laws. Judges should not interpret statutes based on their personal preferences and police should only arrest individuals they believe to have acted illegally.

The eight criteria of generality, publicity, non-retroactivity, clarity, non-contradiction, non-impossibility, constancy, and congruity specify necessary conditions for the activities of lawmakers to count as *lawmaking*. According to Fuller, law is "the enterprise of subjecting human conduct to the governance of rules."[3] When lawmakers respect the eight principles of the rule of law, their laws can influence the practical reasoning of citizens. Citizens can take legal requirements and prohibitions into consideration when deliberating about how to act. They can predict how judges will interpret and apply rules, enabling them to form reliable expectations of the treatment different actions are likely to provoke. When the rule of law is realized, their expectations of congruence will not be disappointed. Taken together with the reasonable expectation that fellow citizens will also obey the law, these expectations justify the belief that the law gives citizens reasons to act or refrain from acting in certain ways.

So long as they avoid complete failure with respect to any one principle, lawmakers can meet the requirements of the rule of law to varying degrees and still succeed in making law. At some point, however, widespread violations of the principles of the rule of law diminish the legal

---

[2] Fuller notes that this generality requirement is consistent with general injunctions on behavior being issued to specific individuals or groups. To meet the generality requirement, laws need not apply to the entire population.

[3] Fuller, *Morality of Law*, p. 106.

character of a system of rules because the laws can no longer figure in the practical reasoning of citizens. Citizens cannot, for example, obey secret rules; if they do not know what the law requires when they deliberate about how to act, they cannot take that requirement into account.

When lawmakers fall far short of the ideal of the rule of law, Fuller argues, citizens start to feel resentment. They rely on knowing how the government expects them to behave in advance. Citizens feel resentment if the expectations are not clear, are contradictory, or demand the impossible. Their actions will be judged according to a standard they had no fair opportunity to meet.[4] Citizens also feel resentment if they cannot form reliable expectations due to frequent divergence between written law and its enforcement. Failures of congruence undermine the confidence with which citizens can look to the written law to determine what officials expect of them. Resentment builds when officials expect citizens to fulfill certain duties, like obedience to law, despite the failure of government officials to fulfill their reciprocal duties.

This resentment is reasonable. Underlying the resentment citizens feel about violations of the rule of law is, according to Fuller, a sense of fairness or reciprocity. For him, the duties involved in social relationships rest on the reciprocal nature of those relationships. In a particular social relationship, each individual forms expectations about how others they are involved in a relationship with will act. These expectations form the basis for the duties that individuals have toward one another. Reciprocity plays a key role in Fuller's account of duty; according to him, the existence of duties depends partly on the behavior of others. In particular, it is fair to expect me to act in certain ways only if similar expectations hold with respect to those judging my behavior. In the legal context, citizens have a duty to follow legal rules provided those rules outline a standard that citizens are knowledgeable of, capable of following, and that is actually used to judge their conduct. Thus, when they respect the rule of law, officials restrain themselves in certain ways. They do not, for example, pursue the goals of government in the most efficient way if efficiency conflicts with the requirements of the rule of law. Citizens similarly restrain themselves, refraining from disobeying directives with which they disagree.

In Fuller's view, then, the rule of law provides some normative grounds for thinking that citizens have a moral obligation to obey the law. However, this obligation is conditional. It is partly conditional upon

---

[4] See Fuller's discussion of Rex: ibid., pp. 33–8.

the actions of government officials. When a government routinely violates the rule of law, passing retrospective legislation or basing their legal rulings on personal whims, then citizens no longer have a duty to obey the dictates of a government.[5] As Fuller states, "Certainly there can be no rational ground for asserting that a man can have a moral obligation to obey a legal rule that does not exist, or is kept secret from him, or that came into existence only after he had acted."[6] Insofar as officials pass clear, prospective, non-contradictory laws and enforce those laws consistently and in accordance with the declared law, citizens have a reason to obey the law, even when the government pursues a particular policy with which individual citizens disagree. Fuller's account helps to explain why it is rational for citizens to participate in the system of cooperation that the legal system establishes. His account also helps us understand the way in which the rule of law limits the arbitrary exercise of power, by setting restrictions on the kind of rules officials can pass as well as on the actions officials legitimately can take.

APPLICATIONS TO ARGENTINA

We can use the theoretical framework of the rule of law to shed new light on *why* some behaviors, exhibited in repressive regimes and universally condemned, are in fact morally problematic.[7] Consider Argentina from 1976 to 1983. During the initial stages of military rule, government officials unofficially conducted an average of thirty kidnappings a day.[8] Over the seven years of military rule, 30,000 individuals disappeared. Disappeared citizens were first abducted by agents of the state or those acting at the request of the state, and were then often tortured and killed. When describing what happened to the *desaparecidos,* or disappeared, Marguerite Feitlowitz writes, "suspected 'subversives' were kidnapped from the streets, tortured in secret concentration camps, and 'disappeared'. Victims died during torture, were machine-gunned at the edge of enormous pits, or were thrown, drugged, from airplanes into the sea."[9]

---

[5] Ibid., p. 40.   [6] Ibid., p. 39.

[7] My claim is not that the rule of law can provide a useful analysis of every problematic behavior characteristic of repressive regimes or conflict-ridden societies. It focuses specifically on violations of the rule of law that affect the relationship between officials and citizens. There are other violations by officials that are captured more accurately by a different moral framework.

[8] Marguerite Feitlowitz, *A Lexicon of Terror: Argentina and the Legacies of Torture* (Oxford University Press, 1998), p. 25. Feitlowitz cites an anonymous judicial source.

[9] Ibid., p. ix.

Individuals "disappear" in the sense that the state refuses to acknowledge that the abduction occurred or provide information on the abductees' whereabouts. In response to allegations of disappearings, governments typically deny a crime has occurred at all, let alone a crime for which they are responsible. In Argentina, some military leaders consistently denied responsibility for the disappearances or the existence of concentration camps. Consider President Jorge Rafael Videla, an army general and leader of the first junta. In 1977, in response to a question by a British journalist, he said, "I emphatically deny that there are concentration camps in Argentina, or military establishments in which people are held longer than is absolutely necessary in this ... fight against subversion ... I live with my family in a military zone and am certain that I don't live in a concentration camp." In 1978 he stated, "In Argentina, political prisoners don't exist. No one is persecuted or constrained on account of his political ideas."[10]

Official disappearing of citizens is widely and correctly condemned. Disappearing individuals involved egregious violations of individual rights. When explaining the wrongness of disappearing in terms of its impact on the direct victim, or the disappeared, this is the most important thing to focus on.[11] However, what the Fullerian analysis provides is an additional insight into the distinctive grounds for moral condemnation of illegal disappearances, drawing our attention to the impact that the actions of officials can have upon the institutional functioning of the legal system, and so to their impact on the relationships between officials and citizens that are structured by law.

Murders pursued in the course of a systematic campaign of state-sanctioned terrorism, as opposed to an ordinary criminal murder, have a differential impact on political relationships, despite the fact that both involve the violation of the murdered individual's rights. When thinking about the damage caused by an ordinary murder, our analysis is normally

---

[10] Ibid., p. 28. Sadly, the practice of disappearing, as well as the use of death squads, is not unique to Argentina. Uruguay, El Salvador, Guatemala, Sri Lanka, South Africa, Ethiopia, and Cambodia are just some of the countries that have employed the disappearance of citizens or operated death squads during periods of civil conflict or repressive rule. Death squads kill individuals at the request of the state, which in turn denies responsibility. However, the location of the body does not remain unknown but is normally "deliberately left where it can be found." Responsibility for such deaths is frequently laid at the door of individuals not associated with, or in conflict with, a regime. See Naomi Roht-Arriaza, "State Responsibility to Investigate and Prosecute Grave Human Rights Violations in International Law," *California Law Review*, 78 (1990), 451–513, at 451–5.

[11] In Chapter 3 I also consider the impact of such rights violations in more detail when I discuss the role that violence plays in undermining central relational and basic capabilities.

restricted to the impact on those immediately affected, such as the victim and his or her family. The effect of such murders on larger communities is usually limited, especially when government officials respond promptly and effectively to such violations, seeking, for example, to apprehend and prosecute those responsible.

However, the impact of a political murder that is extralegal and part of a systematic campaign of terror on political relationships is significantly different. Such murders should not be viewed in isolation, but rather as part of a larger campaign to undermine the stability of the expectations of citizens and, in the process, to undermine the agency of individuals. Unlike ordinary murders, disappearing individuals in Argentina played a pivotal role in undermining the degree to which law structured and defined the contours of political relationships. In both substance and impact, disappearing citizens is incompatible with the overall purpose of law. First, it constitutes a rejection of the implicit commitment of a government that rules by law to hold citizens to the standards expressed by declared rules. Governments "render meaningless legal discourse" when they deny any crime occurred or deny responsibility for crimes that are discovered. Government-sponsored "disappearing" of political dissidents in Argentina violated the congruence requirement of the rule of law. Committed on paper to democratic principles and ideals, Argentine written law nowhere sanctioned the kidnapping of civilians deemed "subversive" by plainclothes police officers. Nor did it sanction the use of torture. Disappearing is "clearly illegal under international law, as well as under the domestic law of every country prohibiting murder and kidnapping."[12] The lengths to which legal officials went to deny responsibility for disappearances and to label abuse of individuals in detention as "regrettable excesses" rather than as torture underline this fact. Thus, the actual activity of law enforcement officials was radically at odds with the picture and description of official behavior sanctioned by the written laws and offered by officials themselves. A government that illegally disappears citizens creates a climate of instability and fear in which citizens cannot turn to declared rules or rely on their interpretation of them to develop stable expectations about what official treatment or response to their actions is likely to be. As Naomi Roht-Arriaza emphasizes, the function of disappearing is to frighten citizens into impotence by terrorizing "broad sections of the population, who live with the uncertainty of not knowing whether their relatives, neighbors, or co-workers

---

[12] Roht-Arriaza, "State Responsibility," 456.

are dead or alive ... The terror and uncertainty create a chilling effect on political activity in general."[13]

By systematically flouting the requirements of the rule of law, Argentine officials failed in their duty to fulfill the expectations of citizens that they would govern by law. However, despite their own disregard for the rule of law, Argentine military leaders emphasized the need for obedience on the part of citizens to eradicate the subversive and corrupting elements of society.[14] Yet officials, through their actions, undermined part of the basis upon which any moral duty of obedience depends. Official "disappearing" of citizens violates the reciprocity at the heart of the relationship among government officials and citizens structured by law. Disappearing individuals enables a government to avoid responsibility for their actions and frustrates the ability of citizens to determine the justifiability of government actions. The absence of due process for those disappeared – indeed, *any* legal process – undermines conditions crucial for realizing congruence, and constitutes a refusal by government officials to be constrained in their actions by what the law permits or prohibits.

It is unsurprising that citizens respond with anger, resentment, and distrust to extralegal disappearances. Officials responsible for disappearings treat those they kidnap, torture, and kill in secret with utter contempt. Furthermore, extralegal kidnapping, torture, and murder erode the trust of citizens and alienate them from the judicial system and law enforcement officials, undermining their faith in law. It is no longer reasonable to trust politicians who lie or security officials who kidnap and torture citizens instead of protecting them from harm. Citizens who learn about such discrepancies between written law and official action have little reason to believe that other written or publicly espoused policies reflect the policies actually enforced by state agents. What we learn from Fuller is that this distrust is in part a product of the absence of reciprocity in the most fundamental political relationships between citizens and lawmakers.

The Fullerian rule of law framework thus provides a new perspective on why certain immoral behaviors are damaging, not only to the individuals concerned but to the fabric of trust and reciprocity that underlies political relationships structured by law. In the process of applying this framework, we acquire a greater appreciation for why political relationships structured by law are of value.

---

[13] Ibid., 451–5.   [14] Feitlowitz, *Lexicon of Terror*, pp. 22–3.

AGAINST THE SIGNIFICANCE OF THE NON-INSTRUMENTAL VALUE OF THE RULE OF LAW

In the previous section I showed how interpreting certain behaviors exhibited in Argentina under the junta as violations of the rule of law reveals a dimension of their damage not often addressed. As such, violations of the rule of law are morally problematic, I argued, because they undermine the reciprocity at the foundation of the moral duties of citizens and officials toward each other. This is a moral wrong distinct from the wrong undeniably done in violating an individual's rights. Mutual respect for the rule of law is one significant aspect of the relationships among citizens and officials that processes of political reconciliation should aim to cultivate, in part because it instantiates the moral value of reciprocity in the relationships among citizens and officials.

In this section I consider one objection to my analysis thus far. A proponent of this objection, while accepting Fuller's core principles of the rule of law, would reject the Fullerian analysis of its moral value provided above. According to the objection, respect for the rule of law is only a dependent value. Respect for the rule of law prevents certain affronts to human freedom and dignity. However, the moral import of the rule of law's respect for human freedom and dignity depends on the substantive ends that law is used to pursue. When law is used to pursue morally valuable ends, then political relationships structured around respect for the rule of law are morally valuable, both because they respect human dignity and freedom, and because they facilitate the efficient achievement of these ends. When the system's aims are immoral, respect for the rule of law has some minimal significance because certain affronts to human freedom and dignity are avoided. However, respect for the rule of law may also be a source of moral concern insofar as such respect facilitates the efficient pursuit of immoral ends. Thus the degree to which the erosion of the rule of law damages political relationships in transitional contexts depends on the moral quality of the ends being pursued by law.

I use the theory of the rule of law offered by Joseph Raz to develop this objection. The essential feature of law, in Raz's view, is that it claims to offer authoritative reasons for action. In other words, we have reason to obey laws simply *because* they are laws. For obedience to be possible, the law must be capable of guiding behavior. For obedience and not mere conformity to occur, law must be able to figure in the practical reasoning of citizens. Thus the basic intuition around which Raz develops his account of the rule of law is, as for Fuller, that laws must be such that they can figure in the practical reasoning of citizens.[15] Raz's principles of the rule of law fall into two categories. The first category of principles specifies what character rules must have in order to be law-like rules.[16] For example, laws should be clear, stable, public, and prospective.[17] The second category of principles is required to ensure that the machinery of law enforcement itself does not deprive law of its ability to guide behavior. Thus, for example, judicial decisions must accord with and be based on the law. As Raz states, "[I]t is obvious that it is futile to guide one's action on the basis of the law if when the matter comes to adjudication the courts will not apply the law and will act for some other reasons . . . people will only be able to be guided by their guesses as to what the courts are likely to do – but these guesses will not be based on the law but on other considerations."[18]

In addition, Raz sets limits on the powers of other law-enforcing agents.[19] Police should not be allowed to ignore the activities of certain kinds of criminals, nor should prosecutors select which individuals to prosecute on the basis of factors not mentioned in the law. Government officials in general should exercise their coercive power only through the channels specified by law.

For Raz, the rule of law is the "specific excellence of the law." Raz draws an analogy between the property of sharpness in knives and the realization of the rule of law in a legal system. Sharpness is the property that enables a knife to perform its function well. When knives are very sharp, they cut well. Absent a certain minimum level of sharpness, an object that looks like a knife is not, strictly speaking, a knife because it cannot perform the function of a knife. Analogously, the rule of law enables the law to actually guide the behavior of individuals. The principles of the rule of law reflect principles of efficacy. Absent a certain minimum level of the rule of law, a system of rules may superficially resemble a legal system but will be unable to guide the behavior of individuals. Thus Raz agrees with Fuller that where lawmakers completely violate one principle of the rule of law, what results is not law. He also agrees that, beyond this, realizing the rule of law is a matter of degree.

Raz argues that there are two virtues realized through respect for the rule of law. The first is respect for individual freedom, or an individual's

---

[15] Joseph Raz, *Authority of Law* (Oxford: Clarendon Press, 1979), p. 213.

[16] Raz notes that the list offered in his chapter "Rule of Law and Its Virtue" is not exhaustive. Depending on the particular circumstances of a society, different additional principles may be necessary in order to produce behavior capable of guiding citizens.

[17] Raz, *Authority of Law*, pp. 214–15.   [18] Ibid., p. 217.   [19] Ibid., p. 218.

"effective ability to choose between as many options as possible."[20] The rule of law facilitates freedom by enhancing the predictability of an individual's environment. The second is respect for human dignity, which entails treating individuals as autonomous agents who have "a right to control their future."[21] Violations of the rule of law are an affront to human dignity insofar as they enhance the uncertainty of an individual's environment or violate the expectations of citizens based on law. Respect for the rule of law is a necessary condition for law to respect human dignity.

Although Raz recognizes these virtues of the rule of law, his enthusiasm for the rule of law is qualified. In his view, neither virtue establishes that there is moral value realized in every legal system, in part because the virtues of the rule of law are negative virtues. That is, respect for the rule of law does not achieve some positive moral good, but merely successfully avoids certain evils that law itself makes possible.[22] The rule of law "is merely designed to minimize the harm to freedom and dignity which the law may cause."[23] Specifically, the rule of law prevents the evil of the exercise of arbitrary power, achieved by violating the requirements of the rule of law, that erodes the predictability and ability to control one's future that the rule of law facilitates.

The moral value of respect for the rule of law is qualified in another sense. Although respect for the rule of law achieves the negative virtues of respect for human freedom and dignity, the significance and extent of the respect for these values will depend importantly on many factors, including the content of laws. The rule of law does not restrict the ends that a legal system can serve. In Raz's view, respecting the rule of law is compatible with the pursuit of iniquity and all kinds of terrible behavior. "Racial, religious, and all manner of discrimination are not only compatible but often institutionalized by general rules."[24] Similarly, there is no particular affinity between respect for the rule of law and types of political regimes. We can make sense of non-democratic societies, like Nazi Germany, realizing the rule of law. Bad regimes can respect the rule of law and good regimes can violate it. As Raz writes:

A non-democratic legal system, based on the denial of human rights, on extensive poverty, on racial segregation, sexual inequalities, and religious persecution may, in principle, conform to the requirements of the rule of law better than any of the legal systems of the more enlightened Western democracies. This does not mean

---

[20] Ibid., p. 220. [21] Ibid., p. 221. [22] Ibid., p. 224. [23] Ibid., p. 229. [24] Ibid., p. 216.

that it will be better than those Western democracies. It will be an immeasurably worse legal system, but it will excel in one respect: in its conformity to the rule of law.[25]

The law is ultimately an instrument, which can be used by all kinds of governments and to achieve a diverse range of ends. In Raz's words:

The law to be law must be capable of guiding behaviour, however inefficiently. Like other instruments, the law has a specific virtue which is morally neutral in being neutral as to the end to which the instrument is put. It is the virtue of efficiency; the virtue of the instrument as an instrument. For the law this virtue is the rule of law. Thus the rule of law is an inherent virtue of the law, but not a moral virtue as such.[26]

Thus, in the context of the legal pursuit of grossly unjust ends, the respect for human dignity and freedom achieved by respect for the rule of law is quite minimal. Indeed, *departures* from the rule of law are precisely what may be required if officials are to maximally respect the dignity of citizens, especially in cases where officials are asked to enforce substantively unjust laws. For instance, police officials would surely have accorded the dignity of black South Africans more respect by violating the congruence require-ment of the rule of law than by abiding by it. Nor do departures from the rule of law in these cases undermine or affront an individual's dignity as a responsible agent.

Since Raz and Fuller agree on the basic criteria for the rule of law, Raz would agree that the examples from Argentina outlined earlier constitute violations of the rule of law. Where there is official denial of illegal practices for which the state is clearly responsible, a discrepancy between the established laws and their enforcement develops. In Raz's view, such violations were an affront to individual freedom and dignity. However, the significance of the violation to individual freedom and dignity depends on whether laws substantively respect individual freedom and dignity as well. In Argentina, the significance of this affront is diminished by the immoral aims that law was being used to achieve. More generally,

[25] Ibid., p. 211. In this chapter, democracy or a democratic legal system will refer to a legal system structured to respect the equal moral and political status of all citizens. References to the pursuit of unjust ends will refer to the pursuit of ends that deny the equal moral and political status of a portion of the citizenry through, for example, the denial of basic human rights. This is consistent with the view of democracy Raz articulates. As the quotation suggests, the criteria for a legal system to be democratic involve more than simply how the legal system structures elections. The characteristics of a non-democratic legal system partly include violations of the rights of individuals.

[26] Ibid., p. 226.

in contexts of repressive rule and civil conflict where arguably many of the aims pursued by governments are immoral, the erosion of the rule of law may be morally valuable insofar as it impedes the efficiency with which immoral ends are achieved.

Although Raz does not explicitly consider the reciprocity at the heart of relationships structured by law, the implications of his analysis are analogous. Consider the case of legislators passing laws to exempt themselves from legal accountability for their actions. Such laws could be clearly written, promulgated, and consistently enforced by officials, and therefore be compatible with the requirements of the rule of law. Yet, in effect, only citizens are being held accountable for their failure to fulfill the expectations that leaders make about their behavior. The significance of the reciprocity realized in such a case is quite minimal. The damage that would stem from violating the rule of law would be minimal as well.

In response to this objection, I want first to emphasize the important insight to which the Razian objection draws attention, namely that the rule of law has important implications for respect for human freedom and dignity. However, I also want to challenge the view of law on which the objection rests. Law is not simply a tool that is morally neutral with respect to the ends that it can be used to pursue, nor are the virtues of law properly conceptualized as negative, virtues that prevent certain abuses that law makes possible. Rather, as I will argue below, law is a distinctive form of social order that has non-instrumental moral value in the sense that there is a necessary connection between governing by law and achieving the moral values of reciprocity and respect for agency in political relationships. The form of social order that law represents is not compatible with the pursuit of any end. Rather, there is a deep tension between the governing by law and the pursuit of injustice. Insofar as the rule of law is eroded during civil conflict and repressive rule, then, political relationships are damaged because important moral values cannot be instantiated in such relationships and because the constraining influence against the pursuit of injustice that law exerts on government officials is diminished. Respect for the rule of law is appropriately viewed as an important dimension of rebuilt relationships because of the moral values such relationships instantiate and because of the important constraining influence that law exercises on government officials.

Raz downplays the significance of the morality of the behavior called for by the rule of law because he views the requirements of the rule of law as preventing violations of individual freedom and dignity that law itself makes possible. However, this view mislocates the danger involved in the exercise of political power by officials. Law itself is not a potential problem, the solution to which is the rule of law. That is, law does not make possible the arbitrary exercise of power by officials. Rather, law itself provides an answer to the problem of the abuse or arbitrary exercise of power by officials, through the constraints that law imposes on officials. Officials govern by law only insofar as they systematically respect the constraints imposed by the requirements of the rule of law. In Jeremy Waldron's words, "The principles of legality aim to correct abuses of power by insisting on a particular mode of the exercise of political power – namely, governance through law – which is thought more apt to protect us against abuse than (say) managerial governance or rule by decree."[27] When a society does not govern by law, it must replace the legal system with some other institution or method of regulating the behavior of citizens. However, it is not obvious what other kind of system of governance could be equally or more restraining of the exercise of political power.

Nor is it clear what other form of governance would direct political power to be exercised in a way that would treat citizens as responsible and self-directed agents and is explicitly premised on the conditional nature of the obligations that citizens owe to officials. As Raz recognizes, the rule of law represents a form of social ordering and governance that is respectful of an individual's moral agency. Fuller recognized this as well. To use Fuller's own language, implicit in the idea of the rule of law is the view that an individual "is or can become a responsible agent capable of understanding and following rules and answerable for his defaults."[28] When officials respect the rule of law, they treat citizens as responsible and self-directed agents. Citizens are judged based on standards of behavior that they had a real opportunity to follow. Thus it is the decisions and actions of individuals, and not the whims of officials, that determine the legal treatment they receive. Departures from the principles of the rule of law, Fuller claims, affront an individual's dignity as a responsible agent. In addition, the overall framework of law is such that it enables citizens to pursue their goals and plans and be appropriately held responsible for their actions. Law's primary purpose is to facilitate self-directed interaction among citizens. The duties involved in respecting the rule of law

---

[27] Jeremy Waldron, "Hart and the Principles of Legality," in Matthew H. Cramer, Claire Grant, Ben Colburn, and Antony Hatzistavrou (eds.), *The Legacy of H.L.A. Hart* (Oxford University Press, 2008), pp. 67–83, at p. 78.

[28] Fuller, *Morality of Law*, p. 162.

are important in part because of the way that officials govern when they govern by law. Finally, as discussed above, law is a form of social order premised on grounding a moral basis of the duties involved in the relationships between citizens and officials. The Fullerian account explicitly recognizes that government officials can legitimately expect or demand obedience from citizens and punish those who disobey only under certain conditions that officials themselves must fulfill, and that the requirements of the rule of law always partially capture those conditions.

I have suggested that it is a mistake to diminish the significance of the moral values realized in political relationships through respect for the rule of law by conceptualizing the virtues of the rule of law as negative virtues. It is also a mistake, I will now argue, to view the law as a mere instrument that can be used to pursue any ends. The Razian objection brings to the fore the *conditional* nature of the non-instrumental value of the rule of law. It may be possible to conceptualize certain contexts in which the reciprocity and respect for moral agency constitutively expressed by relationships structured by the rule of law fail to be realized in any meaningful sense. More importantly, the Razian objection draws attention to the fact that the rule of law, and its constitutive values, can be realized to a greater or lesser degree in different contexts. However, the Razian objection gets its force from a disputable claim: that conceivability entails (real practical) possibility. Conceivability may entail conceptual or logical possibility – that I will not dispute here. What I do dispute is that conceivability *guarantees* real, in our world, possibility. That is, when we conduct thought experiments in which we try to imagine in sufficient detail a dictator pursuing unjust ends by means of a legal system that is fully compliant with the Fullerian account of the rule of law, at a certain point our imagined case loses any plausibility. In Waldron's words, "The outward appearance of the rule of law may be important for the external reputation of a regime. But those who reflect seriously on humanity's experience with tyranny know that, in the real world, this problem of the scrupulously legalistic Nazi is at best a question about the efficacy of cosmetics."[29] That is, it is only if we think of the rule of law as something "cosmetic" that it is compatible with the pursuit of deeply immoral ends. Thus, it is unsurprising that historically there has always been a fundamental tension between the rule of law and repressive rule or the pursuit of unjust ends.

[29] Waldron, "Why Law," 264.

Why does the rule by law sit uneasily with repressive rule? As Waldron notes, if a government wants to "frighten [citizens] into impotence"[30] such that they are willing to do whatever the government demands, then respecting the rule of law is incompatible with that end. According to an influential definition, terror is "the arbitrary use, by organs of the political authority, of severe coercion against individuals or groups, the credible threat of such use or the arbitrary extermination of such individuals or groups."[31] The use of terror can facilitate the creation of an uncertain environment, where citizens cannot predict how the government will respond to their actions. The rule of law, on the other hand, creates a predictable environment, in which citizens are confident about the requirements for their behavior and are unlikely to be "frightened into impotence."

Studies of totalitarian regimes frequently discuss the functional role of terror in such regimes. Political scientist Juan Linz, for example, argues that:

[Terror is used in] establishing the monopoly of authority and organization, eliminating all autonomous subgroups, destroying physically and morally not only actual but potential opponents, creating an atomized society in which individuals feel unable to trust others, disrupting even the most elementary solidarities like the family and friendship, creating a widespread sense of personal insecurity leading to compliance and even overcompliance.[32]

One defining characteristic of totalitarian regimes is that the ruling group or leader identifies with and legitimizes policies based on "an exclusive, autonomous, and more or less intellectually elaborate ideology … The ideology goes beyond a particular program or definition of the boundaries of legitimate political action to provide, presumably, some ultimate meaning, sense of historical purpose, and interpretation of social reality."[33] Totalitarian governments demand the total compliance of citizens with the requirements dictated by their ideological vision. Such compliance is easier to bring about in an environment where citizens fear what will happen if they show any dissent. Terrorizing a population, in other words, can facilitate compliance. Authoritarian regimes hoping to discourage the citizenry from genuine political participation can also more easily achieve

---

[30] The phrase "frighten into impotence" comes from Fuller, *Morality of Law*, p. 40. However, the phrase captures the main point Waldron is making, which is why I include it here.
[31] Juan Linz, *Totalitarian and Authoritarian Regimes* (Boulder, CO: Lynne Rienner Publishers, 2000), p. 100.
[32] Ibid., p. 112.   [33] Ibid., p. 70.

this end in an environment dominated by fear and uncertainty which encourages compliance with government demands.

An additional factor is that the open pursuit of unjust aims or governance via repression makes a government potentially vulnerable to international sanctions.[34] This makes governments very unwilling to make their systematic discrimination as public or explicit as they would have to if they wanted to make it consistent with the rule of law. When the methods of repression and the exact nature of the injustice being pursued are clearly, publicly articulated in laws, then it is more likely that a government will be pressured or feel pressure to change its method of governance or its policies. If the political leadership of a country makes explicit the fact that it is severely repressing its citizenry, it does so at the cost of having to completely isolate itself from the international community. If it is not isolated, then the political elites of other countries will be in communication with its own leaders. However, elites from other countries will not want to be associated with leaders openly responsible for and legally endorsing the repression of their citizenry. In addition, a government that explicitly states the nature of the injustice it is pursuing and legalizes intense repression risks undermining its legitimacy in the eyes of its citizens, for such legal sanctioning makes it very difficult for citizens to deny the brutality and injustice of "their" government officials. So respecting the rule of law will be a very unattractive prospect for such a government.

Despite the fact that the rule of law is often incompatible with the pursuit of unjust ends by repressive regimes, there are significant political costs in the international arenas for governments that openly violate the rule of law.[35] Neil MacCormick echoes a common sentiment when he writes, "A concern for the rule of law is one mark of a civilized society. The independence and dignity of each citizen is predicated on the existence of a 'governance of laws, not men.'"[36] The legitimacy of a government is partially tied to respecting the rule of law. If a state openly violates the rule of law, it risks for this reason becoming a pariah in the

---

[34] The nature and extent of the costs of losing support typically do not correlate directly with the degree to which a state violates the rule of law. National interest or international allegiances may mitigate or exaggerate the sanctions members of the international community place on states that violate the rule of law openly.

[35] David Dyzenhaus discusses the relationship between international legitimacy and the rule of law as well as the political costs involved in violating the rule of law in his *Judging the Judges, Judging Ourselves* (Oxford: Hart Publishing, 1998).

[36] Neil MacCormick, "Rhetoric and the Rule of Law," in David Dyzenhaus (ed.), *Recrafting the Rule of Law: The Limits of Legal Order* (Oxford: Hart Publishing, 1999), pp. 163–178, at p. 163.

international arena. In addition, respect for the rule of law increases the legitimacy of a government in the eyes of its citizens. Leaders who openly violate the rule of law also risk losing part of their standing among citizens. For these reasons, though it is inefficient for dictators or authoritarian rulers to limit their power by *actually* respecting the requirements of the rule of law, there is great reason to maintain the *façade* of legality.

Similar considerations often apply to societies in conflict. Violent conflict frequently strains the rule of law, including in democracies. When analyzing the "Troubles" in Northern Ireland, Brendan O'Leary and John McGarry discuss how "[d]epartures from traditional English legal procedures have become normal as a result of the conflict in Northern Ireland."[37] Particular violations they cite include the fabrication of evidence by police in particularly politically volatile investigations after bombings. Such fabrications led to the wrongful convictions of the Guildford Four and Birmingham Six. Democratic leaders have historically advocated the detention of individuals who might be members of a suspected group, violating normal processes of due law or the presumption of innocence until proven guilty. For certain periods in Northern Ireland detention without trial became customary. The rule of law makes it difficult to adopt policies like internment without trial although such things might be attractive options for ending conflict.

The process of subverting the rule of law is not always overt. While some officials may consciously manipulate the appearance of their rule so that it appears in the international arena to cohere with the requirements of the rule of law, many officials are in denial about or unaware of the corrosive effects of their actions on the legal system. Consider the role of judges in apartheid South Africa. Judicial oaths require judges to swear to uphold justice. As David Dyzenhaus writes, "Judges everywhere claim that their duty is not simply to administer the law, but to administer justice."[38] However, Dyzenhaus argues, the majority of judges in apartheid South Africa endorsed a judicial ideology that had the effect of forcing them to make decisions that resulted in systematic injustice. Judges failed to see how deeply the common law presumptions underpinning the South African legal system were in conflict with the purpose of the apartheid program and the rules passed to enforce the apartheid system. Common law heritage includes a commitment to protect the

---

[37] Brendan O'Leary and John McGarry, *The Politics of Antagonism: Understanding Northern Ireland*, 2nd ed. (London: Athlone Press, 1996), p. 48.
[38] Dyzenhaus, *Judging the Judges*, p. 34.

fundamental rights and freedoms of individuals.[39] Consequently, judges were "at one and the same time being asked to articulate and give effect to equitable common law principles, and to uphold and enforce discriminatory laws: at one and the same time to be an instrument of justice and at another to be an instrument of oppression."[40] Someone might argue that apartheid judges failed in their moral duties, but that would be different than the claim being offered here, which is that judges failed in their role *as judges*. Dyzenhaus argues that judges failed in their role as judges because they failed to expose explicitly the contradiction at the heart of the apartheid legal order. Instead of exposing the deep conflict between the rule of law and the apartheid program, insofar as it contradicted the principles at the very foundation of the apartheid legal system, judges endorsed a judicial ideology that required them to interpret laws as Parliament intended and obscured this fundamental contradiction. They were thus able to convince themselves that they were upholding the rule of law, and defend their actions under apartheid, when in reality their judgments had precisely the opposite effect.

Many of the judges who did appear before the TRC legal hearing tried to rationalize their role in apartheid. They would appeal to the role they had in mitigating the unjust effects of apartheid legislation, when in actuality few judges used the resources at their disposal to reach verdicts of a maximally just sentence. Such denial of complicity in injustice is unsurprising, given our fundamental psychological need to believe that we are moral.[41] Individuals typically recognize their moral shortcomings and imperfections; the crucial thing is to be able to distinguish particular imperfections from the characteristics of evil or amoral persons. However, individuals do not form their identities in isolation. The perceptions of others affect our self-conception. Therefore, it is also important that *others* recognize our moral identity and do not think of us as evil or morally vicious persons. Moreover, individuals have a psychological need for narrative unity. Typically, individuals construct a story or narrative in which they had or have reason to perform certain actions. Such narrative construction both allows us to justify our actions (that seem evil to others) and helps us individually to make sense of our actions.[42]

---

[39] Ibid., p. 15.   [40] Ibid.

[41] For an interesting discussion on denial in a political context see Stanley Cohen, *States of Denial: Knowing About Atrocities and Suffering* (Oxford: Polity Press, 2001).

[42] There is a philosophical tradition of thought that emphasizes the social component of identity formation. Jean-Jacques Rousseau, David Hume, and G. W. F. Hegel, for example, discuss the fundamental human need for recognition.

The above considerations apply metaphorically to nations. No nation thinks of itself as evil or immoral. National identities typically emphasize the virtues and values characteristically exhibited throughout their history. National identities, however, are influenced by the perceptions and judgments of other nations. Thus, it is important that other nations do not think of one's own nation as evil or immoral. Typically, the history of a nation is in part a narrative justifying the actions of that nation. Such narrative construction helps members of a nation make sense of their nation's history and justify their nation's actions that others may perceive as evil or immoral.

Actually fulfilling the requirements of the rule of law makes it very difficult for government officials to deny responsibility for immoral actions or unjust policies, because the rule of law makes injustice known. When government officials respect the requirements of the rule of law, citizens know what actions and policies the government is responsible for committing and enforcing. The requirements of the rule of law set up conditions that ensure open and clear governance. When they respect the rule of law, then, government officials are forced to publicly endorse and implement unjust actions and immoral policies. Yet, given the need for individuals to maintain their moral identity, it is less likely that government officials will pass grossly unjust laws and sanction immoral policies openly. Doing so undermines the perception of goodness, or at least lack of evil, which it is important for individuals to maintain. As Fuller states:

> Even if a man is answerable only to his own conscience, he will answer more responsibly if he is compelled to articulate the principles on which he acts ... It has been said that most of the world's injustices are inflicted, not with the fists, but with the elbows. When we use our fists we use them for a definite purpose, and we are answerable to others and to ourselves for that purpose. Our elbows, we may comfortably suppose, trace a random pattern for which we are not responsible, even though our neighbor may be painfully aware that he is being systematically pushed from his seat. A strong commitment to the principles of legality compels a ruler to answer to himself, not only for his fists, but for his elbows as well.[43]

Eugene de Kock, dubbed "Prime Evil" among South Africans, was a commanding officer of state-sanctioned death squads responsible for killing and torturing ANC activists during apartheid. He is currently serving a 212-year prison sentence for crimes against humanity. When interviewed by psychologist Pumla Godobo-Madikizela, he stated that

---

[43] Fuller, *Morality of Law*, p. 159.

"the dirtiest war you can ever get is the one fought in the shadows ... There are no rules except to win. There are no lines drawn to mark where you cannot cross. So you can go very low – I mean very low – and it still doesn't hit you."[44] Denial of responsibility for atrocities or wrongdoing, or recognition that you are doing wrong, is much easier to maintain when your actions are secret.

I have been arguing against the claim that it is practically possible in our world for a government to fully comply with the requirements of the rule of law while pursuing grossly unjust ends. In the process I have shown another, instrumental reason for valuing the rule of law. Not only does respecting the rule of law involve recognizing the reciprocal nature of the duties officials and citizens have toward one another and respecting the moral agency of citizens, but in practice the rule of law limits the kind of injustice which governments pursue. However, this line of thought may still leave some dissatisfied. Just look, someone might say, at how many regimes *did* openly pursue immoral ends while respecting the rule of law. What about South Africa? Or Argentina?

When you examine these cases carefully, however, you realize that only the *façade* of legality was maintained by these regimes. For example, the Argentine report *Nunca Mas* states about the Argentine judiciary during the dictatorship that "[a]lthough intended by the Supreme Law of the Nation to protect citizens from excesses of authority, it now condoned the usurpation of power and allowed a host of judicial aberrations to take on the appearance of legality."[45] In South Africa, not only was there systematic *de facto* extralegal use of torture and death squads targeting ANC activists, both officially denied, there was at its very foundation a contradiction in the apartheid legal system. There was a program designed to restrict the liberty and rights of the majority of a population legally enacted by a common law legal system, at the foundation of which is a commitment to protect the liberty and rights of all citizens. As Dyzenhaus argues, respect for the rule of law would have required judges to openly recognize and in their rulings articulate the fact that a commitment to apartheid required a rejection of a foundational principle of the common law legal system. South African judges, by obscuring and ignoring this fundamental contradiction, failed to uphold the rule of law.

[44] Pumla Godobo-Madikizela, *A Human Being Died That Night* (Boston: Houghton Mifflin Co., 2003), p. 20.
[45] Argentine National Commission on the Disappeared, *Nunca Mas: The Report of the Argentine National Commission on the Disappeared*, English edition (New York: Farrar Straus Giroux, 1986).

History is replete with examples of repressive regimes and societies in conflict where violations of the rule of law were commonplace. History provides few examples of repressive regimes or civil conflicts where the rule of law flourished alongside the pursuit of systematic injustice. In virtually all, the rule of law was weakened.

It is important to emphasize that I have been arguing against the compatibility of the pursuit of *systematic* injustice and the rule of law. It is of course possible that particular immoral or unjust laws be passed in accordance with the requirements of the rule of law. Respect for the rule of law does not guard against every injustice. In addition, there may be cases where racism or prejudice against a particular group in society makes it likely that actions viewed as impermissible against the dominant group seem justifiable against a minority group. Or there may be certain circumstances, like threats to national security, where actions previously viewed as beyond the pale suddenly become viable options. Even in these cases, however, the rule of law can play an important role in limiting injustice. It is important to recognize that members of a society are forced to be fully aware of what they are sanctioning if they sanction torture or the discriminatory allocation of resources; the rule of law makes the pursuit of injustice publicly knowable. It is likely that even in these cases the rule of law will mitigate or restrict the use of torture. In addition, such a society opens itself up to sanctions from the international community to the extent that its violations of international norms are enshrined in laws.

To summarize the discussion so far, the first objection rejected my claim that respect for the rule of law has significant non-instrumental moral value, and therefore my claim that the erosion of the rule of law is in itself damaging to political relationships in morally significant ways. In response, I argued that it is a mistake to view the law as an instrument and the rule of law as principles that prevent types of abuse that law makes possible. Instead, governance by law represents a distinctive kind of social order, premised on reciprocity among citizens and officials and respect for individual agency, that constrains abuses that the exercise of political power makes possible. In practice there is a deep tension between ruling by law and systematically pursuing unjust ends. Thus appealing to the hypothetical scenarios that Raz sketches does not mitigate the value that the reciprocity and respect for agency internal to law has in practice. The erosion of respect for the rule of law during conflict and repression is appropriately regarded as intrinsically damaging to political relationships insofar as reciprocity and respect for agency are undermined.

AGAINST A FORMAL CONCEPTION OF THE RULE OF LAW

In contrast to the first objection, the second objection grants that structuring political relationships by law is of significant non-instrumental value, and that the erosion or undermining of the rule of law is intrinsically damaging to political relationships. Instead, it challenges the completeness of my account of the requirements of the rule of law. According to the objection, the reciprocity and respect for agency that underpin the requirements of the rule of law discussed in the first section of this chapter have substantive implications. That is, these values also constrain the content law can have, not simply the form law may take. Because my analysis omits any consideration of the content of laws, my account of the role of law in political reconciliation is fundamentally incomplete. In particular, it overlooks important, additional ways in which the erosion of the rule of law that occurs during conflict and repressive rule damages political relationships and provides an overly thin characterization of the rebuilt relationships predicated on respect for the rule of law.

I use an argument advanced by Jennifer Nadler to develop this objection.[46] Nadler suggests that the root of the failure to see the substantive implications of Fuller's conception of the rule of law stems from a mischaracterization of the reciprocity at the heart of the rule of law. This mischaracterization of reciprocity, in turn, is based on a misunderstanding of the question that the articulation of principles of the rule of law is designed to answer.[47] In my discussion so far I have been implicitly assuming that the requirements of the rule of law help us make sense of the conditions that are necessary for the governance of human conduct by rules to be possible. However, according to Nadler, it is the question of "what grounds a legal subject's obligation to obey the law" that is the real issue that the requirements of the rule of law are designed to address.

In the first section, I discussed the implications of the reciprocity underpinning the requirements of the rule of law for a citizen's obligation to obey the law, suggesting that fulfillment of the requirements of the rule of law by officials gives citizens some grounds for obeying the law.

---

[46] Jennifer Nadler, "Hart, Fuller, and the Connection Between Law and Justice," *Law and Philosophy*, 27 (2007), 1–34.

[47] Evan Fox-Decent adopts a similar line of argument, exploring the implications of the respect for agency underpinning the requirements of the rule of law. In his view, the commitment to viewing persons as free and self-determining agents implies a commitment to respect the human dignity of individuals. Such respect underpins, in his view, arguments supporting human rights. See his "Is the Rule of Law Really Indifferent to Human Rights?" *Law and Philosophy*, 27 (2008), 533–81.

Nadler's argument explores this implication in greater detail. First, she notes that for Fuller it is reciprocity that turns a duty into an obligation. In law, the duty of government officials to fulfill the requirements of the rule of law corresponds to the duty of citizens to obey the law. Thus, as I noted in the first section, in order for the duty of citizens to obey the law to become an obligation, officials must fulfill the requirements of the rule of law.

Nadler then asks: how should we understand the principle of reciprocity that underpins the requirements of the rule of law and grounds citizens' obligations to obey the law? One characterization of reciprocity is given by Fuller and is implicit in my earlier discussion. Following Fuller, I characterized the reciprocity at the heart of law as involving a commitment by the government to codify rules that are capable of being followed, and to enforce declared rules combined with a reciprocal commitment by citizens to follow such rules. In Fuller's words, "Government says to the citizen in effect, 'These are the rules we expect you to follow. If you follow them, you have our assurance that they are the rules that will be applied to your conduct.'"[48] But, according to Nadler, this characterization of the ideal of reciprocity will not do. This conception reduces reciprocity to a requirement of fair warning by the government; the government must warn citizens "'of what conduct is to be avoided or performed so that you can avoid punishment.'"[49] The problem is that this conception of reciprocity robs law of its status as a distinctive, morally valuable social order. A gunman could satisfy the requirements of reciprocity, so understood, insofar as he spares my life when given the money he demanded when he ordered, "Your money or your life." Yet it would clearly be a mistake to claim that there is a reciprocal relationship between the gunman and me. According to Nadler, "The implausibility of such a conclusion [that there is a reciprocal relationship] suggests that Fuller must have a more robust conception of reciprocity than he explicitly acknowledges in the 'fair warning' articulation of the meaning of reciprocity."[50] We thus need a better way of characterizing the reciprocity internal to law.

According to Nadler, a more robust conception of reciprocity, and one that is consistent with Fuller's own writings, requires not simply the mutual fulfillment of reciprocal duties but also that the reciprocal duties themselves be, in some sense, equal. The moral force of a duty, its

---

[48] Fuller, *Morality of Law*, p. 40. Nadler cites this passage of Fuller on 26.
[49] Nadler, "Hart, Fuller," 26.   [50] Ibid., 26–7.

obligatoriness, depends "not merely" on reciprocal performances but rather on "equal performances on either side."[51] The demand of equal, reciprocal performances fits with our sense of justice because by requiring equal performance we acknowledge the fundamental equality of each party. "Equal persons can recognize the legitimacy or justice of reciprocal and equal obligations because it is in the equality of the exchange that they are recognized as equals."[52] Thus the reciprocity underpinning the requirements of the rule of law is one in which fair warning on the part of government is coupled with an additional commitment to ensure that laws are consistent with the recognition of the fundamental equality of citizens and officials.

What is required for law to recognize the fundamental equality of citizens and officials? Drawing on Fuller's discussion of the difference between law and managerial direction, Nadler claims that the purpose of law, which provides the rationale for the requirements of the rule of law outlined in the first section of this chapter, is not to further the particular interests or ends of government (or of any particular group of citizens). That is, if law is to recognize the equality of citizens and officials, neither citizens nor officials must be superior, in the sense that their interests dictate the purposes that law (and so those governed by law) serves. Rather, the purpose of law, which provides the rationale for the requirements of the rule of law, is to further autonomy and self-determination, or what I called agency in the previous section. That is, law's purpose must be to further the ability of citizens to pursue their own self-chosen ends in ways that "are consistent with general societal interests." Law provides a framework that makes self-directed inter-action possible.

However, to ensure that law does in fact facilitate such autonomy, it is not enough that the requirements of the rule of law that Fuller outlined be fulfilled. We must also ascertain the substantive purpose being served by law. In Nadler's words, "Orders can violate law's internal morality in their substance – if they are directed only to the lawgiver's ends."[53] Only laws in accordance with public purposes rather than, for example, directed toward particular lawmakers' ends or even the ends of the majority of citizens are sufficiently respectful of the autonomy of citizens. "If a law cannot be justified in terms of public purposes, it can be properly criticized as deficient from the perspective of law."[54] The fundamental difference between law and the gunman situation writ large stems from

---

[51] Ibid., 27.   [52] Ibid.   [53] Ibid., 32.   [54] Ibid.

the purpose that each serves, reflected, Nadler claims, in the substantive content of their demands. A gunman structures his demands to serve his purposes and, in so doing, "unilaterally subordinate[s] the victim to his ends."[55] Such demands fail to meet the demands of the substantive morality at the heart of law. By contrast, laws are formulated to serve public purposes, ensuring that no one is subordinated to the ends of anyone else.

Nadler's analysis has broad implications for understanding the role of law in political reconciliation. It suggests that insofar as the rule of law is undermined during civil conflict and repressive rule, this is a product of a failure to adhere to the formal *and* substantive requirements of the rule of law. Importantly, and something my account fails to acknowledge, the rule of law erodes when laws do not serve public purposes. By failing to address the implications of legality for the ends and goals that governments may legitimately pursue, I fail to capture the depth and extent of the ways that civil conflict and repressive rule undermine the respect for reciprocity and agency at the heart of law. Similarly, my analysis is silent on the need to rebuild law such that public, as opposed to non-public, purposes are pursued. It is silent on the pressing question of what goals and ends laws may legitimately be used to serve.

In response to this objection, I want to explain why, in my view, there is a much simpler way of distinguishing the law from the gunman situation writ large, which does not require the inclusion of substantive requirements of the rule of law or an endorsement of the richer notion of reciprocity Nadler proposes. In brief, Nadler is correct when she claims that the fundamental purpose of law is to respect autonomy, or what I label agency in the previous section, by creating a framework that facilitates self-directed interaction. Respect for agency is thus a necessary dimension of law. As both Nadler and I recognize, for law to facilitate self-directed interaction, the formal requirements of the rule of law outlined in the first section must be systematically met. In so doing, the reciprocity articulated in the original conception Nadler considers is achieved. What Nadler fails to recognize, however, is that the gunman need not fulfill the requirements of the rule of law in order to successfully realize his ends and goals. Any respect for the formal requirements of the rule of law the gunman achieves is simply a contingent and derivative occurrence. Unlike in the case of law, respect for agency or fulfillment of the demands of reciprocity are not fundamental to the gunman situation writ large. Thus the primary difference between law and the gunman

---

[55] Ibid., 29.

situation lies in whether reciprocity and respect for agency are internal to each way of guiding human action.

To see why respect for agency is internal to law we must begin by recognizing that law's primary purpose is to facilitate self-directed interaction among citizens. The social order of law is such that it enables citizens to pursue their goals and plans, and appropriately be held responsible for their actions. On this both Nadler and I agree. What Nadler fails to appreciate, however, is *how* law facilitates self-directed interaction. Individuals pursue their goals in a social context where they interact with others. To pursue their goals successfully, individuals must be able to formulate reliable and stable mutual expectations of how others will behave; such expectations enable individuals to anticipate how others will respond to different actions. Law allows citizens to pursue their own purposes by creating the required stable framework of expectations that makes such self-directed interaction possible. The stable framework of expectations that law creates is possible only insofar as officials systematically adhere to all eight requirements of the rule of law. The commitment to congruence is an especially fundamental principle of the social order that law represents. Congruence allows citizens to be able to understand and successfully predict how others, both inside and outside of government, will respond to their actions. As Fuller writes, "Surely the very essence of the Rule of Law is that in acting upon the citizen (by putting him in jail, for example, or declaring invalid a deed under which he claims title to property) a government will faithfully apply rules previously declared as those to be followed by the citizen and as being determinative of his rights and duties."[56] To understand how law as a form of social order respects the agency of citizens and officials, then, it is not necessary to examine the substantive goals that government officials pursue through law. Furthermore, the original formulation of reciprocity does indeed capture the demands of reciprocity at the core of the relationship between legal officials and citizens, because it articulates the demands that government officials must fulfill if they are to facilitate self-directed interaction. Such demands, reflected in the formal requirements of the rule of law, must be fulfilled systematically for law to be possible.

When we turn to the gunman scenario, however, the situation is fundamentally different. The form of social order represented by the gunman involves a one-way projection of authority; orders are issued by

---

[56] Fuller, *Morality of Law*, p. 210.

a superior to a subordinate in order to achieve the superior's purposes. As Nadler recognizes, unlike law, the defining purpose of the gunman scenario is not to facilitate self-directed interaction and thus agency, but to facilitate the gunman's goals. What Nadler fails to recognize is that this difference in purpose has implications for the formal requirements of the rule of law. Most importantly, it is not necessary that these requirements be fulfilled for the purpose that the gunman's form of social order serves to be achieved. A gunman's purposes may be achieved without, for example, congruence being satisfied. In other words, congruence with prior demands is not an inherent or necessary feature of the social order that the gunman situation represents.[57] In Fuller's words, there is "no room for a formal principle *demanding* that the actions of the superior conform to the rules he has himself announced."[58] It may at times be efficient for a gunman to conform to the demands he has issued to a subordinate. The gunman's ability to motivate a subordinate to fulfill his demand may be affected by the subordinate's belief in the likelihood that the gunman will stick to his word; congruence may sometimes be a good thing. However, often the periodic absence of congruence may be more effective for a gunman's purposes. As we saw when considering the previous objection, the absence of congruence can enhance the coercive power of the gunman over subordinates by increasing their fear and uncertainty over random executions. Thus while we can imagine a situation in which a gunman meets the formal requirements of the rule of law, this is not necessary. In the gunman scenario any satisfaction of the demands of reciprocity, as articulated in the formal requirements of the rule of law, is similarly contingent and accidental. In Fuller's words, "This tacit reciprocity of reasonableness and restraint is something collateral to the basic relation of order-giver and order-executor."[59]

---

[57] Objecting to the formal conception of the rule of law by drawing on a situation in which the gunman satisfies all eight requirements of legality is similar to objecting to inclusive legal positivism by drawing on a case in which legal validity in a particular context is dependent upon morality to demonstrate that the separability thesis is false. Such examples miss the positivist point that it is a contingent matter of fact that there is a link between legal validity and morality in such cases and that the positivist is concerned to deny a necessary connection between law and morality.

[58] Fuller, *Morality of Law*, p. 208, emphasis added. There is also no reason for the generality requirement. While offering general demands may often be expedient for a gunman to issue, there is nothing about the gunman situation that would ground a subordinate's complaint that general demands were not given in a particular context.

[59] Fuller, *Morality of Law*, p. 209.

To this point I have argued that it is not necessary to include substantive requirements of the rule of law in order to articulate the distinctive way in which law instantiates the values of reciprocity and respect for agency. I now want to discuss why, for the purposes of political reconciliation, it is important to draw on a formal conception of the rule of law. Including substantive requirements of legality in our understanding of what the rule of law entails obscures the central insight that Fuller's analysis offers for transitional contexts. That is, focusing on the particular goals and ends that law is used to achieve shifts attention away from Fuller's key insight: that there is non-instrumental value in governing conduct on the basis of declared rules that are actually enforced, regardless of the ends that law is used to pursue. Law represents a distinctive kind of social order, Fuller reminds us, premised on a respect for self-directed interaction that grounds the eight principles of legality. In many societies that are in transition to democracy, this is a fundamental and basic idea that needs to be cultivated. In such contexts the very notion that officials are bound by the publicly articulated, clear, and consistent rules represents a radical shift from the understanding and behavior of officials prior to the transition. Similarly, the idea that the obligation that citizens have to obey officials is conditional on the actions of officials is often absent as well. That there is reciprocity at the heart of this political relationship, like all relationships, is in these circumstances another foundational idea that needs to be articulated and emphasized, and is done so by the ideal of the rule of law I endorse. It would be a mistake to downplay the importance of recognizing and developing the basic reciprocity and respect for agency at the heart of the rule of law I described above as being expressed in the formal requirements of the rule of law because its presence can be taken for granted in stable democratic societies. Nadler's devaluing of the significance of the formal requirements of the rule of law reflects a failure to appreciate how law's purpose provides the rationale for such requirements. This is especially troubling because it is precisely the importance of such formal requirements and of the valuable social order they ground that is undermined during conflict and repressive rule.

A formal account of the rule of law captures the distinctive kind of social order law represents and, at the same time, prevents us from equating all of the demands of political reconciliation with the demands of the rule of law. Thus it guards against a problematic form of legalism in theorizing about political reconciliation. Indeed, an overemphasis on law within the literature is one primary criticism among scholars of transitional justice.[60] The framework of the rule of law draws attention to an important source of damage to political relationships during conflict and repressive rule. It also draws attention to two fundamental values that political relationships should express: reciprocity and respect for agency. Governance by law is a distinctive and important achievement; however, it is not the only achievement (or failure) in political relationships that occurs during civil conflict and repressive rule. Turning to a more substantive conception of the conditions of legality in the context of political reconciliation obscures the limited place of law and the quest for legality in the process of political reconciliation. Looking to the substantive aims and goals that law should pursue as part of the requirements of legality may suggest that law can provide all of the conditions that are required for political relationships based on reciprocity and respect for agency to become possible. However, the implications of reciprocity and respect for agency extend well beyond their implications for the kind of social order and form of governance that law represents and which transitional societies should strive to cultivate. One additional virtue of a formal conception of the rule of law is that it serves as a reminder of the limits of law, both in how it damages and in what way it may serve to rebuild political relations. It is the broader implications of a commitment to reciprocity and respect for agency that I consider in the next two chapters.

---

[60] See, for example, Patricia Lundy and Mark McGovern, "Whose Justice? Rethinking Transitional Justice from the Bottom Up," *Journal of Law and Society*, 35(2) (2008), 265–92; Kieran McEvoy, "Beyond Legalism: Towards a Thicker Understanding of Transitional Justice," *Journal of Law and Society*, 24(4) (2007), 411–40. One consequence of the fact that the rule of law is one ideal of political morality is that there may be situations in which, all things considered, it is best to violate the rule of law or fail to obey those who generally uphold it. What my argument highlights is that, even in these situations, we should still recognize that something morally valuable is thereby lost, even though on balance its loss is justified.

CHAPTER 2

Political trust

INTRODUCTION

In the previous chapter I considered institutional dimensions of the damage to political relationships during civil conflict and repressive rule, which stem from the absence or erosion of the rule of law. In this chapter I concentrate on important attitudinal dimensions of political reconciliation. Deep, pervasive distrust is a prominent feature of political relationships within transitional societies.[1] One significant source of such distrust is the erosion of the rule of law. The objective of this chapter is to articulate why the absence of trust is damaging to political relations and thus why rebuilt political relationships are characterized by reasonable default political trust.

It is puzzling why exactly the absence of trust, as well as the conditions that make trust reasonable, is damaging to political relationships. Academics and politicians within transitional societies frequently claim that it is imperative to build trust. Deep and pervasive distrust is often viewed as an obstacle to peace. Advocates of the importance of trust typically emphasize the instrumental value of trust for political relationships.[2] Trust, for example, bolsters and stabilizes the normative

Earlier versions of this chapter were presented at the Melbern G. Glasscock Center for Humanities Studies at Texas A&M University, an interdisciplinary symposium on reconciliation at the University of Wisconsin-Madison, and the University of Minnesota Duluth. I am particularly indebted to Macalester Bell, Theodore George, Katya Hosking, Nancy Lawrence, Kathleen Murphy, Linda Radzik, Susanne Sreedhar, Daniel Statman, and Sean Walsh for detailed comments and extensive discussion.
[1] Such distrust is not exclusively, or even primarily, a product of the erosion of the rule of law. An important source of distrust is the pursuit of substantive injustice and violations of human rights. I consider these substantive sources of distrust in Chapter 3.
[2] Arguments for the instrumental value of trust can be found in Diego Gambetta (ed.), *Trust: Making and Breaking Cooperative Relations* (Oxford: Basil Blackwell, 1988); Russell Hardin, *Trust and Trustworthiness* (New York: Russell Sage Foundation, 2002); Nicklas Luhmann, *Trust and Power* (Toronto: Wiley Press, 1979); John Hardwig, "The Role of Trust in Knowledge," *The Journal of Philosophy*, 88(12) (1991), 693–708; Karen Jones, "Second-hand Moral Knowledge," *The Journal of*

expectations constitutive of moral political relationships. Reflecting these ideas, philosopher Margaret Urban Walker and the International Center for Transitional Justice (ICTJ) define reconciliation in terms of the rebuilding of civic trust.[3] However, within the literature in philosophy and political science the necessity and value of political trust are increasingly being challenged.[4] Political cooperation, it is claimed, does not depend on trust. Indeed, the virtues of *distrust* of public officials, even in democratic contexts, are often lauded.[5] From such views, the absence of trust is not damaging to political relationships and the promotion of trust is not necessarily morally desirable. Such views challenge the basic idea that cultivating trust is either a necessary or valuable part of the process of political reconciliation.

My argument in this chapter departs from both of these positions. Instead of focusing on whether trust has instrumental value and whether cooperation without trust is possible, I consider what trusting, when reasonable, expresses. I argue that trusting, when reasonable, represents an important way of expressing respect and a commitment to reciprocity in political relationships. The absence of trust or the conditions that make trust reasonable, then, is damaging to political relationships for non-instrumental reasons. The absence of trust or conditions that make trust reasonable are appropriately regarded as damaging to political relationships because one important way of expressing such moral values is not realized. Thus the absence or unreasonableness of default political trust should be of moral concern for its own sake, regardless of whether

Philosophy, 96(2) (1999), 55–78; M. O. Webb, "The Epistemology of Trust and the Politics of Suspicion," *Pacific Philosophical Quarterly*, 73 (1992), 390–440; John Baker, "Trust and Rationality," *Pacific Philosophical Quarterly*, 68 (1996), 1–13; Annette Baier, "Demoralization, Trust, and the Virtues," in Chesire Calhoun (ed.), *Setting the Moral Compass: Essays by Women Philosophers* (New York: Oxford University Press, 2004), pp. 176–90; Philip Pettit, "The Cunning of Trust," *Philosophy and Public Affairs*, 24(3) (1995), 202–25; Daniel Weinstock, "Building Trust in Divided Societies," *The Journal of Political Philosophy*, 7(3) (1999), 287–307. Pettit cites Gambetta (1988), Robert D. Putnam, Robert Leonardi, and Raffaella Y. Nanetti, *Making Democracy Work: Civic Traditions in Modern Italy* (Princeton University Press, 1994), and Francis Fukuyama, *Trust* (New York: Basic Books, 1995).

[3] ICTJ, www.ictj.org/en/tj/784.html. Accessed November 4, 2008.

[4] See, for example, Karen S. Cook, Russell Hardin, and Margaret Levi, *Cooperation Without Trust?* (New York: Russell Sage Foundation Publications, 2007). They write, "trust is no longer the central pillar of social order, and it may not even be very important in most of our cooperative exchanges, which we manage quite effectively even in the absence of interpersonal trust ... Our approach challenges much of the current theorizing about how to improve organizations, governments, business, and societies ... we suggest that distrust may be good in many contexts, since it grounds forms of social structure that help to limit exploitation and protect those who cannot protect themselves" (pp. 1–2).

[5] Russel Hardin (ed.), *Distrust* (New York: Russell Sage Foundation Publications, 2009).

(however unlikely) the instrumental goods that trust facilitates can still be achieved. Relatedly, the cultivation and maintenance of political trust in transitional contexts and of the conditions that make trusting reasonable should be valued for non-instrumental reasons because they enable respect and a commitment to reciprocity to be expressed in the attitudes citizens and officials take toward one another.

This chapter comprises four sections. The first is largely expository and discusses the general understanding of trust provided by Karen Jones in her seminal article "Trust as an Affective Attitude."[6] In the second I analyze one specific kind of trust, political trust among citizens and officials, using Jones's general definition as my starting point. In the third section I argue for the non-instrumental moral value of political trust. The fourth and final section considers the conditional character of political trust's non-instrumental moral value, articulating the conditions under which default political trust is reasonable and thus the moral values of respect and a commitment to reciprocity are achieved.

TRUST IN GENERAL

Trust is widely taken to be an affective attitude or emotion.[7] As such, it reflects a particular way of viewing the object of our trust. This perspective in turn informs our interpretation of the actions of the one trusted. Trust influences which actions or words of the trustee are focused on, and which interpretations of those actions or words of the trustee are viewed as plausible. Plausible interpretations are those consistent with the truster's overall view of the trustee. In interpreting actions and words to maintain such consistency, trusters focus on evidence that confirms or is consistent with their view of the trustee and downplay or resist evidence to the contrary.

More specifically, as Jones argues, trust is an attitude of optimism with respect to the competence and the will of the trustee.[8] The attitude of

---

[6] Karen Jones, "Trust as an Affective Attitude," *Ethics*, 107 (1996), 4–25.

[7] See, for example, Jones, "Trust as an Affective Attitude"; Trudy Govier, "Self-Trust, Autonomy, and Self-Esteem," *Hypatia*, 8 (1993), 99–120; Lawrence C. Becker, "Trust as Noncognitive Security About Motives," *Ethics*, 107(1) (1996), 43–61; Olli Lagerspetz, *Trust: The Tacit Demand* (Dordrecht, the Netherlands: Kluwer Academic Publishers, 1998), p. 34. For a general discussion of the theory of emotions that is the particular basis for the analysis in this chapter, see Ronald de Sousa, *The Rationality of Emotion* (Cambridge, MA: MIT Press, 1987); Amelie Rorty (ed.), *Explaining Emotions* (Los Angeles: University of California Press, 1976); Robert C. Roberts, "What an Emotion Is: A Sketch," *The Philosophical Review*, 97(2) (1988), 183–95.

[8] Jones, "Trust as an Affective Attitude."

optimism refers to the positive or hopeful view we take of the trustee's competence and will. This general analysis of trust can be applied to particular kinds of trusting relationships by identifying the specific domain over which the anticipated competence will extend. We rarely trust individuals completely. Normally, trust covers certain areas or kinds of interaction.[9] Similarly, the anticipated competence could cover a general category of action or subject matter. It can include technical, moral, and/or social competence, depending on the relationship in question. The kind of will anticipated could range from positive goodwill to the absence of ill will.

In addition to its distinctive affective attitude, trust is defined by a certain expectation. The expectation constitutive of trust is that the trustee be, in Jones's words, "directly and favorably moved by the thought" that she is being counted on by the truster. In this sense, the trustee is expected to be *trust-responsive*.[10] The qualification directly captures the idea that the fact that one is being trusted is itself supposed to provide a reason for proving reliable in the domain over which our trust extends, or acting in accordance with the expectation of the truster. This fact and not, for example, the implications or consequences of being relied on are expected to move the trustee. The expectation constitutive of trust is thus not fulfilled if one proves reliable because of a fear of retaliation. Being favorably moved by the thought of being trusted captures the idea that being trusted provides a motivation for responding consistent with how one is being relied on, and not a reason for doing the opposite. The expectation, then, is that the recognition that one is trusted will be given substantial consideration in the deliberation of the trustee, though it need not always be an overriding consideration.

---

[9] This domain consideration is also reflected in a standard formulation of trust as a three-part relation: "A trusts B to do X" (Russell Hardin, "The Street-Level Epistemology of Trust," *Politics & Society*, 21(4) (1993), 505–29, at 506). According to Hardin, "To say 'I trust you' seems almost always to implicitly assume some such phrase as 'to do X' or 'in matters Y'" ("The Street-Level Epistemology of Trust," 506). The specification of X is a reflection of the fact that there are different domains over which our trust extends.

[10] Pettit, "The Cunning of Trust," 203. The term trust-responsiveness is taken from Pettit. As Pettit rightly notes, it is better to refer to trust-responsiveness instead of trustworthiness because trustworthiness is frequently associated with desirable or virtuous character traits. In the political context, individuals need not expect fellow citizens to possess such traits in order to trust them. In this chapter, I use trust-responsiveness to refer to a commitment by the trustee to doing that which she is trusted to do because she is trusted or relied upon to do so. My use is more robust than Pettit's, who defines trust-responsiveness simply as a disposition to prove reliable under the trust of others. My use of "trust-responsiveness," I believe, more directly captures the idea that the trustee is expected to *respond directly* to the trust that is placed in her.

Trust exhibits additional complexities than Jones's general analysis of trust explicitly suggests. First, trusting comes in various degrees and encompasses different scopes. The confidence we have in our attitude of optimism and trusting expectation can differ in strength and degree.[11] At one end of the spectrum, an individual may have unquestioning trust. Alternately, relations may be characterized by absolute distrust. Some threshold degree of confidence in one's expectation and attitude is presumably required for an individual to properly be said to trust. In addition, the scope of our trust, that is, *who* is trusted, may differ among individuals. In the political context, some citizens may trust all political officials. Others may trust only officials from a certain political party or those drawn from members of a given ethnic group.

To be trust-responsive is to be directly and favorably moved by the thought that the truster is counting on you. Unless compelling countervailing considerations obtain, the trust-responsive individual proves reliable, fulfilling the expectation of the truster, within the bounds of discretion that trust permits. This presupposes that those who are trust-responsive are trusted, that is, perceived by the truster as possessing a certain kind of positive will and competence over a given domain of interaction. The trustee normally has some discretion in deciding how to satisfactorily fulfill the expectation of the truster. Such discretion, however, does not leave the truster without any grounds for criticizing the trustee for failing to prove reliable in the appropriate way. The truster also has some discretion in determining what counts as failing to fulfill trust.

In the next section I draw on this general analysis of trust because it can capture key features of the phenomenology of trust. First, this analysis can explain the connection between trusting and the potential for betrayal.[12] The expectation definitive of trust articulates a normative demand, and not merely a scientific prediction of how the trustee will act. The normative aspect of the expectation influences the character of our reactions to violations of trust. Specifically, we feel betrayal, not merely disappointment, when our expectations go unfulfilled. In part because of this vulnerability, trusting involves risk. The truster may be perfectly

---

[11] On this point see Weinstock, "Building Trust," 297–8.
[12] For discussions of the link between trusting and being vulnerable to betrayal and risk, see Pamela Hieronymi, "The Reasons of Trust," *Australasian Journal of Philosophy*, 86(2) (2008), 213–36; Jones, "Trust as an Affective Attitude"; Pettit, "The Cunning of Trust"; Lagerspetz, *Trust: The Tacit Demand*; Annette Baier, "Trust and Antitrust," *Ethics*, 96(2) (1986), 231–60; Nicklas Luhmann, "Familiarity, Confidence, Trust: Problems and Alternatives," in Diego Gambetta (ed.), *Trust: Making and Breaking Cooperative Relations* (Oxford: Basil Blackwell, 1988), pp. 94–107.

assured that the individual on whom she is relying in a distinctively trusting manner will act as she anticipates. Despite this, insofar as the trustee is a free agent, by trusting you take a risk because of the possibility that your trusting reliance could be exploited or ignored.

Second, this analysis can distinguish trust from mere reliance. The attribution of a certain kind of positive will to the trusted is a defining dimension of the Jonesian analysis of the attitude of trust. By contrast, as Jones points out, we can merely rely on other individuals out of necessity or a concern for efficiency without thereby assuming any psychological disposition. Even when we find individuals reliable because of their predictable psychological dispositions, such dispositions need not consist of positive will toward the truster. We can rely on individuals to act in certain ways because of their habitual behavior or disposition, indifference, or even ill will toward oneself.[13]

Finally, the Jonesian analysis has the theoretical resources to distinguish justifiable and unjustifiable (or reasonable and unreasonable) trusting and trust-responsiveness. In the Jonesian view, though trust can give rise to beliefs, it is not defined in terms of particular beliefs. Separating trust

---

[13] Both entrusting and risk-assessment accounts of trust have difficulty explaining why trust involves a vulnerability to betrayal and the difference between trust and reliance. Entrusting accounts of trust define trust in the following way: A trusts B with valued good C. Emphasizing the goods entrusted to the trustee has the consequence of diminishing the significance of the anticipated positive act of the trustee. Yet we can entrust goods in a manner that is merely relying instead of trusting. Indeed, Baier, who offers the paradigmatic entrusting account, writes, "Sensible trust could persist, then, in conditions where truster and trusted suspect each other of willingness to harm the other if they could get away with it, the one by breach of trust, the other by vengeful response to it." See her "Trust and Antitrust," 255.

Risk-assessment views define trust in terms of beliefs or expectations. Very broadly, A trusts B if A believes that B will do X. In this view, we trust when we rely on individuals of whom we believe the risk of such reliance is sufficiently low. Predictions of the trustee's likely action, given the assumption that she will act in her self-interest, form the basis of such risk assessments. Trust is ultimately a matter of strategic choice and represents a "way of managing uncertainty in our dealings with others by representing those situations as risks" (see Becker, "Trust as Noncognitive Security," 45). Examples of theorists who fall into the cognitivist camp include Russell Hardin, "Trustworthiness," *Ethics*, 107(1) (1996), 26–42; Russell Hardin, "The Street-Level Epistemology of Trust"; James S. Coleman, *Foundations of Social Theory* (Cambridge, MA: Harvard University Press, 1990); Luhmann, "Familiarity, Confidence, Trust"; John Dunn, "Trust and Political Agency," in Diego Gambetta (ed.), *Trust: Making and Breaking Cooperative Relations* (Oxford: Basil Blackwell, 1988), pp. 73–93; Partha Dasgupta, "Trust as a Commodity," in Diego Gambetta (ed.), *Trust: Making and Breaking Cooperative Relations* (Oxford: Basil Blackwell, 1988), pp. 49–71.

Risk-assessment accounts cannot explain the vulnerability to betrayal that is distinctive of trust. When calculations of the risk of trusting an individual prove incorrect, the appropriate response is disappointment; there is no normative expectation to ground betrayal. Because trusting does not depend on anticipated positive will from the trustee, risk-assessment accounts cannot explain the difference between trust and reliance.

from belief thus allows us to appeal to different standards when determining the justifiability of trust than those for justified belief. By separating these standards, it becomes possible for trust to be justified in
conditions in which belief cannot.[14] Such a separation of standards of
justification is important for two reasons. First, cases of intuitively justified trust are not always cases of justified belief. The justifiability of belief
depends on the evidence for its truth. Yet justified trusting includes cases
in which our trust outstrips available evidence regarding the trustee.
Relatedly, defining trust in terms of belief renders trust either unjustifiable
or superfluous. If we cannot calculate the risk of relying on an individual,
then it is irrational to believe or rely on those individuals. If we can
calculate the risks, then trusting reliance becomes unnecessary.[15]

POLITICAL TRUST

In this section I develop an account of political trust that builds on the
general analysis of trust outlined in the previous section. My aim is to
characterize political relationships among citizens and officials that are
distinguished by trust in the sense that they generally exhibit default trust
and trust-responsiveness.[16] Trust is the default if the presumptive view
that is taken and the expectations that are made when encountering fellow
citizens and officials in ordinary interaction are trusting. This analysis sets
the stage for the discussion in the next section, where I consider the moral
value of political relationships characterized by trust.

Political trust is defined first by an attitude of optimism with respect
to the competence and will of other citizens and officials. This attitude
refers to a hopeful anticipation that citizens and officials will display the
relevant competence and will in their interactions with others. Focusing
first on citizens, their anticipated competence includes a capacity to
fulfill the duties and responsibilities associated with being a member of

---

[14] On this point see Jones, "Trust as an Affective Attitude," and Richard Holton, "Deciding to Trust,
Coming to Believe," *Australasian Journal of Philosophy*, 72 (1994), 63–76.

[15] Becker, "Trust as Noncognitive Security," 47; Lagerspetz, *Trust: The Tacit Demand*, p. 51.

[16] Different dimensions of trust in a political context are also explored in the literature. Discussions of
distinct but related issues of political trust focus on trust in institutions (e.g., Trudy Govier, *Social
Trust and Human Communities* [Montreal and Kingston: McGill-Queen's University Press, 1997])
and trust in government (e.g., Hardin, *Trust and Trustworthiness*). We should expect connections
among these various dimensions of political trust. Exploring these connections is beyond the scope
of this chapter. I focus on trust among groups of individuals because of my interest in
understanding whether relationships characterized by such political trust have non-instrumental
moral value.

a political community, including following the general rules and norms that structure economic, political, and general social interaction. Law, social convention, and various institutions define such rules and norms. This general competence presupposes the agency of citizens. Thus, citizens are viewed as able to govern their own lives and to interpret and understand the ground rules that regulate interaction within a political community, rather than requiring or needing specific instructions at every moment. By being viewed as agents, citizens are also viewed as responsible, that is, answerable to their conduct and properly held accountable for the choices they make.

The anticipated positive "will" is more accurately characterized as the absence of ill will toward groups of citizens or officials, or the community as a whole. Given that political relationships are fundamentally relationships among strangers, it is unrealistic and unnecessary for political trust to depend on anticipated positive goodwill. The lack of ill will anticipated of trusted citizens first involves the absence of a desire to undermine or overthrow a legitimate social order or government. Lack of ill will is not the same as unquestioningly accepting the status quo; indeed, trusted citizens are trusted to call attention to and push for the reform of the corruption of legitimate social practices and institutions. Second, lack of ill will entails a willingness to play fairly by the norms and rules structuring interaction, coupled with the absence of a desire to exploit the cooperation by others. Finally, lack of ill will reflects the absence of a desire to harm or, in the most extreme cases, eradicate members of certain social, political, or ethnic groups.

The anticipated competence and lack of ill will trusted officials will display in their interaction include the following. Officials act in an administrative capacity, on behalf of a specific community over which they have authority. Given this role, official competence first includes knowledge of what is appropriate and inappropriate for someone in their position to do. Appropriate exercises of authority take into direct consideration the impact on the welfare of the community on whose behalf they are acting when deliberating about which political decisions to make or enforce. The contrast here is with personal interest (primarily) determining official decisions or exercising authority in a way that undermines the well-being of the community. Relatedly, officials understand the appropriate impartiality toward sub-groups within a community that is required if they are to act as representatives of an entire political community. They also understand the limits of the domain over which their authority extends. Second, official competence extends to knowledge required for a particular official role. Lawmakers, for example, understand the requirements of the rule of law. By contrast, examples of these first two kinds of incompetence include the funneling of state resources into private bank accounts, systematic unjustified discrimination toward a segment of the population in the codification or enforcement of law or in the selection of appointed officials, or violations of the requirements of the rule of law.

Finally, official competence implies a real capability to act on the above knowledge. In practice competent officials can exercise their discretionary authority. They are not impotent in the sense of being unable to act in accordance with their best judgment because they are powerless, or rather constrained to act in accordance with the judgment of others. Officials are incompetent if they are unable to ensure enforcement of the rules they pass, have no control over the organization of the society or community they govern, or are unable to regulate interaction.

Trusted officials are seen as lacking ill will toward fellow officials or citizens. Lack of ill will refers to the absence of indifference or active hostility toward the whole or a segment of the political community. For example, trusted officials do not formulate policies that negatively impact the well-being of the population as a whole or sub-groups therein, either intentionally or as a predictable yet unintended consequence. Lack of ill will implies the absence of resentment, hatred, or strong dislike toward any one social group. In its extreme form, such negative emotions are reflected in genocidal or ethnic-cleansing campaigns. Second, officials who lack ill will are willing to abide by the norms and rules structuring the constraints of the permissible exercise of authority. Finally, they have no intention or desire to take advantage of or exploit the cooperation of others.

Like trust in general, the attitude of optimism constitutive of political trust is coupled with an expectation that trusted citizens and officials will be trust-responsive, or directly and favorably moved by the thought that they are being counted on. That is, trusted citizens and officials are expected to be directly responsive to the reliance that citizens and officials make manifest, and are moved to take into consideration and, all other things being equal, act in a way consistent with the expectation of the truster.

Political trust comes in degrees. At one end, citizens may trust their fellow citizens and officials absolutely and unquestioningly, with complete confidence that their trusting expectation will be fulfilled and complete faith in the competence and lack of ill will of others. At the opposite extreme, relationships may be characterized by absolute distrust, with citizens and officials viewing others as incompetent and possessing ill will, and having no expectation that others would be moved by trust were it to be placed in them. At a certain point along this spectrum, relationships can properly be characterized as relationships of trust. Relationships characterized by political trust require a certain threshold level of confidence or optimism regarding the lack of ill will and competence of the trustee. Similarly, there must be the expectation that the trustee will prove trust-responsive along with the trustee regularly proving sufficiently trust-responsive in practice.

Ideally, the scope of political trust should extend to all citizens and officials within a society. In practice, the scope of the trust is often more circumscribed. Some groups of officials, for example judges, may be trusted, while others, including the army and police, may not. Fellow members of a certain ethnic or religious background may be trusted, while members of a different background may not. Citizens as a whole may trust each other, but not trust any government officials. Similarly, only sub-groups within a population may prove trust-responsive.

THE MORAL VALUE OF POLITICAL TRUST

In the previous section I offered an analysis of political trust. In this section I discuss the non-instrumental moral value realized in political relationships characterized by default political trust and trust-responsiveness. Interestingly, the non-instrumental moral value of trust in general or political trust in particular is rarely considered. Part of the reason for this undoubtedly stems from the recognition that trusting makes a truster vulnerable to abuse, terror, deception, and exploitation. Recognition of this fact makes it seemingly difficult to argue that there is moral value in trust per se. It suggests that trust is a helpful tool that, in the right circumstances, can facilitate the realization of important goods for individuals or groups.

My goal in this section is to demonstrate that the value of trust is not reducible to its instrumental role. More specifically, I argue that political relationships predicated on default political trust and trust-responsiveness realize the constitutive values of respect and reciprocity. Default trust implies a presumption of the competence and lack of ill will among officials and citizens, and a presumptive expectation that the trustee will be trust-responsive. Fellow citizens and officials need not prove or give a positive reason to be trusted; rather, a reason or disconfirming evidence is needed to *not* trust citizens or officials. Similarly, default trust-responsiveness implies a presumptive direct and serious consideration of the reliance of others in the deliberation of the trusted. My discussion suggests that political relationships can be damaged when trust and trust-responsiveness are absent because the moral values of respect and a commitment to reciprocity are not expressed in the attitudes of citizens and officials in such relations.

Consider first how default political trust manifests respect. By trusting our fellow citizens and officials as a default position, we presume their competence and basic decency. By definition we are optimistic that citizens understand and are capable of following the basic norms for social interaction and of fulfilling their responsibilities. Citizens are presumed to be moral agents, responsible and capable of governing their own lives. Similarly, officials are presumed to be capable of acting effectively on behalf of the specific community over which they have authority and of possessing the knowledge of what is appropriate and inappropriate for someone in their position to do. Adopting trust as a default position in political relationships is an important way of acknowledging the effective agency of citizens and officials.[17] It is respectful of other citizens and officials to presume this competence, rather than demand that such competence be proven. Indeed, a default basic premise of democracies toward which transitional societies aspire, and one commonly regarded as respectful of citizens and officials, is that all citizens are competent in these ways and all citizens are capable of becoming officials who are competent in the requisite ways. Furthermore, one of the main justifications used by repressive and unjust regimes to deny basic rights to citizens, such as the right to vote, involves an appeal to the incompetence of members of certain groups, who consequently cannot be trusted with the responsibilities of full citizenship. Such actions and justifications are widely regarded as disrespectful; my analysis of the moral value of political trust explains why.

---

[17] The emphasis on the respect for agency achieved in trusting political relationships resonates with points made by Weinstock, who discusses the Kantian respect achieved in relations of trust among citizens who are strangers in civil society. Weinstock agrees that trusting involves an expectation on the part of the truster that the trustee will respond "because of how she stands to me rather than of how she stands to that which I am entrusting to her" ("Building Trust," 293). However, it is important to note that Weinstock's analysis is based on a notion of trust that appeals to the notion of entrusting valued goods as the source of vulnerability definitive of trust and a belief in the lack of ill will, rather than as an attitude that is partly defined by perceiving the trusted in this way; entrusting valued goods is not part of my analysis. Nor does he emphasize the perceived competence attributed to the trustee. In addition, he does not flesh out either of the characteristics of trust as they apply specifically to political relationships. Because of these differences, his analysis of *how* respect gets manifested is correspondingly different.

The presumption of the lack of ill will is an equally significant source of respect. An acknowledgement of agency is a condition for the possibility of trust. Trusting necessarily involves viewing the trustee as possessing an absence of ill will, which presupposes that the trustee has a will. By assuming a default position of trust of citizens and officials, then, we presume that others are agents with wills and do not require this to be proven. This constitutes an acknowledgement of their agency, which is fundamentally respectful.

How the presumption of the lack of ill will demonstrates respect, however, goes beyond the bare recognition of agency.[18] It is also respectful because it assumes basic decency and commitment to fair play. The lack of ill will presumed of citizens is defined by the absence of an active desire to harm others or to undermine a legitimate social order, along with a willingness to abide by rules and norms. It is not difficult for individuals to obey basic social norms regulating their interactions with strangers, such as to avoid harming others arbitrarily; this requires simple basic decency. Similarly, the presumption of lack of ill will of officials involves a presumption of their decency; officials are presumed to have a sufficient concern for the welfare of the political community as a whole. If assuming the basic decency of others is not unreasonable, then the lack of ill will assumption with respect to both citizens and officials seems similarly not unreasonable. A basic commitment to fair play is assumed of citizens, insofar as lack of ill will is defined by a willingness to follow broader legal, economic, and political norms and rules structuring interaction; this requires a basic commitment to fair play. Presuming lack of ill will in officials attributes this same basic commitment, insofar as they are willing to constrain themselves in how they utilize their powers and privileges qua officials. The expectation constitutive of trust expresses a willingness to rely on fellow citizens and officials in a trusting way, confident that this reliance will not be abused. The expectation gives expression to one's belief in the presumed decency and competence of others constitutive of the affective attitude of trust. To demand that citizens or officials prove their decency or commitment to fair play, or to presume they are incompetent, worthy of suspicion, or harboring ill will, is normally fundamentally disrespectful, insulting, and calls out for justification.

---

[18] One may object that distrust acknowledges the agency of the individual distrusted, so there is nothing distinctively respectful about taking a trusting stance toward citizens and officials. While distrust may manifest respect for bare agency, it is not as robustly respectful as trusting because it is coupled with a denial of the basic decency or competence of the distrusted.

Equally importantly, trusting citizens and officials realizes the value of reciprocity. By trusting officials and citizens as a default, we presume of others what we would like them to presume of us (competence, decency, and lack of ill will). Presuming the same of others acknowledges their desire for the same presumption and treats it as equally valid.

To be trust-responsive as a default shows respect because it acknowledges the right of other citizens and officials to make demands on us. When citizens and officials trust, they have certain expectations. They expect that other, trusted citizens and officials will prove trust-responsive, giving significant weight to the fact that they are being counted on. Underlying this expectation is a moral demand that the trustee recognize how the truster's agency influences what counts as appropriate or acceptable behavior. For citizens and officials, fulfilling the expectations of the truster is to acknowledge that other citizens and officials are not mere means that can be treated in whichever way is most effective for the realization of goals. Rather, the expectations of those who trust must be taken into account and given significant weight in the deliberations of those trusted. Proving trust-responsive represents an additional way of acknowledging and respecting the agency of fellow citizens and officials.

Default trust-responsiveness also fulfills the moral demands of reciprocity. By responding to the expectations of the truster as a default, we prove ourselves reliable in the same way that we expect those we trust to be. As a moral principle, reciprocity dictates that it is fair to expect others to act in certain ways only if I am willing to fulfill the reciprocal expectations that others make of me. This suggests that we cannot legitimately expect fellow citizens and officials to be directly and favorably moved by the fact that we are counting on them if we ourselves are not willing to fulfill the expectations of others who trust us. By fulfilling the expectations that others have of us we acknowledge that the legitimacy of our moral demands on others is dependent on what we as individuals do. These are importantly and non-contingently interdependent. Normally, by failing to fulfill the expectations of others who trust us, we fail to acknowledge the moral demands of reciprocity.

Let me conclude by summarizing the argument for the non-instrumental moral value of default trust and trust-responsiveness. By trusting our fellow citizens and officials we respect them, because we presume they are competent and possess basic decency. We demonstrate a commitment to reciprocity by presuming of others what we would like them to presume of us. Trust-responsiveness shows respect because it acknowledges the right of other citizens and officials to make role-specific demands on us. We demonstrate a commitment to reciprocity by proving ourselves reliable in the same way that we necessarily require others to be reliable in order to navigate the social world and pursue our individual ends successfully. In the context of political reconciliation, this discussion suggests that the deep and pervasive distrust characteristic of political relations during periods of civil conflict and repressive rule is appropriately regarded as a source of moral concern and damage to such relations. The attitudes of citizens and officials toward each other fail to express the respect and commitment to reciprocity realized in trusting political relations.

However, someone may object to this analysis of the non-instrumental moral value of political trust in the following way: a default stance of political trust does not always realize the moral values of respect and reciprocity. Indeed, in certain contexts this default stance facilitates exploitation, abuse, and harm. If you live in an environment rife with corruption, failing to prove trust-responsive by ignoring the rules may not fail to respect a commitment to reciprocity; in a context of general bypassing or manipulation of the rules, the conditions in which reciprocity would be realized through your actions are undermined or absent. Similarly, presuming of others that they lack ill will in the sense of being committed to fair play may not be reasonable. Indeed, this presumption may unjustifiably put oneself at risk of exploitation.

Further, in some contexts a default stance of *distrust*, approaching other citizens or officials with suspicion and wariness, seems reasonable. This seems particularly applicable in precisely the contexts in which I am interested – contexts where societies are deeply divided, in the midst of or emerging from civil conflict or repressive unjust rule. In such contexts citizens often cannot reasonably assume that other citizens and officials recognize their agency, either because they are denied rights or legally recognized rights are systematically violated. The absence of a trusting attitude, then, does not fail to express respect and a commitment to reciprocity; such moral values would not be realized in trusting political relations in these contexts. Far from being a source of damage to political relationships, distrust is a way of preventing harm to individuals and damage to political relationships.

In response, I grant that respect and reciprocity are not realized in all political relationships of trust. Default political trust and trust-responsiveness are *conditionally* non-instrumentally valuable. More precisely, respect and reciprocity are realized in relations where default political trust and trust-responsiveness are reasonable. However, it would be a mistake to conclude from the conditional nature of the non-instrumental moral values expressed in political relationships characterized by trust that there is no damage to political relationships when distrust is reasonable. Instead, the reasonableness of distrust in many transitional contexts is an indication of precisely how deep the damage to political relationships is, for the conditions that would make it possible to express respect and a commitment to reciprocity through the attitude one takes toward others do not obtain. In the next section I consider the conditions that influence the reasonableness of default political trust and trust-responsiveness. In the process I demonstrate why we should take the reasonableness of distrust in contexts of civil rule and repressive regimes to be a source of moral concern and why we should take the cultivation of the conditions that make political trust reasonable to be an important aim of processes of political reconciliation.

THE MORAL JUSTIFIABILITY OF DEFAULT POLITICAL TRUST AND TRUST-RESPONSIVENESS

In the previous section I considered an objection to my claim that political relationships characterized by default political trust and trust-responsiveness realize the non-instrumental moral values of respect and reciprocity. According to the objection, there are contexts in which default political trust and trust-responsiveness expose the truster to exploitation and harm. As part of my response, I claimed that default political trust and trust-responsiveness are conditionally non-instrumentally valuable. In this section I consider when political relationships characterized by default political trust and trust-responsiveness express the values of respect and reciprocity. To do this, I examine the circumstances that influence the reasonableness of adopting a default stance of political trust and trust-responsiveness, for it is when default political trust and trust-responsiveness are reasonable that political relationships in which these are the default express respect and a commitment to reciprocity.

How to assess the reasonableness of the default attitude of optimism constitutive of political trust follows straightforwardly from my analysis of what political trust entails. Whether it is reasonable to adopt a default attitude of trust toward a particular official or citizen depends on the general character of the social and political environment. Specifically, it depends on the degree to which officials and citizens generally are competent and lacking ill will as defined in the second section of this chapter. An example of a context where default trust is reasonable, then, would be one in which public officials are generally not powerless but are actually able to enforce declared rules and in which public officials are committed to the rule of law, and so respect the limits on their authority specified by declared rules. On the other hand, widespread and known political incompetence or political ill will among citizens or officials undermines the reasonableness of default trust because there are no grounds to support such an attitude. For example, in societies rife with official corruption it is not reasonable to presume that officials constrain themselves by the lawful regulations attending to their official position. Similarly, governments that deny or violate basic political and social rights demonstrate a failure by officials to recognize and appreciate the agency of all citizens and how that agency should influence and constrain government action.

In Iraq the distrust that increasingly characterizes the relationships between citizens and security forces specifically stems in part from the clear absence of the competence and lack of ill will that would make trust reasonable. As quoted in the *New York Times,* Majid Hamid, a Sunni human rights worker whose brother was abducted and killed by men in police uniform, eloquently captures the reasonable default *distrust* citizens have toward security forces: "Whenever I see uniforms now, I figure they must be militias ... I immediately try to avoid them. If I have my gun, I know I need to be ready to use it." The article explains one source of this distrust when it describes the attitude of Iraqis in Baghdad as "shell-shocked and made fearful by violence that seems to be committed almost daily by men dressed as those who are supposed to protect and serve ... Everywhere Iraqis in uniform go, from ice cream shops to checkpoints, people now flee."[19] By blatantly violating the expectation of citizens that security officials will protect them from harm and instead exploiting their position of power to inflict harm, police officers have undermined the reasonableness of presuming either lack of ill will or competence of officials.

Understanding the reasonableness of presuming that trustees will prove trust-responsive is more complicated. Widespread incompetence and the presence of ill will undermine the reasonableness of expecting that officials and citizens will prove reliable in the anticipated manner. Incompetent officials and citizens may not know how or be able to prove reliable in the anticipated manner. Officials and citizens with ill will toward

[19] Damien Cave, "In Iraq, It's Hard to Trust Anyone in Uniform," *New York Times*, August 3, 2006, www.nytimes.com/2006/08/03/world/middleeast/ 03uniforms.html. Accessed August 3, 2006.

fellow citizens and officials may lack the desire to respond in accordance with the truster's expectation.

Yet it is not obvious that it is reasonable to presume the trust-responsiveness of citizens and officials in contexts in which general political incompetence and ill will are absent. Political relationships are characteristically relationships among strangers, or individuals about whom we do not share an extended history of personal interaction and toward whom we do not have substantial goodwill. Given this, what reasons could ground the presumption that such strangers will prove trust-responsive? That is, why and when is it reasonable to presume that individuals, about whom we know little except that they can be presumed to lack ill will and be competent, will be directly and favorably moved by the thought of being relied on by fellow citizens and officials?

To answer this question, I want to first turn to a discussion by Philip Pettit in "The Cunning of Trust," where he considers the question: why should we think that an individual has goodwill toward us and will prove reliable if we manifest trust, where proving reliable entails attaching greater utility to doing a particular action?[20] Pettit's use of the term "trust-responsiveness" simply requires that the trustee do what the truster is anticipating, but not necessarily be moved by the fact of trust itself.[21] He suggests that appealing to a basic psychological desire of individuals can explain why trustees will be motivated to prove trust-responsive in his sense. Specifically, individuals desire to have the good opinion of others and of themselves,[22] what Pettit labels attitude-dependent goods that a "person can enjoy only so far as they are the object of certain attitudes . . . on the part of others" (or themselves).[23] Generally speaking, individuals care about attaining attitude-dependent goods and consequently seek the good opinion of others. It is this desire, Pettit argues, that motivates trust-responsiveness.

Pettit's key insight is that trusting has an expressive and communicative character. It is trust's expressive character that motivates an individual to prove herself reliable. Trusting normally expresses that the truster thinks well of the trustee (or will continue to think well insofar as the trustee

---

[20] Pettit, "The Cunning of Trust."

[21] In this way Pettit's understanding of trust-responsiveness departs from my understanding, in which to be trust-responsive is to be directly and favorably moved by the demands of trust itself. I will return to this difference below.

[22] Interestingly, in Chapter 1 I appeal to this same basic psychological disposition in connection with understanding how the rule of law influences behavior in practice.

[23] Pettit, "The Cunning of Trust," 212.

proves trust-responsive). However, the trustee will only continue to enjoy
the good opinion of the trusted, and realize this attitude-dependent good,
to the extent that she proves trust-responsive in an appropriate manner.
By ignoring or exploiting trust, the trustee risks losing the good opinion
of the truster and the attitude-dependent good that trusting makes
possible. The good opinion of third parties, Pettit notes, is also impacted
by whether the trustee proves trust-responsive. Trusting communicates
the good opinion that the truster has of the trustee in a general manner.
Fulfilling the trust of others can enhance the good opinion of third parties
of the trustee. By implication, Pettit argues, ignoring or exploiting the
truster's trust, especially in a public manner, has a negative impact on the
good opinion of the trustee by third parties.

In my view, the public dimensions of the act of trusting and of
proving trust-responsive that Pettit emphasizes are especially important
in the context of political relationships. These relationships are conducted within government and within civil society, all of which can be
especially open to public view and the subject of public concern. This
feature of political trust, coupled with an appeal to the desire for the
good opinion of others, offers a compelling way of understanding the
motivational force of being trusted in a political sense. However, to help
us understand why it is reasonable to formulate the expectation constitutive of political trust, it is necessary to fill out and modify Pettit's
analysis in two important ways.

First, the content of the good opinion that political trusting expresses
needs to be specified. Second, the reasonableness of expecting that
citizens and officials will prove trust-responsive in the sense articulated
in the second section of this chapter needs to be shown. Pettit's use of
"trust-responsiveness" simply requires that the trustee do what the truster
is anticipating, and in this sense prove reliable.[24] An individual may
prove trust-responsive if she acts in the way the truster is anticipating
because she wants to maintain the good opinion of the truster and third
parties, but *not* because of the fact that she is being relied on itself.
We merely rely on individuals when we presume they will act in a
specific way out of fear or out of the desire for the good opinion of
others. We *trust*, on the other hand, when we expect that the trustee be
moved directly and favorably by the fact of being trusted itself. Proving
trust-responsive requires that the trustee be moved directly and favorably
by the fact that she is being relied upon. We need to demonstrate that it

---

[24] In footnote 10 I noted our divergent understandings of trust-responsiveness.

is reasonable to expect this of citizens and officials and link this with the desire for the good opinion of others in the appropriate way. In so doing, the role that the desire for the good opinion of others plays in explaining the reasonableness of presuming trust-responsiveness must be modified to distinguish trust from mere reliance.

In my view, the content of the good opinion that political trust expresses follows from the analysis of political trust offered in the previous section.[25] By trusting in a political sense, we express our view of fellow citizens and officials as competent, basically decent, and lacking ill will. Political trust also conveys the hopeful anticipation that the trustee will prove trust-responsive. Presuming trust-responsiveness expresses the judgment that the trustee will recognize and respect you as an agent, and will recognize and respect the demands of reciprocity. To view an individual in this way is normally to think well of her and thus trusting communicates the good opinion that the truster has of the trustee. By proving trust-responsive, an individual confirms this opinion and demonstrates in practice that she respects and acknowledges the truster and the demands of reciprocity.

The remaining challenge, then, is to explain the reasonableness of anticipating that fellow citizens and officials will prove trust-responsive in the sense that they are directly and favorably responsive to the fact that they are trusted. To do this, I want to clarify the role that the appeal to the desire for the good opinion of others should play in explaining the reasonableness of default political trust. In my view, appealing to this desire gives us a reason to think that other citizens and officials will be directly and favorably moved by the thought that

---

[25] Pettit has an alternative understanding of the content of the good opinion that trusting expresses. According to Pettit, when you trust you communicate the belief that the trustee is trustworthy, or at least a presumption of trustworthiness that will be confirmed or denied depending on how the trustee responds. Pettit defines trustworthiness as proving reliable because of a desirable character trait, like loyalty and virtue. For example, if you think the trustee is virtuous, then you have reason to believe that manifesting your reliance will motivate the trustee to respond to your trust for its own sake. To respond to trust is a virtuous action; it is the right thing to do (Pettit, "The Cunning of Trust," 209–12). In Pettit's view, the explanation of how the desire for the good opinion of others motivates trust is "parasitic on these mechanisms for trust." To think of someone as trustworthy is normally to think well of them. The desire for the good opinion of others can generate a motivation to prove trust-responsive among those not independently trustworthy, loyal, or virtuous, because doing what the truster expects is a way to maintain the truster's good opinion. However, it is problematic to adopt this analysis of what trusting expresses in the political context. Pettit's analysis relies on overly optimistic presumptions of deep loyalty or virtue of fellow citizens and officials that reasonable trust-responsiveness is parasitic on. It is also unnecessary. As the discussion below shows, there is a simpler and more direct way to link the good opinion expressed in political trusting with the content of political trust.

they are being counted on in a distinctively trusting way. This desire is not the *reason* why the trustee proves reliable. Rather, the reason to prove oneself reliable is because one is being relied on in a trusting manner. The recognition that trusting expresses the good opinion that the truster has of the trustee explains *why* one might be motivated to prove trust-responsive in this way toward those to whom one simply lacks ill will. The key point is that to maintain the good opinion of the truster, the trustee must prove trust-responsive by responding *to the demands of trust itself.* If citizens and officials want to achieve the attitude-dependent goods of trust, they must *not* be motivated directly by the desire for the good opinion of the trustee. Such reliability fails to fulfill the expectation constitutive of trust and so fails to satisfy the conditions under which the desire for the good opinion of the truster and third parties can be maintained.

It may be objected that appealing to the desire for the good opinion of others is unnecessary to explain why citizens and officials are moved by the demands of trust. The fact that being relied on in a trusting manner motivates individuals to prove themselves trust-responsive is not mysterious. Proving trust-responsive is simply the right thing to do. This is why, as Pettit notes, individuals who are loyal and virtuous *are* trust-responsive in my sense. According to the objection, citizens and officials should be expected to be moved by trust in the same way they can be expected to be moved by the demands of morality more generally. Expecting citizens to respond to the demands of trust is analogous to expecting citizens to be concerned about or motivated by the demands of morality more generally. If it is not unreasonable to expect citizens and officials to not be amoral but to be moved by the demands of morality, at least to a minimum degree, then it is not unreasonable to expect citizens and officials to be moved by the demands of trust.

The problem with this explanation is that it provides an unilluminating (and often incorrect) analysis of why, in certain political contexts, default political trust is or becomes unreasonable. Implicit in the objection is the assumption that in certain contexts, citizens or officials can become so morally corrupt that they no longer care about doing the right thing or are no longer moved by the demands of morality. However, this explanation is in tension with the characteristically deep and pervasive forms of official and unofficial denial and/or rationalization for immoral actions practiced in contexts where default political trust is not reasonable. This is especially true in contexts of civil conflict or repressive rule. Immorality is rarely openly admitted and responsibility for incompetence or ill will is rarely accepted. Instead, to return to an example discussed in Chapter 1, official responsibility for disappearing citizens is denied and torture is labeled as necessary for victory in a battle to save civilization. Such patterns suggest that a lack of concern for morality is not primarily the reason that trust-responsiveness becomes unreasonable to expect.

A more fruitful line of inquiry suggested by the above analysis is: why do people stop caring about maintaining or having the good opinion of certain individuals or groups of potential or actual trusters? Determining when it is reasonable to expect that citizens and officials will prove trust-responsive depends partly on understanding how and why the general desire for the good opinion of others gets blunted, qualified, or limited in certain social contexts such that the motivation to be trust-responsive and, by extension, the reasonableness of trust get undermined. Pettit himself offers useful guidance on precisely this issue, which highlights the relevance of this line of inquiry for social contexts in which trust is in fact unreasonable, such as divided societies or societies in the midst of civil conflict or repressive rule. The desire for the good opinion of others, he writes, may be limited to a certain sub-group of the population, which occurs in deeply divided social contexts or in contexts in which there is a "grossly inferior minority" population. Absent a desire for the good opinion of such marginalized groups, there will be a correspondingly lessened (or absent) motivation to prove trust-responsive.[26] Second, the absence of conditions of publicity and transparency, which guarantee access to information, can undermine the motivation to prove trust-responsive. Failing to prove trust-responsive in such conditions will not lead to the lessening of the good view of trusters and third parties, since such others will not have relevant information about how you acted. Third, the absence of a context in which trusting plays the relevant "signaling function" can prove problematic. Using the above framework, trusting is assumed to signal the view of the trusted as trust-responsive, competent, and lacking ill will. When this expressive function is not realized because of, for example, known general corruption, then trusting can no longer plausibly be said to convey this view of the trustee.

A different objection that may be raised to my analysis is that I have shown why and when the expectation constitutive of trust is reasonable and why it is reasonable to prove trust-responsive, but in so doing I have

---

[26] Indeed, in divided contexts proving trust-responsive toward trusters from an antagonistic population can undermine the good opinion of the trustee in the minds of members of their own population.

undermined my claim that trust has a non-instrumental moral value. According to Pettit, the desire for the good opinion of others that motivates trust-responsiveness is not a very noble desire, but rather one of which we should be ashamed. He writes, "The desire for the good opinion of others ... counts by most people's lights, not as a desirable feature for which they need to strive, but rather as a disposition – a neutral or even shameful one – that it is hard to shed."[27] If the desire for the good opinion of others is a rather base desire, and it is the desire that motivates individuals to be moved by trust itself, then that calls into question whether respect and reciprocity are conveyed by proving to be trust-responsive.

In response, I want to suggest that the desire for the good opinion of others is, in its non-pathological forms, deeply moral. This desire reflects a desire to be recognized as good, as well as a care of, concern for, and a sense of interconnectedness to others in the world. Individuals want not simply the esteem of others, but to be well thought of in a moral sense. It is this desire that helps us understand the lengths to which individuals and groups will go to deny or rationalize wrongdoing. In addition, ignoring or being indifferent to the opinion of others can represent a form of narcissism and arrogance. To suggest that it is a matter of indifference is to suggest that we have complete access to the standards for doing well and for how well we are in fact doing. To care about the good opinion of others and to use their opinions as a partial barometer for how well we fare reflects a certain kind of humility. It also reflects a concern about how our interactions in the world impact others. Here a default concern about the good opinion of others seems appropriate; that is, unless countervailing considerations (which include considerations of context) are present, we should care about the view of others and assume that they have knowledge or guidance as to how well we are doing.

Finally, given how thinly the affective attitude of trust is specified as attributing basic decency and competence to officials and citizens, and given that trust-responsiveness is grounded in a very basic psychological desire (for the good opinion of others), it is clear that there needs to be a serious erosion in the moral fabric of a society for political trust to be eroded as well. In contexts where general trusting is not reasonable, we can explain why moral problems are at the foundation of the breakdown of trust. If it is no longer reasonable to assume the basic decency, lack of ill will, competence, or general desire for the good opinion of other

---

[27] Pettit, "The Cunning of Trust," 203.

citizens and officials, a significant breakdown in moral relations and corruption of the general moral environment has occurred. Basic decency, competence, and desire for the goodwill of others – the features that define and underpin default reasonable trust – do not reflect a utopian point of view and should not be impossible to maintain. My framework of trust helps to highlight the deep moral problems at the foundation of the breakdown of trust.

Recognition of such problems puts us in a position to understand why the fact that distrust is reasonable in contexts of civil conflict and repressive rule should be a source of moral concern. Distrust, even when reasonable, is appropriately regarded as an important source of damage and moral concern, both because respect and a commitment to reciprocity are not expressed in political relationships and because the conditions that would make it possible for political relationships to express such values – general basic decency, lack of ill will, competence, and concern about the good opinion of others – do not obtain. Appreciating the conditional non-instrumental value of political trust illuminates *why* we have significant reason to view reasonable default political trust as an important characteristic of rebuilt political relationships.

CHAPTER 3

Capabilities

INTRODUCTION

The theoretical frameworks of the rule of law and reasonable default political trust discussed in Chapters 1 and 2 enrich our understanding of some of the important moral issues that are expressed in many of the actions during civil conflict and repressive rule that are widely regarded as morally problematic. However, they do not address all of the issues that should be of moral concern. Indeed, many of the most obvious and deeply troubling aspects of political relationships, like normalized and systematic violence, do not seem best described as failures of the rule of law or trust. An appeal to the relational problems associated with the absence of enforced rules and distrust does not seem sufficient for explaining how systematic violence afflicts relationships within a community, nor does conceptualizing the tasks of processes of reconciliation strictly in terms of the establishment of the rule of law and the cultivation of reasonable trust seem to capture all that we care about achieving in the rebuilding of political relationships.

The central thesis of this chapter is that many intuitively damaging characteristics of relationships during civil conflict and repressive rule are helpfully analyzed using the capability framework. The capability framework enables us to understand the various kinds of harm involved in common unjust institutional structures and patterns of interaction, and the ways in which it may be possible to repair them. It highlights the deeper changes, both official and unofficial, in political relationships required by political reconciliation that neither the frameworks of the rule of law nor of political trust can adequately capture.

Capability refers to the effective freedom or genuine opportunity of individuals to achieve valuable doings and beings, or functionings.

I am grateful to Linda Radzik and Susanne Sreedhar for their comments on earlier drafts of this chapter.

My discussion in this chapter concentrates on four capabilities that are constitutive of political relationships and especially impacted by civil conflict and repressive rule: the capabilities of being respected; being recognized as a member of a political community; being an effective participant in the economic, social, and political life of the community; and fulfilling basic functionings that are necessary in order to survive and to escape poverty.

There are three sections in this chapter. The first provides a brief overview of the basic concept of capability and discusses the moral significance of four particular capabilities relevant for the present discussion. The second considers the important ways in which capabilities are systematically diminished during civil conflict and repressive rule. The third addresses the relationship between the undermining of capabilities, the breakdown of the rule of law, and the reasonableness of trust.

CAPABILITIES

General description

The economist Amartya Sen and the philosopher Martha Nussbaum first developed the capability approach.[1] According to Sen and Nussbaum, there are a range of valuable doings and beings that are constituents of individual well-being, which an individual may or may not be in a position to achieve. Being respected, adequately nourished, and educated are examples of such doings or beings. Sen and Nussbaum label such doings and beings as functionings. An individual's overall capability is a function of the various combinations of functionings that she has a genuine opportunity to achieve in a secure manner.[2]

To claim that an individual has a given capability, and so a genuine opportunity to achieve a particular functioning, is to say more than

---

[1] Amartya Sen and Martha Nussbaum are the pioneers of the concept of capabilities. See, for example, Martha Nussbaum, "Aristotle, Politics, and Human Capabilities: A Response to Antony, Arneson, Charlesworth, and Mulgan," *Ethics*, 111(1) (2000a), 102–40; Martha Nussbaum, *Women and Human Development: The Capabilities Approach* (Cambridge University Press, 2000b); Martha Nussbaum, "Adaptive Preferences and Women's Options," *Economics and Philosophy*, 17 (2001), 67–88; Amartya Sen, "Development as Capabilities Expansion," *Journal of Development Planning*, 19 (1989), 41–58; Amartya Sen, *Inequality Reexamined*, (Cambridge, MA: Harvard University Press, 1992); Amartya Sen, "Capability and Well-Being," in Martha Nussbaum and Amartya Sen (eds.), *The Quality of Life* (Oxford: Clarendon Press, 1993); Amartya Sen, *Commodities and Capabilities* (Oxford University Press, 1999a); Amartya Sen, *Development as Freedom* (New York: Anchor Books, 1999b); Amartya Sen, "Elements of a Theory of Human Rights," *Philosophy and Public Affairs*, 32(4) (2004), 315–56.
[2] Sen, *Inequality Reexamined*.

that she will not be interfered with in specific ways. An individual can be free from external interference and still be unable to realistically pursue and achieve any valuable options. For example, an individual who is malnourished may not have the capability of being nourished, though no one is violating her negative rights by preventing her from getting food.[3] An individual may simply not have the resources required to purchase food. Although this example highlights the importance of resources for capabilities, the capability of an individual is not strictly a function of her resources. Individuals vary in terms of what they can achieve with a given resource.[4] A bike can be a resource for mobility. However, whether an individual can achieve mobility by having a bike depends on facts about an individual (e.g., whether they are able-bodied, disabled, or otherwise physically unable to operate a bike); the condition of the physical infrastructure (e.g., whether there are paved roads or a path on which a bike can travel); and social norms (e.g., whether there are formal or informal restrictions on who may use a bike).[5] Thus an assessment of an individual's capability must take into consideration what Sen calls interpersonal conversion rates, or differences in the ability of individuals to achieve functionings with a given amount of resources; such differences will be a function of personal factors, social norms, public policies, and legal, political, and economic institutions.[6]

Following the philosophers Jonathan Wolff and Avner de-Shalit, we can summarize the two general factors that shape the capabilities of individuals as: what a person has, and what a person can do with what she has.[7] The first category is broadly understood to encompass both internal and external resources. Internal resources capture what the individual herself possesses, such as talents, skills, and psychological well-being. External resources refer to outside means that an individual

---

[3] Amartya Sen, "Freedom of Choice: Concept and Content," *European Economic Review*, 32(2–3) (1988), 269–94, at 272. Indeed, precisely this phenomenon is currently playing itself out in the world community, where the spike in food prices and lower supplies of food are contributing to an increase in global hunger. See Marc Lacey, "Across Globe, Empty Bellies Bring Rising Anger," *New York Times*, December 4, 2008, www.nytimes.com/2008/04/18/world/americas/18food.html. Accessed December 4, 2008.

[4] Sen, "Capability and Well-Being," p. 33; Sen, *Development as Freedom*, pp. 70–1.

[5] Conversion factors impact whether and how commodities contribute to functionings. Two general types of conversion factors are personal and social. Examples of social conversion factors include public policies and social norms. Ingrid Robeyns, "The Capability Approach: A Theoretical Survey," *Journal of Human Development*, 6(1) (2005), 93–114, at 99.

[6] Sen, *Commodities and Capabilities*.

[7] Jonathan Wolff and Avner de-Shalit, *Disadvantage* (Oxford University Press, 2007), pp. 172–3.

enjoys, including wealth and income or family support. The second category is the social and material structure that determines what an individual can do or become with the resources she has. Law, customs and tradition, religion, language, culture, the physical infrastructure, and the natural environment are all part of the social and material structure.

As noted above, an individual has a capability only if she is free to achieve a given functioning in a secure manner. Security of functioning achievement implies that the achievement of a functioning is not temporary or at undue risk; the functioning achievement is one that an individual is able to maintain. One only has a genuine capability, then, if the achievement of a given functioning is not a temporary or unstable achievement and if the achievement is not put at undue risk by the pursuit of other functionings. The risks of particular moral concern are those that are involuntary, or risks that an individual "would not have taken had they had the option, or are forced to take risks that in one way or another are bigger than others are being exposed to or take."[8] By contrast, in some cases the achievement of a particular functioning may represent only a temporary accomplishment.[9] For an individual who faces the constant threat of eviction due to unsteady employment and a corresponding shifting ability to pay her rent, the continued achievement of being sheltered is constantly at risk. Alternatively, the possibility of achieving certain functionings may necessitate putting other functionings at risk. This occurs when, for example, all feasible available employment options are in dangerous occupations. In this case employment and a concern for securing nourishment and shelter through employment force an individual to put her bodily integrity at risk.

Paolo Gardoni and I have argued that to determine which genuine opportunities a particular individual has, we should consider what she has chosen and achieved, as well as what other individuals who are similarly situated have chosen and achieved. Information about the functionings of these other people tells us which choices are genuinely open to an individual. Statistical data can provide a picture of the opportunities that an individual may have, based on the opportunities others have taken. Such information allows us to distinguish between a situation in which an individual has a genuine opportunity that is not actually taken advantage of and a situation in which such a genuine

---

[8] Ibid., p. 66.
[9] Wolff and de-Shalit first emphasized the importance of security for capabilities in ibid., pp. 63–73.

opportunity does not exist.[10] For example, higher rates of unemployment or higher concentrations in low-wage or low-skilled forms of employment among individuals from a sub-group within society suggests a diminished or restricted capability to work. Statistical information can also provide an insight into the security of achieved functionings. According to Wolff and de-Shalit, we can infer the security of functionings from the statistical trends for certain sub-groups over time in terms of their mobility within a sector. In their words, "Imagine that among certain groups – perhaps the young, recent immigrants, or the low paid – there is a high degree of mobility in employment or housing, with those moving jobs or homes also experiencing periods of unemployment or homelessness. This, then, gives a prima facie reason to believe these functionings are not achieved securely by people within these groups."[11]

When systematic differences in terms of the range, quality, and security of genuine opportunities available can be found among sub-groups within a society, we have *prima facie* reason to believe that a structural barrier to achieving a particular functioning exists for members of a particular social group. That is, we have reason to attribute differences in the functionings achieved not simply to personal preference, individual choice, or individual resources, but rather to systematic, for example, institutional considerations that constrain the genuine options of individuals.

Capabilities have both an instrumental and a non-instrumental moral value. The instrumental value of capabilities stems from the connection between capabilities and freedom. Capabilities reflect the genuine opportunities open to an individual; the greater the capability of an individual, then, the freer she is to achieve what she desires or values. Conversely, the absence of capabilities impedes the freedom of individuals to achieve what they desire or value. Capabilities also have non-instrumental value because of their relationship with freedom. As Sen notes, having genuine opportunities is an important constitutive dimension of freedom; to deny a woman an opportunity to do what she values is to interfere with her freedom.[12]

---

[10] For a more detailed discussion of the assessment of capabilities, see Colleen Murphy and Paolo Gardoni, "Assessing Capability Instead of Achieved Functionings in Risk Analysis," *Journal of Risk Research*, 13(2) (2010), 137–47.

[11] Wolff and de-Shalit, *Disadvantage*, pp. 116–17.

[12] Amartya Sen, *Rationality and Freedom* (Cambridge, MA: Harvard University Press, 2004), p. 585.

The non-instrumental value of capabilities stems from the view of the human being implicit in capabilities, and the relationship between capabilities and justice. First, the idea of capabilities is premised on a view of human beings as agents, able to shape how their lives go and the terms of their interaction with others. In Nussbaum's words, "The core idea is that of the human being as a dignified free being who shapes his or her life in cooperation and reciprocity with others."[13] To have a capability means that an individual is genuinely free to choose whether or not to strive to achieve a particular doing or being, or dimension of well-being in her life.[14] Thus, having capabilities means that an individual is in a position to shape who and what she becomes. The conception of the person underpinning the capabilities framework is the same conception implicit in the frameworks of the rule of law and trust. Indeed, it is out of respect for the agency of individuals that proponents of capabilities for public policy purposes have emphasized the importance of promoting capabilities and not functionings in public policy; the guiding idea is that the role of public policy should not be to ensure that certain choices are made, but to ensure that the conditions are in place from which an individual can choose from among a number of valuable options how her life will go. Having a genuine opportunity to achieve valuable functionings is a constitutive component of individual well-being. Second, capabilities have non-instrumental value because they define important dimensions of justice. The lack of certain capabilities can constitute a violation of justice.[15] Conceptualizing the demands of justice in terms of capabilities focuses on what is of fundamental, non-instrumental concern, namely,

---

[13] Nussbaum, *Women and Human Development*, p. 72.

[14] Sen, "Capability and Well-Being," p. 39. Sen claims that capabilities as positive freedom represent one or two dimensions of freedom. Opportunities are one dimension of freedom. The second dimension of freedom is what Sen labels the process dimension and is broadly concerned with freedom of choice and *how* an individual fulfills opportunities or *why* an opportunity is not available. The foreclosure of an opportunity that stems from a direct violation of negative freedom thus raises, in Sen's view, a distinct issue of justice that the foreclosure of that same opportunity due to illness does not. However, in both cases the capability of an individual might be reduced by the same amount. This example is taken from Sen, "Elements of a Theory of Human Rights," 330–1. However, in this chapter I focus only on capabilities. In practice, the two types of freedoms are deeply interconnected. Individuals may consider the freedom to choose as constitutive of the opportunities she values. Thus the way we define opportunities can in many cases incorporate the process aspect of freedom. Furthermore, an individual is likely to have better opportunities if she is able to participate in the political and economic processes that determine the opportunities she will have.

[15] See Nussbaum, *Women and Human Development*, especially pp. 70–3; Wolff and de-Shalit, *Disadvantage*; Sen, *Development as Freedom*.

the freedom of individuals to achieve important dimensions of well-being. Thinking of the demands of justice in terms of a required distribution of commodities, like income or resources, fails to acknowledge that such resources are of value instrumentally because of their role in facilitating the capabilities of individuals.

Application to political reconciliation

As I illustrate in the next section, the capabilities framework is useful in thinking about political reconciliation because it helps us to properly conceptualize important sources of damage to political relationships during civil conflict and repression. In so doing, the capabilities framework puts us in a position to understand what the repair of political relationships in transitional contexts requires. Before discussing the particular capabilities, I offer two initial reasons for assuming that the capabilities framework is promising for understanding what political reconciliation entails. First, the concept of capabilities focuses our attention on the role that institutions play in defining and structuring the genuine opportunities of individuals. It explicitly recognizes that institutional norms and institutionally defined roles and relationships fundamentally affect what individuals are free to do or become. Thus the capabilities framework is uniquely positioned to capture the institutional implications of political reconciliation that are broader than the implications of a legal system. Second, the emphasis of the capabilities framework on the influence of personal resources, external resources, and the social and material structure on an individual's capability creates a broad conceptual space for locating injustice in relationships and understanding how political relationships are damaged during periods of civil conflict or repressive rule.

In the next section I focus on four capabilities that are impacted by civil conflict and repressive rule: the capabilities of being respected by others; of participating in the social, economic, and political life of a community; of being recognized as a member of a political community; and of surviving and escaping poverty. The first three capabilities are fundamentally relational, in the sense that they implicate doings and beings that are necessarily achieved in relationships. The fourth capability captures a necessary condition for achieving central relational capabilities.

Although other capabilities may also be impacted by civil conflict and repressive rule, my interest is restricted to these four because they are constitutive of relationships among equals within a political community. Sen highlights the deep connection between the ideals of justice and equality in the modern imagination, which is a product of the assumption in the modern world of the moral equality of all human beings.[16] The equality of political relationships depends on everyone within such relationships being effectively free to achieve these particular functionings. The most basic capability that is definitive of political relationships is the capability of being recognized as a member of a political community, where the absence of such recognition would include being ostracized or regarded as fundamentally and permanently an outsider. This capability is often a condition for certain kinds of political relationships to be possible, and is impacted by how membership in a political community is conceptualized. Insofar as one cannot relate as a member of a political community with others, one cannot by implication relate as an equal member. Second, relationships among equals are premised on respect. Thus the second capability of concern is the capability of being respected by others.[17] Disrespect, humiliation, and degradation signal the lack of recognition of the standing and dignity of others. Third, political relationships encompass the interaction of members of a society in the social, economic, and political domains. Exclusion from these domains or an inability to shape the character of these domains signals that one is inferior relative to other members of society. Thus the capability of being a participant in the political, economic, and social processes of one's community is critical for political relationships of equality.[18] The fourth and final capability of interest is not fundamentally relational, but is in practice often a condition for respect and participation.

[16] Sen writes that each normative theory of justice has a view of basal equality or "equality in some individual feature that is taken to be basic in that particular conception of social justice": *Inequality Reexamined*, p. 131. Theorists, from libertarians to Rawlsians to utilitarians, all argue that there is something "which everyone should have and which is quite crucial to their own particular approach." Sen, *Inequality Reexaminded*, p. ix.

[17] This corresponds to one aspect of the capability for affiliation proposed by Nussbaum. Nussbaum writes that part of affiliation involves "having the social bases of self-respect and non-humiliation; being able to be treated as a dignified being whose worth is equal to that of others": *Women and Human Development*, p. 79.

[18] This resonates with Nussbaum's capability of having control over one's environment, but is broader than the category she proposes. Nussbaum describes the components of this capability in the following terms: "**A. Political**. Being able to participate effectively in political choices that govern one's life; having the right of political participation, protections of free speech and association. **B. Material**. Being able to hold property (both land and movable goods), not just formally but in terms of real opportunity; and having property rights on an equal basis with others; having the right to seek employment on an equal basis with others; having freedom from unwarranted search and seizure." Ibid., p. 80.

The basic capability of, in Sen's words, doing "certain basic things necessary for survival or to avoid poverty"[19] includes the capabilities of maintaining bodily health, being adequately nourished, and having sufficient income.

In the next section I argue that important sources of damage during civil conflict and repressive rule are usefully conceptualized as damage to the four capabilities discussed above. That is, the capabilities framework helps us better understand the various kinds of harm that are involved in obviously unjust actions, and gives us a better sense of how to fix such damage. Concentrating on select capabilities draws our attention to what is of particular concern when considering questions of justice in the context of political relationships, that is, what an individual is able to do and become through her interactions with others. Common patterns of and conditions for interaction during civil conflict and repressive rule are damaging because they lead to the systematic, involuntary diminishment of central and important relational capabilities and, consequently, undermine relationships of equality.[20] By seeing how these capabilities get undermined, we are in a position to see why civil conflict and repressive rule undermine the ability of individuals to relate as equals.

GENERAL PATTERNS OF DIMINISHMENT OF CAPABILITIES DURING CONFLICT OR REPRESSIVE RULE

This section focuses on three different categories of unjust acts or structures prevalent in contexts of civil conflict and repressive rule: violence, economic oppression, and the inequitable construction of group identity. In each case I discuss the harm or damage, in terms of capabilities, that stems from this kind of injustice. I consider how each undermines or diminishes capabilities by its impact on the internal resources, external resources, or social and material structure on which capabilities depend. Some of the effects on capabilities are obvious; others are less obvious but

---

[19] This general capability covers many of the dimensions captured by Nussbaum's first three capabilities: "**1. Life**. Being able to live to the end of a human life of normal length; not dying prematurely, or before one's life is so reduced as to be not worth living. **2. Bodily health**. Being able to have good health, including reproductive health; to be adequately nourished; to have adequate shelter. **3. Bodily integrity**. Being able to move freely from place to place; having one's bodily boundaries treated as sovereign, i.e. being able to be secure against assault." Ibid., p. 78.

[20] That I focus on the four capabilities mentioned above does not suggest that the other capabilities mentioned by Nussbaum, for example, are not important or central to individual well-being. Rather, they are not constitutive of relationships among equals in a political community and are not centrally impacted in the same way as the four capabilities on which I focus.

just as important to attend to if political relationships are to be transformed into relationships among equals. Particular emphasis is placed on how the expressive function of unjust practices and institutional structures impacts capabilities.

Violence

As noted in the introduction, violence is perhaps the most prominent and important characteristic of societies under repressive rule or in the midst of civil conflict, and so constitutes a paradigmatic example of injustice. Violence in general refers to the use of force in order to harm or abuse an individual. Violence takes many different forms. In this section I consider four such forms: rape, limb amputation, torture, and killing. After briefly describing each kind of violence, I then discuss the impact of such violence on capabilities.

Rape and sexual violence have been used historically as tools of warfare and repression. The widespread and systematic rape, torture, and impregnation of women as part of civil war, campaigns of ethnic cleansing, or genocide occurred during the Rape of Nanking by Japanese soldiers in Nanking, China from 1937 to 1938; in Rwanda during the genocide; in Sierra Leone during its civil war, where as many as 275,000 women are estimated to have been raped; during the ethnic cleansing campaign against Bosnian Muslims in Bosnia-Herzegovina; and in the current ongoing conflict in the Democratic Republic of the Congo and genocide in Darfur. One of the features of sexual violence is that it is meant to have many victims; the woman's relatives are usually intended to be among the targets. In the ten-year-old conflict in the Congo, tens of thousands of women of all ages have been "systematically raped and mutilated," some while being held as sex slaves, while others have been raped in front of their husbands.[21]

Another characteristic form that violence takes is the torture and killing of members of a political opposition group or, more broadly, perceived threats to a particular regime. South Africa during apartheid, Argentina during the military junta, Chile under Pinochet, and Northern Ireland are some of the many places where torture of political dissidents was systematic. As the South African TRC noted in its Final Report, "When the South

---

[21] DeNeen L. Brown, "The Brutal Truth: A Filmmaker Confronts the Rapists of the Congo and Finds No Remorse," *Washington Post*, April 8, 2008, www.washingtonpost.com/wpdyn/content/article/2008/04/07/AR2008040702782.html. Accessed April 10, 2008.

African Police (SAP) shot several hundred black protestors in the weeks following the June 16 events at Soweto, they were operating in terms of a well-established tradition of excessive or unjustifiable use of force against government opponents."[22] Violence is also playing a central role in the current political crisis in Zimbabwe.

In civil wars, violence increasingly directly targets civilian populations and is especially heinous in character. In describing the civil war in Sierra Leone from 1991 to 2002, Human Rights Watch notes that it "was characterized by unspeakable brutality and serious crimes. Forces failed to distinguish between civilians and combatants. Families were gunned down in the street, children and adults had their limbs hacked off with machetes, and girls and women were taken to rebel bases and subjected to sexual violence. The civil war was notable for the systematic use of mutilation, abduction, sexual violence, and murder of civilians. Tens of thousands of civilians were killed and up to one-quarter of the population was displaced."[23] One notorious form of violence was limb amputation; "limbs are the deliberate targets of land mines and machetes, weapons purposefully used to butcher and immobilize their victims ... Without mobility one is at the mercy of the enemy, and there has been no mercy in Sierra Leone, where thousands of civilians have lost limbs since 1992 ... As the tragedy of this country has become known to the rest of the world, the savagery of the RUF [the Liberian-supported Revolutionary United Front] has grown notorious ... [the] hallmark [of their raids] is crude amputations: feet, hands, ears, lips and noses."[24]

Violence first undermines capabilities by diminishing the personal resources required for the four capabilities of interest. The direct and lingering physical effects of violence like rape, torture, and limb amputation undermine the personal resources needed to achieve very basic human functionings. Rape and torture by definition constitute a violation of bodily integrity and health, and so by definition undermine the achievement of these functionings. The immediate suffering that forms of violence inflict constitutes one layer of harm. Brutal rape or sexual mutilation can further impede the capability of controlling urination

[22] TRC, *Truth and Reconciliation Commission of South Africa Report*, vol. 1, ch. 2, p. 26.
[23] Human Rights Watch, "Sowing Terror: Atrocities Against Civilians in Sierra Leone," *A Human Rights Watch Report*, 10(3)(A) (July 1998), http://hrw.org/reports/2004/sierraleone0904/1.htm#_Toc81830567; Human Rights Watch, "Getting Away with Murder, Mutilation and Rape," *A Human Rights Watch Report*, 11(3)(A) (June 1999).
[24] Editorial, "The War Amputees of Sierra Leone," *CMAJ* (*Canadian Medical Association Journal*), 162(13) (2000), www.cmaj.ca/cgi/content/full/162/13/1797?ck=nck. Accessed April 10, 2010.

and defecation. Chronic physical pain from torture can permanently compromise bodily health.

The physical and psychological effects of violence like rape and torture characteristically impact the capabilities of being recognized as a member of a community, being respected, and participating in the economic, political, and social life of a community. Feeling shamed and humiliated are common responses to the experience of being raped or tortured; certain physical after-effects (e.g., an inability to urinate normally) may serve as an additional source of shame and humiliation. Such shame and humiliation may in turn lessen victims' basic sense of self-respect. Violence undercuts the capability to participate in the economic, political, and social life of a community in multiple ways. For one thing, when severe enough, the physical effects of rape or torture may effectively foreclose certain areas of employment from an individual. In addition, a natural response to shame and humiliation is withdrawal from interaction as a way of protecting oneself against future humiliation and degrading treatment. Violence can also deeply traumatize victims, undermining their basic trust in other human beings and causing a general fear of the social world, both of which erode an individual's willingness to engage in the social world. Indeed, the erosion of agency is a central purpose of torture. As a Uruguay therapist notes of the torture regularly carried out on political prisoners during the military regime from 1973 to 1985, "The original point of torture was to take various individuals who had been politically or socially active, on behalf of their various causes, in a particular location at a particular moment and to gouge out their capacity for such activism: to leave them as if dead, unable any longer to aspire, let alone to act."[25]

Violent acts are also expressive and have a social meaning.[26] Implicit in the act of rape and torture is the message that this form of treatment is acceptable, that the victim is entitled to no better, and that the perpetrator is entitled to treat the victim in these ways. When this message is internalized, the victim's sense of self-worth may be lowered or reinforce an already low opinion. Lacking a robust sense of self-worth or a sense of the treatment appropriate to and compatible with her actual, basic human dignity and value may undermine the victim's sense that she should demand better treatment, or that she is entitled to participate politically and socially in her community.

[25] Lawrence Weschler quoted in Walker, *Moral Repair*, p. 41.
[26] On the expressive character of wrongs from which this account draws inspiration, see Murphy and Hampton, *Forgiveness and Mercy*.

Violence also affects the personal resources required for capabilities by influencing the preferences of direct victims and members of targeted groups. Victims and members of a targeted group may alter their preferences to choose and pursue actions and avenues that will enable them to avoid future violence. When violence is directed against political opponents, torture or limb amputation can create an incentive and strong preference to avoid politics in particular or the public realm in general, or to cease supporting an opposition movement or regime. Violence enhances the incentive among members of oppressed groups to passively accept tyranny, injustice, or defeat in a conflict. As Sen aptly notes, "Tyrannies operate not just by violating freedoms, but by making collaborators out of victims. It may turn out to be difficult or even impossible for the hopelessly oppressed to bring about a change (at least acting as individuals), and under these circumstances, they may even decide that it is 'silly' to bemoan constantly their lack of freedom and to desire a radical change that will not occur. Such passive tolerance of tyranny, which, alas, has been observed across the world, can exist even when a clear realization that there is a genuine prospect for change would generate strong public support for such a change."[27]

Violence reduces the external resources required for relational and basic capabilities. If the physical and psychological effects of violence or social stigma associated with being a victim are such that they preclude employment, this in turn diminishes their opportunity to acquire income and wealth. Being socially stigmatized or unable to trust can erode familial relationships and friendships, a different kind of external resource. If needed, medical and psychiatric care can further reduce the external monetary resources available for achieving the basic functionings of adequate nourishment and shelter.

Violence also shapes the social and material structure of a society in ways that lessen relational and basic capabilities. The message implicit in systematic violence – that rape, limb amputation, or torture constitutes a permissible form of treatment toward certain individuals or members of targeted groups – is communicated to the wider society. Consequently, such treatment may become viewed as permissible in general, or as a permissible response to specified infractions (e.g., supporting an opposition movement or party; challenging certain established economic, political, or social norms or roles). Insofar as this message is widely accepted

---

[27] Sen, *Rationality and Freedom*, p. 635.

and such violence becomes normalized, this enhances the role that violence can play in undermining the social bases for respect and in reinforcing restrictive social norms and roles. When social roles and constraints effectively exclude certain groups from participation, for example, when legal institutions bar certain groups from full participation (e.g., through the legal denial of civil and political rights or through gerrymandering), then violence reinforces inequalities in the capability of individuals to participate in the political, economic, or social life of their community. An individual is likely to have better opportunities if she is able to participate in the political and economic processes that determine the opportunities she will have. By supporting and maintaining the marginalization of groups in political and economic processes, then, violence supports and maintains their subsequent restricted opportunities. Finally, when being a victim of violence like rape is viewed socially as constituting a reason for ostracization, it can weaken the social conditions necessary for interaction and recognition as a full member of a community.

Violence during periods of civil conflict or repressive regimes frequently has a broader target than the direct victim, for example, the family of victims, members of a particular social group, or citizens generally. For instance, a major factor in the use of rape in war is to assault the sense of manhood of men within a community. The women are harmed in part to harm the men and reduce the personal resources required to successfully participate in a campaign of war or opposition. In campaigns of ethnic cleansing, violence by one ethnic group against individuals from a targeted ethnic group is designed to motivate other members of the targeted ethnic group to flee from their homes and communities, thereby allowing the persecutors to achieve ethnic homogeneity in a particular territory.

There are distinct ways in which violence affects the capabilities of those who are part of a social group or community that is broadly targeted, but are not themselves direct victims. First, those who are not direct victims of violence suffer from the threat of violence, the knowledge that they are at risk of being a future victim of violence.[28] The threat of violence draws attention to the fundamental insecurity of the ability to maintain certain functionings, including bodily integrity, of members of targeted groups. This threat constitutes a direct diminishment of the

---

[28] Ann E. Cudd, *Analyzing Oppression* (New York: Oxford University Press, 2006), especially pp. 90, 116–17.

security of their achieved functionings, and so a direct erosion of basic capabilities. The threat of violence can additionally diminish the personal resources on which capabilities depend. Although they do not experience direct physical harm, the threat of violence can constrain and restrict action. Members of a targeted group alter their actions and preferences to avoid becoming a victim (and so avoid going to certain places or avoid contact with certain individuals), or else face the constriction of their capabilities in the ways discussed above if the threat of violence is realized. In particular, instead of contesting unjust restrictions on participation in the political and economic life of the community, or unequal enforcement of the law, violence can create an incentive for members of a targeted group to passively submit to such restrictions. More generally, participation in the life of the community may be restricted out of fear of the risks of venturing into the public or political domain. Individuals may instead retreat to their private life and relationships. Further, the threat of violence draws attention to the fact that functionings achievements currently enjoyed, such as bodily integrity, may not be enjoyed in the short- or long-term future. This knowledge can itself be a source of constant stress and anxiety.

The threat of violence may also indirectly reduce the external resources of individuals. The stress and anxiety inherent in the threat of violence may in turn erode the success of individuals to use their skills and talents to participate and compete in the economic, social, or political arena. This ineffective participation as well as diminished participation in the economic and political life of a community in turn reduce the external resources, like income and wealth, available to individuals. Chronic stress and anxiety can further strain familial relationships and diminish family support, another kind of external resource for capabilities.

Furthermore, the threat of violence shapes the social and material environment in ways that diminish the capabilities of members of a targeted group. Some of these effects are identical to those for direct victims. Insofar as violence and the message about the acceptability of violence toward certain individuals or communities become commonplace, violence erodes the general social bases for respect for a targeted population. The threat of violence is often sufficient to reinforce restrictive social norms and roles that restrict the capability of some to participate in the life of the community by providing a strong incentive to refrain from challenging them. The South African clinical psychologist Nomfundo Walaza summarizes the impact of violence and the threat of violence on the capabilities of members of a targeted group in her description of life for black South Africans during apartheid: "What happened to your next-door neighbor and in your area affected you – you lived in a constant vibration of fear and insecurity, of being utterly deprived in all kinds of ways, of knowing you could never develop your full potential. So some paid more, others paid less, others paid differently – but every black person in this country did pay a price."[29]

Finally, there are general ways in which violence diminishes the capabilities of all members of a society where systematic violence takes place through its impact on the social and material structure and infrastructure of a society. As noted in the introduction, conflict and repression impact every aspect of life. Education is constrained. For example, in 2006 43 million children were unable to attend school for conflict-related reasons.[30] The quality and availability of health care diminishes. Civil wars reduce the public funds available for public health and often destroy the physical health care infrastructure of a community, including hospitals and clinics, and may lead to the exodus of medical professionals.[31] During the civil war in El Salvador the health care budget was reduced by 50 percent, and neonatal mortality rose from 20/1,000 to 23/1,000.[32] This impacts the availability and equality of basic care needed by everyone and special care needed by those injured by violence. This can diminish the ability of all members of a society to satisfy basic functionings. Further, economies suffer. An Oxfam report in 2007 estimated the economic cost of conflict in Africa since 1990 at $300 billion, a sum equal to the aid from international donors over the same period of time. Conflict was reportedly responsible for a 15 percent decrease on average in an African nation's economy.[33] Putting these figures into perspective, the report notes that "if

---

[29] Krog, *Country of My Skull*, p. 214.
[30] Save the Children, "Armed Conflict Creating Crisis in Education for 43 Million Children, New Save the Children Report Finds," September 12, 2006, www.savethechildren.org/newsroom/2006/armed-conflict-creating-crisis-in-education.html. Accessed November 6, 2008.
[31] Hazem Adam Ghobarah, Paul Huth, and Bruce Russett, "Civil Wars Kill and Maim People – Long after the Shooting Stops," *The American Political Science Review*, 97(2) (May 2003), 189–202.
[32] Antonio Ugalde, Ernesto Selva-Sutter, Carolina Casatillo, Carolina Paz, and Sergio Canas, "The Health Costs of War: Can They Be Measured? Lessons from El Salvador," *BJM*, 321(7254) (2000), 169–72.
[33] Oxfam, "Africa's Missing Billions: International Arms Flows and the Cost of Conflict," October 2007, www.oxfam.org.uk/resources/policy/conflict_disasters/bp107_africasmissingbillions.html. Accessed November 6, 2008. Countries considered include Algeria, Angola, Burundi, Central African Republic, Chad, Democratic Republic of Congo (DRC), Republic of Congo, Côte d'Ivoire, Djibouti, Eritrea, Ethiopia, Ghana, Guinea, Guinea-Bissau, Liberia, Niger, Nigeria, Rwanda, Senegal, Sierra Leone, South Africa, Sudan, and Uganda.

this money was not lost due to armed conflict, it could solve the problems of HIV and AIDS in Africa, or it could address Africa's needs in education, clean water and sanitation, and prevent tuberculosis and malaria."[34] At a very basic level, civil wars can undermine fundamental economic institutions, which require a relatively stable social context in order to function.[35] Reduced economic activity both results from and contributes to diminished investment, the closure of businesses, and the loss of human capital due to those who have died as well as those who are injured or displaced. Diminished economic activity in turn contributes to rising unemployment, reduced income, lost opportunities, and increased difficulty in meeting basic needs. When sources of employment and economic resources are undermined, this can contribute to the monetary impoverishment of individuals, which can further impede their ability to satisfy basic capabilities, and diminishes their capability to be a participant in the economic life of a community.

Economic oppression

Economic oppression occurs when the relative poverty of members of certain, targeted social group(s) is maintained through practices such as employment discrimination; wage discrimination; and segregation in employment, education, housing, and social interaction. Segregation refers to the *de facto* or *de jure* "enforced clustering of persons by social group status in certain residential areas, educational institutions, and occupations or jobs."[36] Repressive regimes often engage in economic oppression, and such repression can in turn become a source of civil conflict. In order to illustrate the impact of economic oppression on capabilities, I consider the case of apartheid in South Africa, a paradigm case of economic oppression.

Defining features of economic oppression are institutional and structural, and so I begin by discussing how the social and material structure of apartheid impacted capabilities. *De jure* segregation marked every aspect of life during apartheid. "Laws and regulations confirmed or imposed segregation for taxis, ambulances, hearses, buses, trains, elevators, benches, lavatories, parks, church halls, town halls, cinemas, theaters, cafes, restaurants, and

---

[34] Ibid.
[35] For a description of such impact, see Yekutiel Gershoni, "From War Without End and an End to a War: The Prolonged Wars in Liberia and Sierra Leone," *African Studies Review*, 40(3) (1997), 55–76, at 55.
[36] Cudd, *Analyzing Oppression.*

hotels, as well as schools and universities."[37] In each context, segregation in practice resulted in inferior facilities and public funding, lower-paying and lower-status employment opportunities, and greater social and legal restrictions for non-white South Africans. In particular, Africans were required to live in designated rural Homelands that lacked the amenities found in white areas, such as running water and electricity, and in which white capitalists were forbidden from investing. Most employment opportunities existed outside the Homelands, but legal obstacles made leaving the Homelands difficult and risky for Africans. Pass laws, which required Africans who lived or traveled outside the Homelands to carry documentation at all times proving they had permission to do so, "were vigorously enforced and resulted in tens of thousands of arrests each year."[38] As a consequence of the difficulties of finding employment, higher levels of unemployment were found in African communities.[39] Black South Africans who did find employment were concentrated in lower-status and lower-paying occupations and faced rampant wage discrimination. For example, by 1970 white manufacturing and construction workers earned six times as much as Africans, while white mine workers earned twenty-one times as much as Africans.[40]

The institutionalized dimensions of apartheid limited the capabilities of black South Africans in multiple ways. Legal institutions severely restricted their opportunities to participate in the social and economic life of the community. The forced relocation of Africans to the Homelands, coupled with pass laws, posed substantive structural constraints on the capability of seeking and securing employment as a form of participation in the economic life of a community. *De facto* or *de jure* employment discrimination and segregation directly reduced the kinds of participation in the economic life of the community that were possible, and effectively foreclosed various types of employment. The costs of seeking and obtaining employment included increased risks to other capabilities. Because employment opportunities existed primarily outside of the Homelands, many black Africans spent extended periods of time away from family and friends, thereby forgoing the capability to participate in their shared social life. When residing outside the

---

[37] Thompson, *A History of South Africa*, p. 197. Generally the government privileged Coloreds and Indians over Africans, p. 201.

[38] Ibid., p. 193.

[39] Ibid., p. 195; unemployment increased substantially during the 1970s, and by 1977 26 percent of Africans were estimated to be unemployed.

[40] Ibid. By 1982 this gap had reduced, though it still existed.

Homelands illegally, Africans had to remain under the radar of police officials, creating an incentive to avoid participation in the broader social life of the area where they resided. Participating in the economic life of a community and, through employment, securing the external resources instrumental for achieving adequate nourishment and shelter often came at the price of sacrificing the capability for affiliation. Illegal status often increased the risk to the security of bodily integrity and risked the complete inability to participate in the life of the community if arrested.

The expressive message of the institutional structure and justification of apartheid undermined the capabilities to be respected and recognized as a member of a community. The experiences of apartheid for black South Africans were humiliating and degrading. As Nussbaum highlights, it is always humiliating to be denied capabilities because of who we are.[41] Such institutionalized humiliation directly undermined the social bases for respect and self-respect. The intentional marginalization of black South Africans – educationally, economically, and socially – reflected, reinforced, and was justified by appeal to their status as neither full nor equal participants in South African society. The government's view of Africans in particular as less than full and equal members is reflected in the 1967 circular of the Department of Bantu Administration and Development: "It is accepted Government policy that the Bantu are only temporarily resident in the European areas of the Republic for as long as they offer their labour there. As soon as they become, for one reason or another, no longer fit for work or superfluous in the labour market, they are expected to return to their country of origin or territory of the national unity where they fit ethnically even if they were not born and bred in the homeland."[42]

The cumulative impact of structural constraints constitutive of the economic oppression during apartheid was the reduction of the external resources of black South Africans. The success of such oppression in maintaining the relative poverty and diminished external resources of black South Africans is demonstrated by the fact that by 1980, South Africa had the most inequitable distribution of wealth of ninety countries studied by the World Bank. Whereas white South Africans "were as prosperous as the middle and upper classes in Europe and North America,"[43] according to the Second Carnegie Inquiry into Poverty and

---

[41] See Nussbaum, *Women and Human Development*.
[42] Thompson, *A History of South Africa*, p. 193.   [43] Ibid., p. 200.

Development during apartheid in South Africa at that time, "nearly two-thirds of the African population had incomes below the Minimum Living Level (MLL), defined as the lowest sum on which a household could possibly live in South African social circumstances."[44] In the Homelands, 80 percent of the people lived below the MLL. Reduced external resources in turn undermined the capability to achieve basic functionings, such as being adequately nourished and sheltered. Unsurprisingly, lack of income combined with poor health services resulted in high levels of undernutrition, disease, and infant mortality rates among black South Africans.[45] Reduced external resources put at risk the security of those basic functionings that were achieved, insofar as limited and unstable monetary resources needed to be constantly divided so as to achieve multiple basic functionings. Further, an additional, important source of reduced external resources stemmed from the separation of families over extended periods of time.

Lastly, the personal resources of black South Africans directly suffered because of the structure of economic oppression. Separation from families reduced the family support that is critical for competing successfully in the economic and political arena and, more generally, for dealing with the stress and anxiety of life under apartheid in a way that enabled the exercise of agency. In education, teachers were paid less and were less qualified, and government spending was exponentially less for black South Africans.[46] Undereducation, illness, and lack of adequate health care diminished the cultivation of the personal resources and skills needed to compete successfully in the economic marketplace. Psychological resources needed to successfully exercise one's agency in the pursuit of various functionings were undermined. The inability to provide the resources needed to secure the basic functionings for oneself and one's family can be deeply humiliating, and undermines the respect one feels toward oneself and is given by others. The chronic absence or insecurity of basic functionings can be a chronic source of stress and anxiety. The lack of self-respect, stress, fear, and humiliation can in turn undermine the motivation and confidence needed to exercise agency. Given its comprehensive effects, the South African TRC aptly described apartheid in its Final Report as "a grim reality for every black South African ... Dumped in the 'national states' without jobs, communities experienced powerlessness, vulnerability, fear and injustice ... One did not need to be a political

---

[44] Ibid., p. 202.   [45] Ibid., p. 195.   [46] Ibid., p. 197.

activist to become a victim of apartheid; it was sufficient to be black, alive and seeking the basic necessities of life that whites took for granted and enjoyed by right."[47]

The inequitable construction of group identity

Group identities and membership in social groups exercise an important influence on individuals' capabilities during repressive rule and civil conflict, especially in deeply divided societies. After first discussing the relationship between identity and violence, I focus in the remainder of this section on the impact of the construction of the identity of the political community and of severe stereotyping on capabilities.

One way in which group identity can have a direct impact on capabilities is by making individuals vulnerable to violence and economic oppression because of their group affiliation. In contexts of civil conflict, especially ethnic conflict, group identity can make an individual more vulnerable to violence and killing. Insofar as individuals are victims of violence and suffer from the threat of violence because of their group identity, either in a civil war or in a campaign of repression, identity can facilitate the undermining of the capabilities in the ways discussed above in connection with violence. Similarly, when economic oppression is targeted toward a particular group, sharing the identity of the targeted group can in turn make an individual vulnerable to such oppression.

Group identity affects capabilities in additional ways. Depending on how the notion of citizenship is defined within a political community and reflected in the general social and material structure, the group identity of an individual can undermine her capability to be recognized as a member of a political community; participate in the political, economic, and social life of a community; and be respected. Conflicts over language policy, the historical narrative delineated in textbooks, and the permissibility of forms of cultural expression are prevalent in deeply divided societies, especially in the contexts of ethnic conflict. Cultural practices, rituals, customs, public monuments, music, drama, art, and language policies all help to delineate the shared worldview, memories, and interests of a particular social group and bolster a sense of shared identity. Cultural expression thus plays an important role in preserving group identity and recognizing a community. This is why "battles over cultural expressions

---

[47] TRC, *Truth and Reconciliation Commission of South Africa Report*, vol. 1, ch. 2, p. 34.

and the symbolic landscape are central to group recognition and identity."[48]
Given the role that cultural expression and policies play in defining
what it means to be a member of a particular group and demonstrating
that a group is recognized by others, how conflicts over culture are
resolved within a political community have important implications for
what it means to be a member of a community and for who will be seen
as full or legitimate members of a community. Insofar as public policies
dealing with cultural expression, such as the official language policy of a
political community, exclude or refuse to acknowledge the expressions
of some social groups by, for example, refusing to grant certain languages an official status, such policies can implicitly communicate that
members of such groups are not full or legitimate members of a
community.

The construction of identity in a political community can also erode
the personal and social resources required for respect. According to social
identity theory, individuals attach value and emotional significance to the
part of their identity that is based on membership of a group.[49] Our
personal sense of worth and respect, for example, is often intimately tied
up with our sense of the worth or value and respect shown to the groups
of which we are a part. The outcome of cultural contestations has
implications for the capability of being respected, insofar as the outcome
is interpreted as demonstrating the relative respect that various groups
within society enjoy.

In the contexts of deeply divided societies or civil conflict, there are
additional ways in which the social and material structure can limit the
capability of individuals from certain groups to participate in social,
economic, and political processes. Deep divisions among communities
and antagonistic relations can support social norms or legal rules that
limit who it is acceptable for members of a particular social group to
interact with socially, economically, or politically. Thus it is unsurprising
that in Northern Ireland the rate of intermarriage between Catholics and
Protestants has historically been extremely low and interdenominational
couples have often been targets of violence during especially intense
periods of conflict.

Insofar as a group identity makes one subject to stereotyping,
capabilities can be undermined in further ways. Stereotyping is a process

---

[48] Marc Howard Ross, *Cultural Contestation in Ethnic Conflict* (New York: Cambridge University
Press, 2007), pp. 1–2, 15.
[49] Ross, *Cultural Contestation*, and Cudd, *Analyzing Oppression*.

of categorization in which we make generalizations concerning individuals about whom we know little on the basis of features that they share with other members of some identifiable group.[50] Stereotyping is a way to categorize individuals on the basis of their similarity to or distance from a prototype representative of each category or group. Stereotypes are socially learned, and knowledge of commonly held stereotypes influences interaction. When acting, individuals will take stereotypical expectations into consideration. Stereotypes also influence how actions are seen and interpreted.

Stereotype categorization is not an unbiased process. Individuals tend to favor the groups to which they belong, recognizing the heterogeneity within their group and viewing it in a positive light. One way to maintain a positive self-identity is by maintaining a positive image of one's group. Out-groups to which an individual does not belong are disfavored and often viewed as homogeneous. Positive images of one's own group are often maintained by manipulating one's image and beliefs about one's group and other groups, especially in the face of countervailing evidence. Thus privileged groups rationalize social injustice by the stereotypes they make of individuals in disadvantaged groups. Privilege is rationalized by obscuring external factors or the fact of social disadvantage, and instead attributing it to hard work (and harder work relative to those who do not succeed) and personal merit.[51]

To illustrate such stereotyping, consider Northern Ireland. Severe stereotyping among Catholics and Protestants is well documented in Northern Ireland. The political scientists Brendan O'Leary and John McGarry illustrate one particular stereotype in the course of summarizing and then subsequently dismissing one explanation sometimes offered for the disposition to violence in both communities in Northern Ireland. They write:

The first, "culturalist" theory of Irish violence does not merit any serious analytical attention, though its popular resonance in Great Britain should not be underestimated. It is the dogma of "the Fighting Irish." In this folklore, throughout the world, from the bar-rooms of Chicago to the bar-rooms of Melbourne, the Irish male can be found displaying the alleged traits of his people: aggressive and unreasoning violence, facilitated by excessive alcohol consumption. It is a very old stereotype – indeed a colonial stereotype. The English maintained that the Irish were murderous savages in the course of

---

[50] Cudd, *Analyzing Oppression*, p. 69.   [51] Ibid., p. 72.

murdering and savaging the natives – this indeed was how they welcomed Ireland into "peaceful civilization."[52]

Such stereotyping can be damaging in itself and because of its consequences for the social and material structure. Stereotypes can motivate and justify the construction of an unjust social and material environment, which in turn diminishes the capabilities of disadvantaged groups. Stereotypes are used to justify, rationalize, and reinforce oppressive social practices. Individuals from stereotyped groups can face discrimination and social obstacles to employment; lower numbers of employed individuals within a group can then strengthen the perception of the members of that group as lazy and so justify a refusal to hire. Such rationalization further curtails the ability of members of such groups to participate in the economic and political life of a community. When individuals are viewed as aggressive and unreasoning, this then undermines the legitimacy of the complaints they can articulate about the overall social structure. It may also motivate the violent treatment of such social groups, insofar as violence and force is taken to be the only thing that members of such groups "listen to." When stereotypes call into question the agency or autonomy of members of certain social groups, they can then undermine the capability of individuals to be respected. It is less likely that those with stereotypical beliefs will recognize the necessity of respecting the rights of members of an oppressed social group, or will acknowledge the legitimacy of complaints or demands from such groups. Stereotypes that question the competence of members of social groups can be used to ground a general social distrust of individuals from an oppressed group; such distrust can be socially humiliating when someone is viewed as less trustworthy because of their membership of a suspect social group. When stereotyped negatively, individuals can feel humiliation and shame because of the unappealing stereotypes applied to members of their groups, which portray them as inadequate or inferior relative to another social group.[53]

In addition, stereotypes can serve as an obstacle to the capability of individuals to participate in the political, economic, and social life of a community by undermining the personal resources of members of

---

[52] John McGarry and Brendan O'Leary, *Explaining Northern Ireland: Broken Images* (Oxford: Wiley-Blackwell, 1995), p. 234, endnote 476. The psychologist cited is E. E. O'Donnell, *Northern Irish Stereotypes* (Dublin: College of Industrial Relations, 1977).

[53] Cudd, *Analyzing Oppression*, p. 163.

stereotyped communities. Stereotypes can become self-fulfilling.[54] Those subject to stereotyping can internalize stereotypes, adopting the view of themselves as inferior, weak, incompetent, lazy, or violent. As a result of the internalization of stereotypes, which may call into question the agency, autonomy, or dignity of members of an oppressed group, individuals may come to question their own autonomy, agency, or moral dignity as persons.[55] Such internalized views will in turn inhibit an individual's ability to participate successfully in the economic, political, and social arenas.

DAMAGED POLITICAL RELATIONSHIPS

The previous section considered the ways in which three characteristic unjust structures or practices during civil conflict and repressive rule (violence, economic oppression, and the inequitable construction of group identity) systematically diminish four capabilities constitutive of relationships among equals within a political community. In practice, of course, it is rare to find only one of these unjust actions or structures in the contexts of civil conflict or repressive rule. Violence often accompanies and is sparked by political marginalization or economic oppression. Violence in turn further reduces political participation and reinforces economic inequality and oppression.

One important lesson from this discussion, which will inform my discussion in the next chapter, is that the sources of damage to individuals and political relationships during periods of civil conflict and repressive rule are widespread and implicate legal, political, economic, educational, and cultural institutions and practices. This implies that there will be numerous and widespread areas of communal life to address if efforts at reconciliation are to successfully rebuild political relationships. Restricting our focus to attitudes and legal institutions will overlook important dimensions of political interaction that should be the focus of moral concern and the subject of processes of reconciliation.

By way of conclusion, I want to summarize why the damage to the three relational basic capabilities discussed in this chapter should be of serious moral concern. Some sources of concern are intrinsic to the nature of capabilities. First, the systematic diminishment of capabilities has

---

[54] Ibid., p. 163.
[55] This point is also emphasized by Paul Benson, "Free Agency and Self-Worth," *The Journal of Philosophy*, 91(12) (1994), 650–68, and Cudd, *Analyzing Oppression*.

implications for the well-being of individuals and for justice. Being respected, being a participant in the political, economic, and social life of a community, being recognized as a member of a community, and satisfying basic functionings are all important constitutive dimensions of well-being. Thus, undermining the genuine opportunity or capability that individuals have to achieve these functionings diminishes their opportunity to achieve important aspects of well-being. Furthermore, these capabilities are constitutive of relationships among equals within a political community. Insofar as relating as an equal with others within an individual's community is a basic requirement of justice, the systematic diminishment of the four capabilities discussed above involves injustice. Finally, the systematic diminishment of central capabilities fails to respect the agency of human beings, who should be in a position to shape their lives and the terms of their interaction with others, but instead have diminished control over their lives and interactions. Such diminishment reflects the loss of freedom that the unjust actions and structures discussed above produce.

There are additional reasons to be concerned about the diminishment of capabilities, which stem from the relationship between capabilities, the rule of law, and trust. For example, as Wolff and de-Shalit highlight, an inability to achieve basic capabilities can negatively impact the ability of an individual to live within the law and so fulfill the reciprocal responsibilities that respect for the rule of law requires. Wolff and de-Shalit illustrate this point powerfully when they consider someone who is earning the minimum wage in a Western country. "If he is concerned about his children's well-being and if he wants to guarantee for them clothes they will not be ashamed to wear, and good nutrition, and perhaps to have a modicum of social life, he may have no option but tax evasion, buying goods he knows are stolen, claiming benefits while working, and the like. He might hate what he has to do both because of the risks and because it makes him an outsider . . . a society that is constructed in a way that in effect forces some people to break the law in order to live a materially decent life is especially incompetent or unjust."[56] This relationship will be explored in greater detail in the next chapter as I consider what processes of reconciliation must do in order to rebuild relationships in the requisite ways and in a manner that is morally justifiable.

[56] Wolff and de-Shalit, *Disadvantage.*

PART II

Promoting Political Reconciliation

Evaluating processes of political reconciliation

INTRODUCTION

In Chapters 1, 2, and 3 I argued that the frameworks of the rule of law, political trust, and capabilities provide important theoretical resources for understanding how relationships go wrong during civil conflict and repressive rule, as well as how relationships should be rebuilt. Each framework drew attention to the deeper moral issues that are expressed in actions widely regarded as morally problematic during civil conflict and repressive rule. However, for my analysis of political reconciliation to be complete it is necessary to discuss the general question of how transitional societies should foster the desired transformation. In this chapter I concentrate on what it would mean for a putative process to be successful in contributing to the desired transformation of political relationships and pursuing this transformation in a morally permissible manner.

My first objective is to develop a general framework for evaluating whether and in what ways a particular process contributes to the rebuilding and transformation of political relationships. The proposed framework is not a substitute for public policy analysis or political judgment in particular transitional societies; my goal is thus not to outline a general formula for pursuing political reconciliation. Indeed, the determination of which process would be appropriate to pursue in a particular context depends on a detailed understanding of how relationships have gone wrong, what kinds of transformation are the most pressing, and what kinds of damage particular processes are in a position to repair. Rather, the framework is designed to guide policy making in transitional contexts by clarifying the considerations that should inform decisions about how to pursue political reconciliation.

My second objective is to outline normative constraints on the pursuit of political reconciliation, and so describe the general characteristics of permissible processes. My interest is in the moral side constraints that delimit acceptable ways of rebuilding political relationships. My goal is thus not to reach an all-things-considered judgment regarding, for example, the justifiability of establishing a truth commission in a particular transitional context. While the permissibility of a process is a necessary condition for reaching this judgment, the overall justifiability of a process will also depend on understanding the role of reconciliation in transitional justice, and on how to balance the value of pursuing reconciliation against other kinds of values, including retributive justice.

There are two sections in this chapter. The first discusses the indirect and direct contributions that a process can have on the transformation of political relationships. The second considers the normative constraints that should be respected if reconciliation is going to be pursued in a morally permissible manner, as well as the factors that should inform policy decisions regarding the pursuit of political reconciliation.

EFFECTIVENESS

There are two general ways in which a process might rebuild political relationships. The first is by directly cultivating the characteristics of rebuilt political relationships. A process would be effective in this sense if, for example, it increased political trust among citizens and officials or enhanced capabilities. Processes that directly cultivate the characteristics of rebuilt relationships can impact one dimension of transformation, such as respect for the rule of law. However, it is possible for a process to contribute to more than one dimension. For example, a process may facilitate respect for the requirements of the rule of law and in so doing cultivate trust and trust-responsiveness.

A process might also promote the transformation of political relationships in a more indirect manner. Processes can foster the social or moral conditions for the rule of law or political trust. Alternatively, a process that directly contributes to one kind of transformation may have as an auxiliary consequence the encouragement of another characteristic. As I discuss below, certain capabilities are fertile in the sense that they support other capabilities. As is the case with direct contributions to political transformation, the indirect contributions of a process may be limited, affecting only one dimension of transformation such as the rule of law. The indirect contribution of a process may also be more diffuse, for example, facilitating shared conditions for all three dimensions of repair, namely, the rule of law, trust, and capabilities.

In this section I first consider the indirect contributions of a process to political reconciliation connected to the cultivation of the conditions necessary for change to become possible. I then turn to the direct contributions a process can have on political transformation. Finally, I highlight the auxiliary consequences of the indirect or direct pursuit of the transformation of political relationships.

Indirect effectiveness

The most basic contribution a process of reconciliation can have is to make the pursuit of the transformation of political relationships possible. There are two conditions that influence this possibility: hope and the acknowledgement of the need for repair. I begin my discussion of the indirect contributions of processes of reconciliation with these two conditions.

Hope

Hope plays a critical role in facilitating the conditions that enable the general transformation of relationships. Hope reflects an attitude of optimism about the possibility of achieving or realizing a desired, though uncertain, state of affairs or object.[1] This optimistic attitude involves more than wishful thinking, or simply imagining or envisioning a desired situation or goal. For an individual to say that she hopes that a situation comes about, it must also be the case that she is actively working toward its realization by, for example, telling others of her hopes, seizing opportunities to promote what is hoped for, and working "to sustain and augment the feelings that will carry them through to some course of action."[2] Actions that stem from hope differ from other kinds of actions in that the pursuit of the hoped-for goal is always conditioned by the recognition of the deep uncertainty of the outcome of our actions, that what we hope for may not be achieved; if the outcome was guaranteed, there would be no need for hope. To hope, therefore, is to take an "agential stance" toward the world, even despite or in the face of extreme limitations, and to take concrete steps toward the realization of the hoped-for goal.[3]

---

[1] I take this general idea from Margaret Urban Walker, *Moral Repair*, pp. 44–9; Walker also mentions beliefs and desires as constitutive of hope.

[2] Ibid., p. 53.

[3] Victoria McGeer, "Trust, hope, and empowerment," *Australasian Journal of Philosophy*, 86(2) (2008), 237–54. See also Walker, *Moral Repair*, p. 27.

Hope influences our motivation to act by energizing us and inspiring us to pursue an end. It also influences our actions, insofar as it leads us to look for and become aware of ways in which what is hoped for can be achieved.[4] Hope presupposes a certain level of creativity and imaginative capacities in the one who is hopeful. Hoping thus depends on an ability to imagine alternative ways of responding to a situation or set of limitations in order to achieve the hoped-for end. To hope we must be able to see our limitations and constraints "as boundary conditions that we can act constructively in the face of, often pushing beyond those conditions in surprising ways and thereby enhancing our capacities."[5]

Hope is critical for the transformation of political relations because of its influence on agency. Hope both reflects and encourages optimism about the possibility of transforming political relations, and as a result motivates the exercise of agency to achieve this goal. By definition, when members of a transitional society are hopeful about the possibility of reconciliation, they are motivated and strive to act so as to achieve this transformation. The agential stance toward the world that is constitutive of hope is required for political transformation because the transformation of relations becomes a reality only insofar as members of transitional societies act to rebuild relationships.

The kind of agency that hope encourages is also critical for the successful transformation of political relations. When we hope, we use our imaginative capacities to envision what we might do to achieve the hoped-for end. In the context of political reconciliation this implies envisioning what might be done to achieve more peaceful and just political interaction. Hoping thus fosters creativity and the identification of alternative ways of interacting. It can facilitate the shifting or altering of the dynamics of interaction. Hoping can, for example, motivate members of antagonistic communities to attempt to work together for the sake of the shared hoped-for end of reconciliation. Hoping may also regulate and constrain our responses to others so as to not foreclose future interaction and cooperation.[6]

If hope plays the critical role in making the pursuit of reconciliation possible, then it is critical to know what conditions contribute to or

---

[4] Walker, *Moral Repair*, p. 50; McGeer, "Trust," 246.
[5] McGeer, "Trust," 246. This imagining of how things could be otherwise is true even in cases where what we hope for cannot be brought about solely by our actions. As Margaret Urban Walker notes, "People have varied and characteristic ways they try to invite, affect, or produce an outcome for which they hope, *even when the outcome is not directly, or at all, to their own effort.*" On this point see Walker, *Moral Repair*, p. 49.
[6] See McGeer, "Trust" on this point.

undermine hope in transitional contexts. There are at least two conditions that are important in this regard. The first is the cessation of violence. This creates a space in which imagining more peaceful forms of inter-action becomes easier, and less dangerous or risky to act on. It is challenging to be optimistic and imagine pursuing peaceful interactions with members of antagonistic communities or groups when an individual remains a target of violence. Similarly, it becomes dangerous and risky to act on hope insofar as it can put an individual's life in danger. The second condition that underpins hope is the shared commitment to be part of the same society. Insofar as it remains unclear that those with whom one is now in conflict will in the future be members of the same political community, it becomes difficult to envision or be motivated to work toward the repair and transformation of shared political relationships. On the other hand, a commitment to remain part of the same political community opens up the possibility that others within a transitional society have the same goal, namely, to shape a shared future. This minimal commitment can encourage the imagining of what this shared future will be like. When the commitment to be part of the same society is coupled with an endorsement of the new institutional order, then the prospects of hope are even greater. In this latter case, the vision of the future that is shared is even more robust, and motivates in others the commitment to repair and transform political relationships so as to make this institutional order function successfully.

The impact of hope on the possibility of achieving reconciliation need not be restricted to providing an initial, motivational impulse to pursue the transformation and change of political relationships. Hope can also sustain and further that process of transformation once it has begun. Hope can directly enhance the capability of individuals by increasing the personal resources needed to exercise agency to achieve certain relational or basic capabilities. Hope can encourage or underpin the motivation to trust others. As McGeer notes, "Substantial trust in others is critically dependent upon our capacity to feel hopeful about them, about their capacities and dispositions as agents, as well as hopeful about how these capacities and dispositions can be positively affected by our actively and explicitly putting trust in them."[7] To the extent that hope encourages trust, it can also contribute to the social conditions required for the cooperative interaction needed to sustain the rule of law by, for example, motivating citizens to have faith in the law.

---

[7] McGeer, "Trust," 243. See also Walker, *Moral Repair*, p. 44 on this point.

Acknowledgement of the need for repair

With hope, the exercise of agency needed to rebuild political relationships becomes possible. However, for hope to translate into efforts to rebuild political relationships, the need for such rebuilding must be recognized and acknowledged. Denial refers to a refusal to acknowledge difficult or unpleasant facts. One contribution that a process may make to reconciliation, then, is to counter denial about the necessity of rebuilding political relationships that stems from a failure to acknowledge the ways in which civil conflict and repressive rule damaged relationships. Denial may occur at either the level of officials or the general citizenry, both during as well as after civil conflict and repressive rule. Denial may be general or specific in character, reflecting either a wholesale repudiation of the idea that political relationships need to be rebuilt or a more specific, targeted refusal to acknowledge particular forms of damage.

The sociologist Stanley Cohen categorizes three general forms that political denial may take at the level of officials or citizens.[8] His categorization provides important theoretical resources both for identifying denial when it occurs and for understanding what forms acknowledgement must take if denial is to be counteracted. The first category, literal denial, involves disputing the truth or accuracy of factual claims. For example, frequently officials and citizens literally deny claims by fellow citizens of torture by officials during periods of civil conflict or repressive rule. Chapter 1 illustrated instances of literal denial in Argentina, including the refusal of military leaders to acknowledge the existence of political prisoners. In the contexts of repressive regimes, Cohen notes, citizens retreat into their private life so as to avoid being confronted with certain facts about what is occurring within their society and to be able to literally deny what is occurring.

Interpretive denial applies to cases in which actions or events are redescribed so as to appear less troubling or controversial; in Cohen's words, "by euphemism, by technical jargon, the observer disputes the cognitive meaning given to an event and re-allocates it to another class of event."[9] Calling official abuse of prisoners "regrettable excesses" instead of "torture" or labeling forced expulsions "transfers of population" are examples of this kind of denial.

Implicatory denial consists in a failure to recognize and acknowledge the significance or implications of what one witnesses, knows about, or

---

[8] For a comprehensive discussion of political denial, see Stanley Cohen, *States of Denial: Knowing about Atrocities and Suffering* (Cambridge: Polity Press, 2001).
[9] Cohen, *States of Denial*, p. 8.

does. Practices that citizens know about but do not directly participate in may be acknowledged to constitute torture. However, citizens may view such practices as normal and so not feel moral indignation. Alternatively, citizens and officials may downplay the significance of such practices because they take torture to be justified in the face of a threat or because they are indifferent to torture insofar as the practice has little to do with them personally. A rejection of personal responsibility for actions or practices is one way of denying their significance. Even when their actions are implicated in morally troublesome practices, citizens or officials may deny responsibility by claiming not to have known or understood the ends and projects to which their actions or jobs contributed.

The relationship between denial at the level of officials and at the level of citizens is often complicated and mutually reinforcing. Cases of official denial are characteristically public in character and highly organized, "initiated, structured and sustained by the massive resources of the modern state."[10] Official denial can have a significant influence on the beliefs and actions of citizens. Cohen notes that the official techniques used to deny atrocities or their significance contribute to social conditions that facilitate atrocities; official denial impacts how observers and perpetrators interpret and understand what is going on around them or what they are doing. However, denial among citizens is not only a byproduct of official action. Societies often have unofficial, "unwritten agreements about what can be publicly remembered and acknowledged" and social norms against telling truth in certain domains.[11] In addition, the possibility and plausibility of these various forms of official denial depend on the social and political context of a society. As Cohen writes, "Denials draw on shared cultural vocabularies to be credible. They may also be shared in another powerful sense: the commitment between people – whether partners or an entire organization back-up and collude in each other's denials."[12] The plausibility of the Argentine government's denial of disappearances depended on the presence of a receptive audience that wanted to hear that such actions were not occurring. The ability of officials to commit, justify, or refuse to acknowledge responsibility for human rights abuses is dependent on the attitudes and actions of citizens within a community.

Denial is a source of concern in transitional contexts. The changes required to rebuild political relationships in ways that support capabilities, the rule of law, and reasonable political trust depend on

[10] Ibid., p. 10. [11] Ibid., p. 11. [12] Ibid., p. 64.

cooperative efforts among both officials and citizens. Denial and resistance from either citizens or officials may undermine the ability of transitional societies to work toward such change.[13] Thus it is important to counter denial at both levels.

Acknowledgement, or "what happens to knowledge when it becomes officially sanctioned and enters the public discourse," is needed to counter denial in transitional contexts.[14] Official forms of acknowledgement are a direct way to counteract official denial. They can often also set the stage for countering denial among citizens insofar as they change the contours of public discussion and debate, and influence public discourse.[15] There are a variety of forms that official acknowledgement may take. The particular form that acknowledgement should take is context-dependent; what form is appropriate in a given context depends on what kind of denial the acknowledgement is designed to counter.

Official fact-finding investigations are one way to counter the first and second forms of denial. Such investigations can document systematic patterns of abuse and attribute responsibility for such abuses when possible, establishing who did what to whom. The reports issued from such investigations can constitute an official acknowledgement of abuses and of responsibility for abuses. Fact-finding investigations are less suited to countering cases in which the occurrence of specific events or practices, or responsibility for such practices, is not contested. Rather, in the face of implicatory denial of the significance of events, memorialization or apology may be more appropriate. Memorializing victims and their suffering can serve as a corrective to indifference with respect to what occurred. Official apologies for practices and actions may challenge and counter denial of their unjustifiability.

Although it is important to foster hope and acknowledge the need for reconciliation when it is denied, the successful cultivation of the rule of law and political trust, as well as relational and basic capabilities, will depend on more than hope and acknowledgement of the need for such repair. The rebuilding of political relationships also requires the development of the social and moral context that supports each of these dimensions of political relationships. After discussing two general conditions

---

[13] Walker recognizes a similar point: *Moral Repair*, p. 203.
[14] Cohen, *States of Denial*, p. 225.
[15] I discuss some of the conditions which influence whether such forms of acknowledgement lead to changes in public discourse in Chapter 5 on truth commissions.

that underpin all three dimensions of political relationships, I consider the social and moral conditions unique to each aspect.

Respect for moral agency

The undermining of the rule of law, deep distrust or the unreasonableness of political trust, and the diminishment of central capabilities each represent a way of undermining or eroding respect for the moral agency of others. The erosion of such respect should thus be a general source of moral concern. Below I highlight why processes of political reconciliation must cultivate general respect for moral agency if the rule of law, trust, and relational and basic capabilities are to be encouraged.

Consider first the systematic violation of the requirements of the rule of law. The rule of law refers broadly to the governance of the conduct of citizens and officials on the basis of legal rules that are knowable, able to be followed, and enforced in practice. As I discussed in Chapter 1, the rule of law is characteristically undermined, albeit to different degrees, during periods of civil conflict and repressive rule. As a matter of practice, what written rules declare does not guide the actions of officials who enforce such statutes, and so the congruence requirement is systematically violated. For example, though officially proscribed, the torture of individuals arrested on suspicion of violating the law may be systematic.

Such violations exhibit a failure of respect for agency. Implicit in the rule of law is a view of individuals as agents who are appropriately held responsible and answerable for their actions. When functioning as it should, law enforcement officials' responses to individuals is determined by whether individuals are believed to have followed or violated legal rules. Similarly, the character of such an official response is determined by the constraints specified in declared rules. However, official whim, not what declared rules dictate, determines the character of the legal response to individuals who have violated the law insofar as practices like torture are engaged in, though proscribed by declared rules. In such circumstances, an institution founded on respect for agency fails to respect agency in practice. Alternatively, specifying rules so vaguely that it is impossible for individuals to know which actions constitute a violation of the declared rule means that individuals are not in a position to determine their conduct in a way that avoids official reprimand. It is the will and whim of officials that will instead dictate whether what is done is in violation of declared rules.

In contexts of civil conflict and repressive rule, default political trust is typically neither present nor reasonable. The absence or unreasonableness of a default stance of political trust also reflects a systematic failure of respect for agency. Political trust refers first to an attitude of optimism about the competence and lack of ill will of fellow citizens and officials, coupled with an expectation that those we trust will be directly and favorably moved to prove reliable when trust is placed in them. When it is unreasonable to take an optimistic view of the competence and lack of ill will of others, one cannot reasonably assume that they are basically decent in the sense of both understanding and being willing to follow norms for social and political interaction, including norms that forbid wantonly harming others. The absence of basic decency implies a failure to respect the boundaries or constraints on permissible interaction with our fellows. Similarly, when it cannot reasonably be assumed that others will prove trust-responsive, using the fact that others are relying on them to provide a reason for proving reliable, fellow citizens and officials will fail to acknowledge or be motivated by the demands and expectations that we can impose on others by virtue of our agency. Given the connection between being motivated to prove trust-responsive and being concerned with the opinion that others have of you, the unreasonableness of expecting others to prove trust-responsive indicates a deeper failure to be concerned with the opinions that others have of you.

When individuals refuse to trust others, even when it is reasonable to do so, this reflects a rebuff of the agency of others who are capable of exercising the responsibilities associated with citizenship. Such a refusal is reflected in governments' denial of civil and political rights to certain groups within a political community or generally. Distrust can also reflect a refusal or inability to see that others are willing to play fairly by rules structuring interaction and are not driven by a desire to harm others within society, and to see that others recognize and are motivated to respond to the demands that their fellow officials and citizens make of them. Such distrust, especially when unreasonable, reflects a failure to respect that others are able and are willing to exercise their agency responsibly and appropriately.

Finally, the systematic diminishment of the capabilities to be respected, to be recognized as a member of a political community, and to participate in the social, economic, and political life of a community is also a product of a general failure to respect the agency of others. Capabilities represent different ways that individuals may choose to exercise their agency, capturing the various doings and beings they have a real opportunity to achieve. Civil conflict and repressive rule reduce the freedom of individuals to exercise their agency because they affect the personal and external resources as well as the social and institutional conditions required for individuals to have genuine opportunities to exercise the capabilities constitutive of membership in a political community.

Given that interaction during periods of civil conflict and repressive rule systematically disrespects and disregards the moral agency of others, such respect must be cultivated if relationships are to be transformed and rebuilt. The effective cultivation of such respect depends in turn on understanding the conditions that undermine or encourage it. In the next chapter I discuss these conditions in detail when I consider three capacities that are exercised by agents when interacting with others as agents – the capacities to care about, to empathize with, and to acknowledge the second-personal reasons of others – and explain how the construction of group identity can undermine the exercise of these capacities toward others.

Reciprocity

The erosion of a commitment to reciprocity is a second underlying theme of the discussion of the normative issues expressed in features of political relations during civil conflict and repressive rule. As a moral principle, reciprocity prescribes that it is fair to expect others to act in certain ways only if one is willing to fulfill their reciprocal expectations of oneself. For example, law is maintained and regulates behavior only to the degree that the reciprocal constraint on the part of citizens and officials required by the rule of law is systematically respected. Such restraint requires that officials govern by outlining a standard that citizens are knowledgeable of and capable of following, and that is actually used to judge their conduct. As noted in Chapter 1, the idea that officials are bound by the publicly articulated, clear and consistent rules or that the obligation of citizens to obey the law is conditional on the actions of officials is missing within many transitional societies. The systematic disregard for the requirements of the rule of law undermines the reciprocity at the core of law and reflects the need for the cultivation of a commitment to this value.

Similarly, the reciprocity expressed in mutual default trust and trust-responsiveness is absent in transitional contexts, which are characterized by an absence of trust and of conditions that make trust reasonable. Trusting others as a default presumes of others what we would like them to presume of us – namely, our competence, lack of ill will, and general decency. Adopting trust as a default effectively treats as equally valid the desire of others to be recognized as competent, lacking ill will, and decent. Likewise, proving trust-responsive as a default entails responding to the demands of others as we would have them respond to our demands of them, by proving reliable in the anticipated way. Such trust-responsiveness in effect acknowledges that the legitimacy of our moral demands on others is dependent on what we as individuals do.

Given that both the rule of law and political trust represent ways of structuring relationships based on reciprocity, their stable and long-term cultivation depend on fostering a recognition and commitment to reciprocity in transitional contexts. That is, the general understanding that the validity of my demands on others depends partly on what I as an individual am willing to do is often in need of development.

In addition to the general commitment to respecting the agency of others and to reciprocity that underpin the rule of law, reasonable default trust, and capabilities, distinctive social and moral conditions underpin each characteristic. After considering the conditions for the rule of law I discuss those required for trust and capabilities.

Conditions for the rule of law

Law is the process of submitting human conduct to the authority of rules.[16] The success of this process depends on four conditions that Fuller discusses throughout his writings: ongoing cooperative interaction between citizens and officials; systematic congruence between the law and informal social practices; legal decency and good judgment; and faith in the law.[17] My discussion of international criminal trials in Chapter 6 considers each of these conditions in detail, and goes on to show how international criminal trials can foster their development. For the purposes of this chapter it is sufficient to describe each condition and offer initial reasons for its necessity for the maintenance of law.

The first condition of law is ongoing cooperative activity between citizens and officials. Officials cannot maintain a legal system solely through their own activity. The passage of clear and prospective legal rules will not regulate and guide conduct if citizens are not willing to obey them. For legal rules to actually govern and regulate conduct, citizens must be willing to submit to such rules. A widespread disregard for law renders the activities of legal officials futile. Similarly, citizens cannot govern their conduct according to legal rules solely through their own

---

[16] Fuller, *Morality of Law*, p. 106.
[17] Fuller refers to these conditions in *The Morality of Law*; Lon Fuller, *Anatomy of the Law* (Westport: Greenwood Press Publishers, 1968); Lon Fuller, "Human Interaction and the Law," in Kenneth Winston (ed.), *The Principles of Social Order: Selected Essays of Lon F. Fuller*, rev. ed. (Portland: Hart Publishing, 2001), pp. 231–66.

efforts. Citizens cannot govern their conduct according to legal rules if they do not know what such rules permit or prohibit or if such rules are not actually enforced. Officials must thus be willing to systematically adhere to the requirements of the rule of law for law to be possible.

Three further conditions must hold for the cooperative activity at the core of law to be successful in the sense that regulating conduct according to rules is such that an environment conducive to the exercise of agency is realized. The first is congruence between law and informal social practices. This condition enhances the likelihood that citizens and officials will interpret general rules in a similar way, ensuring that citizens will be held to a standard that they were in a position to determine and had a genuine opportunity to follow.[18] The ability of law to facilitate self-directed interaction also depends on the legal decency and good judgment of officials. Officials must be decent in the sense of being willing to constrain themselves according to the rule of law. There is no simple formula that legal officials can follow in order to maintain law, and it is impossible to fulfill all the requirements of the rule of law perfectly; good judgment is thus required to guarantee that the requirements of the rule of law are balanced in an appropriate way. Finally, citizens must have faith in the law. Such faith underpins the willingness of citizens to restrict their conduct in the way that law demands.

Conditions for political trust

When a distrustful view of certain groups within society or of officials is entrenched, the process of building trust requires first cultivating a willingness and openness to change the view an individual has of others, especially those currently distrusted. For this willingness and openness to successfully result in trust, the circumstances and conditions that prevent one from seeing other members of society or officials as competent, decent, and lacking ill will must be countered. For example, severe stereotyping or the dehumanizing of members of certain groups may reinforce the view of members of certain groups as fundamentally unable to exercise the responsibilities associated with citizenship, or as motivated by an intense ill will toward others.

The conditions required for trust-responsiveness to become a default in interaction are threefold. First, trusting must in practice have the expressive character discussed in Chapter 2. That is, trusting must reflect a view of the trusted as competent, lacking ill will, and decent. Only then can the

---

[18] Postema, "Implicit Law," 365.

desire to maintain the good opinion of others by proving trust-responsive motivate trust-responsiveness. Certain practices like ongoing violence and widespread corruption can undermine the expressive function of trust, rendering it implausible to think that by trusting another an individual is viewing the trustee as decent, competent, and lacking ill will. Ensuring that trusting has the expressive character that normally motivates trust-responsiveness, however, is not sufficient to motivate trust. An individual will be motivated to prove trust-responsive only if she values the good opinion of the truster. Thus in transitional contexts it is also necessary to address the conditions, like the systematic marginalization of members of a certain social group, that prevent individuals from caring about the good opinion of (some other) members of society. Finally, trust-responsiveness depends on conditions of transparency, so that by violating the expectations of the truster, the trusted runs a genuine risk of losing the good opinion of another.

Countering the conditions that undermine default trust and trust-responsiveness at the same time enhances the reasonableness of trust and trust-responsiveness. For example, countering marginalization as a condition that prevents individuals from viewing others as competent and from being concerned about the good opinion of others puts those who are marginalized in a position to prove trust-responsive and to change their view of those who had been responsible for marginalization in the past. Similarly, violations of the rule of law and the denial of basic civil and political rights are obstacles to recognizing the agency of others and ground the reasonableness of distrust among those whose rights are violated. Restoring the rule of law and respecting basic civil and political rights may cultivate a view of those whose rights were denied as competent and decent individuals and at the same time demonstrate that officials can be trust-responsive, thus making trust of officials more reasonable.

Conditions for relational and basic capabilities

A general condition for the cultivation of the relational and basic capabilities of all citizens is the cessation and reform of unjust actions and structures that systematically diminish such capabilities. The unjust actions and structures considered include violence, economic oppression, severe stereotyping, and the construction of the identity of a political community in terms that by definition exclude from membership individuals who are from that society. In each case, the unjust action or structure diminishes capabilities because of how they affect the personal resources, external resources, and social and material structure of a society. To enhance relational capabilities, then, it is necessary to address the conditions that contribute to their diminishment. In some cases, what this entails is relatively straightforward. For example, the cessation of violence requires the termination of the use of force to harm or abuse others. For other types of injustice, the prescriptions for reconciliation will be less obvious. Economic oppression, for example, is maintained by a range of factors, including employment and wage discrimination as well as segregation.

Direct effectiveness

My discussion up to this point has examined ways in which processes can contribute to political reconciliation indirectly, by cultivating the conditions required for the rebuilding of political relationships to be possible and successful. However, processes can more directly repair the damage that civil conflict and repressive rule inflict on political relationships by promoting the characteristics of transformed and rebuilt relationships. Consider first the rule of law. Processes might directly contribute to the transformation of political relations by producing an increase in the subjection of conduct to governance by legal rules. This could be the product of an increase in the rate of obedience of legal rules by citizens who constrain their conduct according to what declared rules permit or prohibit. Alternatively, processes might produce a greater degree of restraint among officials by confining them to arresting only those who are believed to have violated declared rules or by working to ensure that declared rules are capable of being followed because they are clear, prospective, general, and do not require the impossible. There will be differences within transitional contexts in terms of both the need for and the extent of the task involved in promoting the rule of law. In cases where the rule of law is eroded, these direct contributions will entail reforming practices that are inconsistent with the rule of law, or reforming declared rules that fail to fulfill the rule of law's requirements. However, where law is absent in a more wholesale manner, the tasks needed to establish law are more substantial and widespread, including the crafting of a system of declared rules and the ability of officials to see to their actual enforcement.

Processes of reconciliation may directly contribute to political trust by changing the way in which citizens and officials view and respond to each other's demands. Insofar as processes result in citizens or officials viewing each other as competent, lacking ill will, and decent where such views were not taken before, a process can facilitate the attitude constitutive of political trust.[19] Processes may also cultivate the expectation that fellow citizens and officials will prove trust-responsive if trust is placed in them. Relatedly, processes may contribute to trust by promoting trust-responsiveness, by leading citizens and officials to take into direct consideration the fact that fellow citizens are relying on them when deliberating on how to act.

Finally, processes can directly enhance the capabilities of individuals by virtue of how they increase their personal and external resources or change the social and material structure such that the genuine opportunity of individuals to be respected, be recognized as members of a community, participate in the social, economic, and political processes, and achieve basic functionings increases. Processes may increase personal resources through psychological medical intervention, which can address the trauma, stress, and anxiety that inhibited and undermined the successful exercise of agency.[20] Education and training can develop the talents and skills of individuals. External resources can be directly increased through cash compensation or cash with certain restrictions, such as using it only to purchase certain necessities like food. The social network and familial support system of individuals may be strengthened. Finally, the social and material structure may be altered by changing laws that sanction discrimination, or enforcing laws that prohibit discrimination or language policies that preclude recognition of the primary language of part of a community, social attitudes like stereotypes, or social norms that preclude interaction or sanction violence.

Auxiliary consequences

Processes that facilitate political reconciliation by indirectly or directly transforming political interaction in the ways discussed above may have broader, less-intended impacts. Thus, an additional way in which processes may indirectly contribute to the pursuit of reconciliation is through the auxiliary consequences they have on other dimensions of change.

Some processes may influence other dimensions of relationships positively. For example, what Wolff and de-Shalit label fertile functionings "spread their good effects over several categories, either directly or by

---

[19] I discuss below how the reasonableness constraint impacts our understanding of the permissibility of a process bringing about such change.
[20] This discussion of how we might enhance capabilities draws on Wolff and de-Shalit, *Disadvantage*.

reducing the risks to other functionings."[21] Empirical research has shown that affiliation provides a certain kind of immunization against certain types of harm or stress, enhancing the ability of individuals to deal with their problems and the security of their functionings. If individuals feel a sense of belonging to a community, they often have an enhanced sense of self-esteem.[22] Promoting one particular capability may thus enhance other capabilities as a result.

The general conditions underpinning the rule of law, trust, and capabilities may themselves be strengthened by the enhancement of these aspects of political relationships. For example, an important source of the erosion of hope is injustice, which in turn is designed to undermine an individual's conviction in her own agency and competence. As Walker notes, "the exclusion of certain people or whole groups from exercising forms of competence and the denial and stereotyping that teach that some kinds of people cannot be competent in certain ways, can damage or pre-empt hopes if people themselves can be made to accept that verdict. It can have a negative impact on hopes and efforts if people can be intimidated by the fear that it is true ... Often people can be successfully discouraged, threatened, punished, and humiliated out of their hopes by persistently belittling their competence or thwarting their agency ... Some gross harms are intended precisely to create hopelessness and humiliation of types that will destroy important hopes."[23] Insofar as processes rectify injustice and establish the social and material structure in which hope can flourish, the promotion of political reconciliation may in turn strengthen and enhance hope.

Conversely, the pursuit of one kind of change may negatively impact other dimensions of political relationships. The choice of achieving one functioning may limit the ability of an individual to achieve a different functioning, and thus her capability to achieve that functioning. Limited external resources may be used to achieve nourishment or shelter, but not always both. In practice, individuals have open to them various vectors of achieved functionings that they are in a position to pursue. Similarly, the pursuit of one kind of policy by a government may have certain costs or benefits for other dimensions of relationships. For example, attempting to increase the external resources of individuals may undermine the social bases of respect. This would occur if, for example, the receipt of cash compensation from the government humiliates those who receive it.[24]

---

[21] Ibid., pp. 121–2.   [22] Ibid., p. 140.   [23] Walker, *Moral Repair*, p. 64.
[24] This example is taken from Wolff and de-Shalit, *Disadvantage*.

The failure to address certain dimensions of relationships may also impact prospects for change and transformation in other dimensions. Corrosive functionings are those whose absence has a negative impact on other functionings. In this way the disadvantages to individuals may be cumulative over time. Consider education. "In general, the less one is educated, the worse one's chances of finding employment. In other words the risks to the functionings connected with employment (such as affiliation, control over one's environment, and practical reason), which we know from our interviews are functionings likely to be damaged if one does not work."[25]

Similarly, the erosion of the capability for affiliation, or to be recognized as a member of the political community, can undermine the rule of law. Wolff and de-Shalit cite empirical evidence in which "once there is a loss of a sense of community, respect for these rules drains away, and they become increasingly difficult to enforce."[26] Similarly, the diminishment of the rule of law can erode the capabilities of participating in the political, economic, and social life of a community and of satisfying basic functionings. The erosion of the rule of law increases the control individuals have over their actions and environment; absent a clear system of rules, it becomes more difficult to predict what the consequences of one's actions will be and to formulate plans on that basis. The erosion of the rule of law, then, makes it correspondingly difficult for individuals to know what they must do in order to, for example, procure certain kinds of employment or avoid sanctions from government officials. The motivation to prove trust-responsive is impacted by the rule of law; when the publicity and transparence supported by the law are not present, then failing to prove trust-responsive does not risk lessening others' view of one. Others may not be in a position to know that their trust was violated or by whom it was violated.

SELECTING PROCESSES AND PRIORITIZING CHANGE

In the previous section I considered how we should conceptualize what should count as success for a given process of reconciliation. I outlined what a process would need to do in order to promote the desired repair and transformation of political relationships. I now want to turn to the question of the general considerations that should factor into decisions about which kind(s) of process(es) to use to promote political reconciliation in particular transitional contexts.

[25] Ibid., p. 144.   [26] Ibid., p. 140.

The first consideration is the particular character of civil conflict and the nature of a repressive regime. Chapters 1, 2, and 3 canvassed general ways in which relationships are characteristically damaged. However, transitional societies will differ in many respects – for example, the extent to which violence is group-based and what particular group was targeted. The extent to which the rule of law breaks down will also vary across societies, as will the depth of distrust and the conditions missing for trust to be reasonable. Knowing which process(es) is (are) appropriate to adopt in a particular transitional context depends on understanding the character of the damage to relationships, and thus the areas where transformation is needed.

The second consideration that should inform the choice of the particular way to pursue political reconciliation is which types of transformation a particular process does and does not facilitate. Such knowledge is imperative for understanding whether a process will respond to the particular needs of a specific transitional context. One way to determine how a particular process will impact political relationships is to consider its function (social, expressive, or moral), and demonstrate how that function facilitates or is constitutive of specific kinds of transformation. Jean Hampton offers an argument of this kind in her defense of retributive punishment. Hampton discusses the expressive function of punishment and how that function directly addresses and counters the claim implicit in wrongdoing, namely, that the victim does not deserve better treatment and that she is lower than the perpetrator.[27] In Chapter 5 I develop this kind of argument to support the claim that truth commissions promote political reconciliation. I consider the expressive function of acknowledging past wrongs through truth commissions and how this function can foster respect for moral agency.

Social scientific research can also offer empirical support for conceptual arguments in defense of particular processes. For example, the political scientist James Gibson examines the claim that truth had a positive impact on reconciliation in the South African context; he measures changes in levels of intergroup trust in South Africa, using indicators to see how the view of members of different racial groups changed as a result of the TRC.[28] Relatedly, social scientific research can enrich our understanding of the conditions that must be in place for a process to actually foster a

---

[27] See Murphy and Hampton, *Forgiveness and Mercy*, especially Chapter 4.
[28] James Gibson, *Overcoming Apartheid: Can Truth Reconcile a Divided Nation?* (New York: Russell Sage Foundation, 2004).

change or transformation of political relationships as it should. Normally, the realization of the function of a particular process in a specific transitional context depends on certain conditions. In the next two chapters I offer theoretical arguments to support specific claims about the contributions of truth commissions and criminal trials to reconciliation, and highlight important conditions for these contributions to be realized in practice. In my argument I explicitly recognize the role that empirical research can play in confirming or refuting my claims.

The third issue that should feature in the selection of a particular process of reconciliation is whether a process rebuilds political relationships in a morally permissible manner. Processes should respect the normative constraints that should govern the pursuit of political reconciliation. One general constraint on processes is that they do not violate the core moral values that are realized in political relationships characterized by respect for the rule of law, mutual reasonable trust, and relational as well as basic capabilities.

This general constraint will be satisfied to the extent that processes abide by the two moral values underpinning the frameworks of the rule of law, trust, and capabilities: respect for moral agency and reciprocity. Respect for moral agency implies that the pursuit of political reconciliation should not trample on or overlook individuals who will participate in and be impacted by such processes. That is, policies for reconciliation should not treat citizens or officials as mere means, but as distinct individuals whose autonomy and dignity should be respected. Thus the pursuit of reconciliation should take into account the impact on individuals of a particular process, and not simply the impact on society as a whole. Similarly, the pursuit of reconciliation should not require the elimination of disagreement and discussion within transitional societies about the merits of pursuing alternative ways of pursuing reconciliation or about the results of pursuits that are taken. Making the pursuit of reconciliation a democratic pursuit, in the sense of being one in which all individuals can be a part and have a say, ensures that reconciliation is not imposed on but is pursued and achieved by members of a transitional society.

The second moral value that processes of reconciliation should embody is reciprocity. Processes should be premised on the recognition that the justifiability of imposing demands and expectations on others is conditioned by what individuals themselves do. Processes can embody this conviction in terms of how the burdens of the pursuit of reconciliation are distributed. Where the burden of the pursuit of reconciliation should fall must take into consideration who has directly or indirectly benefited from the wrongdoing and damage to relationships in the past, as well as who has been directly and indirectly harmed by it. Thus those who benefit from violence and economic oppression, for example, may appropriately be expected to bear to a greater degree the burden of responsibility for achieving political reconciliation than those who were harmed by the structure of relationships in the past.

A fourth and final consideration that should govern policy making in transitional contexts is connected to the question of prioritization. In the conclusion I return to the issue of prioritization in transitional contexts. For the purposes of this chapter, it is sufficient to define the issue of prioritization. Transitional societies do not have an unlimited amount of resources to devote to the pursuit of reconciliation, and there are issues other than the pursuit of reconciliation that require attention. Thus there are two kinds of prioritization that need to occur in transitional contexts. The first involves prioritizing particular dimensions of relationships to repair and transform. When choosing between processes that address a particular dimension of repair, the choice should take into account the auxiliary consequences of a particular process. That is, the impact that a particular process will have on other dimensions of required transformation should be considered.

The second type of prioritization regards the pursuit of reconciliation against other demands in transitional contexts. One purpose of this book is to increase our understanding of how this broader prioritization should be accomplished by clarifying what is at stake in the pursuit and achievement of political reconciliation. My analysis helps us make informed judgments about how to balance the pursuit of reconciliation against the pursuit of other objectives.

CHAPTER 5

Truth commissions

INTRODUCTION

This chapter focuses on the role of truth commissions in promoting political reconciliation. Truth commissions are official, temporary bodies charged with investigating and reporting on human rights abuses in a society's past.[1] While the TRC (mentioned in Chapter 1) established in South Africa following apartheid is the most well known, in fact there have been dozens of truth commissions established around the world in the past three decades. Others include those in Argentina, Sri Lanka, Ghana, Haiti, Guatemala, Chile, the Philippines, Uganda, El Salvador, Peru, and Sierra Leone.[2]

An earlier version of this chapter was presented at a symposium on "Place, Time, and Texts: How *Do We Keep Knowing?*" sponsored by the Melbern G. Glasscock Center at Texas A&M University. I am grateful for the very helpful comments that I received from the participants in that symposium.

[1] Truth commissions differ in the specific types of human rights abuse investigated and the length of the time period of abuse examined. Sometimes hearings of perpetrators and victims are public. Truth commissions also differ in the kinds of investigative powers they have; some have had the powers of search and seizure. In some cases the final report of a truth commission is made public. See Priscilla Hayner, "Same Species, Different Animal: How South Africa Compares to Truth Commissions Worldwide," in Charles Villa-Vicencio and Wilhelm Verwoerd (eds.), *Looking Back, Reaching Forward: Reflections on the Truth and Reconciliation Commission of South Africa* (University of Cape Town Press, 2000), pp. 32–41.

[2] As noted in the introduction, truth commissions do not hold perpetrators accountable in the same way that criminal trials do, and are morally controversial because of this. Not only do truth commissions lack the power to punish perpetrators, they also often function in conjunction with some type of amnesty provision. For example, in South Africa individual perpetrators could be granted amnesty and be immune from civil and criminal prosecution if they made a full disclosure of the acts for which they were responsible and showed that such acts were done for political reasons. Unsurprisingly, many discussions of truth commissions focus on the moral justifiability of such commissions, offering explanations as to why the (apparent) sacrifice of justice is justifiable. For some especially good discussions of this, see Jennifer Llewellyn and Robert House, "Institutions for Restorative Justice: The South African Truth and Reconciliation Commission," *University of Toronto Law Journal,* 49 (1999), 355–88; Amy Gutmann and Dennis Thompson, "The Moral Foundations of Truth Commissions," in Robert I. Rotberg and Dennis Thompson (eds.), *Truth v. Justice: The Morality of Truth Commissions* (Princeton University Press, 2000), pp. 22–44, at p. 22; Jonathan Allen, "Balancing Justice and Social Utility: Political Theory and the Idea of a Truth and

My interest in this chapter is in the contributions of truth commissions to political reconciliation, and is thus narrower in scope than discussions in the literature. The thesis I defend is that truth commissions can contribute to political reconciliation by fostering respect for moral agency. In defending this thesis, I set aside questions about whether truth commissions sacrifice justice and how the values of reconciliation can be balanced against other moral considerations and values. This is not to suggest that such additional or larger questions are unimportant. Rather, my hope is to clarify the contributions truth commissions make, morally speaking, as a first step in understanding and assessing their overall justifiability in the context of transitions and transitional justice.

There are four sections in this chapter. As I discussed in Chapter 4, a general moral failing illustrated by the breakdown of the rule of law, absence and unreasonableness of political trust, and diminishment of central capabilities is a failure to respect the moral agency of certain individuals or groups of individuals within society. This insight leads me to focus on respect for moral agency in the first section of this chapter. In particular, I discuss three capacities exercised by individuals who successfully respect the agency of others. I then illustrate how these capacities are characteristically absent or undermined during periods of civil conflict and repressive rule.[3] The second section concentrates on understanding what is responsible for the undermining of these capacities and argues that the construction of group identity can play a critical role in this process. The third section discusses how the acknowledgement of past atrocities by truth commissions can contribute to the formation of a more inclusive understanding of membership in a political community and, in the process, foster the capacities of moral agents that are undermined during periods of civil conflict and repressive rule. The fourth and final section considers and responds to skepticism that truth commissions can contribute to changes in the definition of group identity and respect for moral agency.

THE CAPACITIES OF MORAL AGENTS

The particular ways in which relationships tend to go wrong during periods of civil conflict and repressive rule share a common feature: they involve a failure to respect the moral agency of others. This suggests that

---

Reconciliation Commission," *University of Toronto Law Journal*, 49 (1999), 315–53; Dyzenhaus, "The South African TRC."

[3] I do not claim that these capacities are undermined globally, but that they are often undermined or not exercised with respect to members of certain groups within society.

one important task of processes of reconciliation is to cultivate the recognition of and respect for agency, in particular toward those to whom such respect was previously not shown. To cultivate such respect, it is important to understand how and why failures of respect, especially when systematic, became possible. This section develops my answer to this question. Drawing on a discussion by the philosopher David Shoemaker, I first summarize three central capacities of moral agents. Shoemaker's analysis of the capacities that moral agents exercise in their relationships with others is important because it provides resources for understanding what gets undermined. This explains systematic failures to respect the agency of others. After discussing Shoemaker's view, I then suggest that these capacities of moral agents are absent or undermined during periods of civil conflict and repressive rule.

Members of the moral community are moral agents.[4] As moral agents, Shoemaker suggests, they possess a general capacity to enter into fundamentally interpersonal relationships with others. Such relationships are characterized by reactive attitudes, like resentment, gratitude, indignation, and love, which express our feelings toward others. Such attitudes also represent a way of holding others responsible for their actions, insofar as they express our views with respect to the success or failure of the objects of our attitude in fulfilling the moral demands we make of them.

There are three moral capacities that individuals must have in order to enter into such relationships. The first is the capacity to "recognize and apply second-personal moral reasons."[5] Second-personal reasons derive their authority from the person expressing the reason. The authority of the demand expressed in reactive attitudes stems from the authority of the individual expressing the attitude. Thus the demand expressed in second-personal reasons is important insofar as the demander is important. This is why it makes sense to think of individuals who wrong us as being responsible *to us*; individuals fail each other, and not simply morally, by wrongdoing. Similarly, the second-personal character of authority explains why individuals have a claim for seeing their demands fulfilled. To be able to engage with others interpersonally, individuals must be able to recognize the demands that others make of them and to recognize the normative authority of others to make such demands. Recognition of this

[4] David Shoemaker, "Moral Address, Moral Responsibility, and the Boundaries of the Moral Community," *Ethics*, 118 (2007), 70–108, at 71–5.
[5] Ibid., 86–9.

fact by others is reflected in part by how individuals respond when the demands of others go unfulfilled and, in particular, if they feel guilt and remorse over this fact.

The second capacity of moral agents is to be susceptible to the emotional address of others, which in turn depends on the capacity to identify empathetically with others. Interpersonal interaction is unavoidably emotional and the reactive attitudes constitutive of such relationships are forms of "emotional address."[6] When expressing negative reactive attitudes like resentment, for example, we call on the target of our resentment to feel what they have done to us. The expectation is that by understanding how they have made us feel, individuals will respond in part emotionally. Insofar as they recognize what they did as wrong, individuals will feel remorse and regret and be moved to make appropriate amends. To be able to participate in such emotional engagement and interaction, an individual must be able first to understand what another individual is communicating through her attitudes and emotions. Insofar as reactive attitudes like resentment or indignation call on an individual to feel what she has made someone go through, the target of resentment must be able to do precisely this: to understand how a person has been affected by her actions. This understanding depends on an ability to identify empathetically with others, to be "emotionally vulnerable with respect to the fortunes of the items the person with whom one empathizes cares about, and vulnerable in a roughly similar way to the person with whom one empathizes."[7] By understanding the emotional address of others, individuals are also in a position to respond to that emotional engagement in the appropriate, anticipated manner. The contrast with the fundamentally emotional, interpersonal engagement of individuals would be interaction that is characterized by viewing and treating others objectively, listening to and acting on the reasons or demands they make on us but not hearing fully what they express in their attitudes, and not engaging with them in a fundamentally personal way.

The third capacity of moral agents is the capacity to be motivated by second-personal reasons and to respond to the emotional address of others. According to Shoemaker, this motivational capacity in turn depends on an ability to care about the source of such reasons and appeals. Shoemaker defines care in terms of a "disposition to experience mature, complex emotions corresponding to the up-and-down fortunes of X."[8] Thus, if I care for an individual I will be happy when

---

[6] Ibid., 91.   [7] Ibid., 98.   [8] Ibid., 83.

things go well for that person and sad when things go poorly for her. According to Shoemaker, the connection between caring and motivation is something we implicitly assume when evaluating and interacting with others. Normally, we assume that if an individual is in a position to preserve and promote some good, X, through her actions, and is not motivated to so act, this indicates that she does not care about the good in question. If this connection between caring and motivation is correct, then one source of the failure to be motivated to respond to the demands and emotional address of others is an absence of care. If an individual does not care about another, then she will not care about or be moved by the other's demands and emotional appeals. The other's demands "simply have no motivational grip on him."[9] Nor will an individual be moved to understand how her actions have impacted the other person.

The three capacities exercised by moral agents in their interactions with others provide a promising starting point for understanding how the failure of respect for moral agency exhibited during civil conflict and repressive rule becomes possible. They suggest that one source of the failure to respect agency can stem from the erosion or undermining of the capacities to recognize and act on second-personal reasons, to be susceptible to the emotional appeals of others, and to care about them. In my view, while perhaps not global, there is often a broad erosion of these capacities during periods of civil conflict and repressive rule, frequently with respect to members of certain social groups and ideological adversaries, as well as members of a different ethnic, religious, or regional group.

To illustrate this point, consider Antjie Krog's moving account of South Africa in her *Country of My Skull: Guilt, Sorrow, and the Limits of Forgiveness in the New South Africa*. Krog is an Afrikaner journalist who covered the proceedings of the TRC in South Africa. When writing of a conversation she had with a Xhosa intellectual, Professor Kondlo, and her impressions of the TRC, Krog captures the erosion of the capacities to recognize the second-personal reasons of others, to be susceptible to the emotional appeals of others, and to care. She writes:

"How could we lose our humanity like that? The word 'apartheid' suddenly sounds like a euphemism!" I battle with my voice.

"Whites," says Kondlo, throwing back the last of his drink with a grimace, "have no *ubuntu* ... they choke on all their rights, but they have no human compassion."

---

[9] Ibid., 91.

Wordless, lost. While Afrikaner surnames like Barnard, Nieuwoudt, Van Zyl, Van Wyk, peel off victims' lips. The question they keep asking: What kind of person, what kind of human being, keeps another's hand in a fruit jar on his desk? What kind of hatred makes animals of people?

It is the ordinary people who appear before the Truth Commission. People you meet daily in the street, on the bus and train – people with the signs of poverty and hard work on their bodies and their clothes. In their faces, you can read astonishment, bewilderment, sown by the callousness of the security police and the unfairness of the justice system. "We were treated like garbage: worse than dogs. Even ants were treated better than us."

And everyone wants to know: Who? Why? Out of the sighing arises more than the need for facts or the longing to get closure on someone's life. The victims ask the hardest of all the questions: How is it possible that the person I loved so much lit no spark of humanity in you?[10]

The "hardest of all" the questions that victims asked at the South African TRC directly invokes the capacity to care, which moral agents possess and exercise in their interactions with others. Another way of formulating the fundamental question that victims who have been subjected to indifference, brutality, and injustice ask is: how did it become possible for others to fail to care about someone that I cared about so deeply, and so consequently fail to be moved by their emotional appeals and normative second-personal demands for decent, humane treatment? This question is echoed in the testimonies of other victims of human rights abuse, violence, and brutality in different contexts, who wonder how their torturers or rapists failed to be moved by their cries of pain to cease the infliction of suffering. The coldness and lack of sympathy that black South Africans in particular faced from the security forces and officials of the apartheid regime, who were characterized as largely indifferent and callous, further reinforces the notion of an absence of care and subsequent indifference to emotional pleas. That indifference and lack of susceptibility to certain emotional appeals was not restricted to the security forces. The deep sense of injustice, resentment, and in some cases rage felt among black South Africans remained largely unacknowledged among the wider white South African community and the state during apartheid. This failure to understand what life was like under apartheid and how black South Africans felt reflected a more general failure to empathize in an identifying way with their experiences. Finally, both the widespread violence as well as the general structure of the apartheid state, premised on the widespread denial of basic civil and political rights, were

[10] Krog, *Country of My Skull*, pp. 59–60.

symptomatic of the general failure to recognize the normative authority of black South Africans to make demands on officials and fellow members of society. That is, the legitimacy of the demands being expressed in the resentment, cries, and protests during apartheid went unheeded and often unrecognized.

These failures were not unique to South Africa, nor were the questions asked by victims of the South African TRC. What Krog's words powerfully convey are the failures to exercise the capacities of moral agents that can be found during contexts of civil conflict and repressive rule, where violence and human rights abuses are frequently widespread and systematic.

THE ROLE OF IDENTITY

The previous section discussed three capacities that moral agents exercise when they interact with other members of the moral community in a manner that is respectful of the moral agency of others: the capacity to recognize and apply second-personal moral reasons, the capacity to care about and to empathize with others, and the capacity to respond to the emotional address of others. I also discussed a poignant illustration of the failure to exercise these capacities in contexts of civil conflict and repressive rule. The erosion of the capacities of moral agents is an important source of the absence of respect for moral agency during civil conflict and repressive rule. If the analysis of the previous section is correct, it suggests that a key question that processes of political reconciliation must address to be successful is: *what undermines the capacity of individuals to care about, empathize with, and acknowledge the second-personal reasons of others?*

In this section, I suggest that one important source of the erosion of respect for the moral agency of others stems from how group identity is understood. The construction of group identity plays an important role in the cultivation of the moral capacities that underpin respect for moral agency and in determining the scope of individuals toward whom these capacities are exercised. Conversely, definitions of group identity can be such that the three capacities of moral agents are not developed and exercised, or are developed and exercised toward only part of a population. Finally, I consider how truth commissions can influence the construction of group identity in a way that is conducive to the cultivation of respect for moral agency.

Psychocultural dramas offer a useful starting point for understanding the relationship between group identity and the capacities to care about, empathize with, and acknowledge the second-personal moral reasons of others.[11] Such dramas involve intensely emotional conflicts over social policy, language, or resources in situations of ethnic conflict. Consider the example of parading in Northern Ireland given by the political scientist Marc Howard Ross. There are numerous parades held in Northern Ireland each year; for example, 3,100 were held in 2003. Most parades mark historical events important to either the Catholic or Protestant community. Ross describes the parade season in the following way: "Following time-honored traditions, throughout the 'marching season' in Northern Ireland Protestant men in dark suits and bowler hats assemble at local lodges, attend church services, and hold parades to mark various sacred days, with a particular emphasis on two dates in the first half of July: July 1, the anniversary of the Battle of the Somme in 1916, in which many soldiers from Northern Ireland died; and July 12, the day when, in 1690, William of Orange's Protestant forces defeated Catholic King James' troops at the Battle of the Boyne."[12] The parade season in Northern Ireland is an ongoing source of intense contestation. In response to resentment about some Protestant parade routes going through Catholic neighborhoods, Catholics decided to lobby the government to change the routes. A Parade Commission was formed in 1997 to consider complaints about parades each year. Parades have sparked violence, conflict with police, and sometimes deaths.

Parades are not often a source of such intense emotion, protest, and violence, nor is a commission normally established to deal with parades. To understand why parades are so contentious in Northern Ireland, Ross suggests, we need to understand their place in the narrative understandings of the Catholic and Protestant communities. Many philosophers and political scientists emphasize the narrative character of social group identity.[13] Narratives help an individual or social groups make sense of who they are, where they have come from, and their place in and the meaning of the social world. Narratives construct and reflect how social groups view reality, providing interpretations, for example, of a group's experiences and interactions with other social groups.

There are three important aspects of a social group's narrative understanding that illuminate the relationship between group identity and the capacities of moral agents. First, a social group's history is understood

---

[11] The term "psychocultural dramas" comes from Ross, *Cultural Contestation*, pp. 25–6.
[12] Ibid., p. 6.
[13] See, for example, Susan Dwyer, "Reconciliation for Realists," *Ethics & International Affairs*, 13 (1999), 81–98; Jeffrey Bluestein, *The Moral Demands of Memory* (New York: Cambridge University Press, 2008); Ross, *Cultural Contestation*.

normatively in two different ways. Past experiences can be seen as providing important lessons for the present and future. A social group's understanding of the appropriate way to act in a particular situation can be influenced by considering parallels with the present situation and the past.[14] Also, the collective memory of a community includes judgments about the justifiability of its past actions and the actions of other groups with which it has been involved, as well as judgments about the character of its motivations and the motivations of others.[15] Elements of bias often inform these normative judgments. Group narratives "portray a group's experiences in a favorable light emphasizing moral qualities the group has displayed in overcoming enemies and threats to its existence over time."[16] By contrast, judgments of the actions and motivations of other groups, especially antagonistic groups, are informed by stereotypes. As discussed in Chapter 3, stereotyping is a process of categorization in which we make biased generalizations, or generalizations that put our social group in a favorable light, about individuals of whom we know very little based on their presumed resemblance to a group in a way that favors the groups to which an individual herself belongs.[17] Thus, unsurprisingly, in Northern Ireland "both groups see themselves as decent, fine, ordinary people, but each other as bitter and brainwashed."[18]

Second, the narrative of a community importantly contributes to a sense of a shared or common fate among the members of the social group. Expectations for future treatment are formed on the basis of an understanding of how a group has fared in the past. Judgments of the motivations and past actions of members of other groups similarly influence the shared expectations of likely treatment in the future. Such shared expectations reflect a group's basic shared hopes and fears (e.g., about the physical safety of members of a group, the potential for future humiliation, and the loss of political power) as well as deepest suspicions of antagonistic social groups.

Third, the narrative understanding of a community is shaped and maintained by forms of what Ross calls cultural enactment, which are

---

[14] Ross, *Cultural Contestation*, pp. 32–4. In the context of the recent economic crisis in the United States, an example of such looking to the past for normative lessons for the present can be seen in the invocations of the Great Depression in which analysts look to see in what respects our situation today is similar to the situation then, and how the government can respond to avoid the same pitfalls of the past and to replicate the successes of past responses.
[15] Ibid., p. 32.   [16] Ibid., p. 42.   [17] Cudd, *Analyzing Oppression*, p. 69.
[18] McGarry and O'Leary, *Explaining Northern Ireland*.

emotionally powerful for members of a social group. Cultural enactment refers to various ways in which a social group expresses its culture and thus its interpretation of the social world. Some forms of cultural enactment reconnect a group with its collective past and historical events. This can serve as "an occasion for communal celebration, for an outpouring of communal grief, a source of communal pride, and so forth."[19] Commemorated events may include historical triumphs in battle as well as humiliating defeats, periods of political dominance as well as periods of humiliating subordination to others. Part of what is remembered and communicated by such cultural enactment can be basic hopes and fears.[20] Such expressions are often selective, incorporating events that are emotionally symbolic and often not attempting to understand another group's perspective.

With this understanding of the narrative character of social group identity, we are now in a position to understand both why parades are a source of such powerful emotions and how identity influences the capacities of moral agents. First, parades are a source of intense emotion for both communities because they call to mind key events of triumph and defeat and invoke deeply held fears and suspicions in the process. Parades commemorating Catholic defeat, sometimes conjoined with songs featuring anti-Catholic lyrics, that are permitted to march through Catholic neighborhoods spark resentment among Catholics and evoke fears of a return to a period of Protestant domination politically and economically similar to that of the early twentieth century. The refusal to permit such parades evokes Protestant fears of a loss of religious and political rights were Ireland to be reunited. For some, the denial of important forms of cultural expression, such as the parades, represents the first step in the eventual marginalization of the Protestant people and Protestant culture. Such fears help to explain why an issue like parades can become fraught with such emotional significance and power. It also helps to explain why the return to self-government in 1998 faced difficulties.[21]

How does the role of a narrative structure of group identity help us understand ways in which the capacities to care about, empathize with, or acknowledge the authority of others to make moral demands on us get undermined? Consider the capacity to recognize and act on the second-personal moral reasons offered by members of a different, especially antagonistic, social group. Culturally defined and reinforced views of others can

[19] Bluestein, *Moral Demands of Memory,* p. 188.
[20] Ross, *Cultural Contestation,* p. 21.   [21] Ibid., p. 14.

serve to undermine the recognition of the second-personal reasons of others, or of the authority of such reasons. First, viewing members of a social group as "bitter and brainwashed," as prone to violence, or as unreasonable is to see them as moral agents who do not act reasonably (but engage in "unreasoning" violence) and do not think rationally (but are "brainwashed"). Such views delegitimize their demands, making such demands seem illegitimate and unreasonable. Demands that stem from "brainwashing" do not express compelling reasons in the same way that demands expressed in reasonable reactive attitudes do.

In addition, the delegitimization of demands can become more pronounced when full citizenship or membership in the political community is associated with a particular social group within a population, either *de facto* or *de jure*. Such associations imply that members of other social groups are not full citizens or members of the political community. For example, restricting full South African citizenship to whites or associating Britishness with Protestantism and Catholicism with Irishness undermines the full membership status of non-white South Africans, Catholic Brits, or Protestant Irish. This relationship diminishes the authority of the demands of such groups because of the relationship between citizenship and rights and obligations.[22] Insofar as rights and the authority to make certain claims on others are tied to citizenship, those viewed as less than full members of a community will be considered to have less than full authority to make certain demands. The corresponding obligations and responsibilities that the government and fellow members have with respect to the treatment of those viewed as less than full members may also be challenged.

Finally, feeling threatened by a social group can inhibit the ability to acknowledge the demands of members of the threatening group. Social groups can be threatening in different ways. They may evoke fears of physical harm or subordination, or they may challenge a group's interpretation of its past actions and experiences. Feeling threatened may contribute to or motivate a refusal to engage with the demands and claims of other social groups out of a desire for self-protection, physically or psychologically. Ross's description of Northern Ireland illustrates this latter point: "Protestants and Catholics in Northern Ireland ... have trouble acknowledging the other's parallel perceptions. This is because each party's emotional concerns make it very difficult to hear, let alone

---

[22] See, for example, Bluestein, citing Joseph Raz, *Moral Demands of Memory*, p. 46.

acknowledge, the other's account, especially when their own actions may be the root cause of an adversary's feelings and behavior."[23]

The narrative structure of group identity also helps us understand how individuals' susceptibility to the emotional appeals of and ability to empathize with others can be undermined. A precondition for interacting with others interpersonally and thus being susceptible to their emotional address is that we view them as reasonable moral agents. For me to take seriously the emotional appeals of another I must believe that there is *prima facie* reason to believe that her appeal to me is legitimate or appropriate. I must believe that there is *prima facie* reason to believe that I have wronged an individual who is resentful toward me, or that it is reasonable for her to have this belief. Anger or indignation that is the product of brainwashing or expresses an unreasonable disposition to violence will not be seen as emotions that I can identify with or understand. I may not be able to see or respond to an emotional plea that I understand how I have made another feel. Insofar as her emotional and motivational life is unreasonable, I will not be able to envision how I have made her feel. Identifying empathy will seem impossible to achieve. Instead, I will view her objectively as a curious, foreign sort of object, or strange, sometimes deeply disturbing, phenomenon.

Finally, narrative understanding can undermine the ability to care. Insofar as I view members of another group as less than full members of a political community, my care and concern for them may be less than the care and concern I have for those who are full members of my society. Insofar as I view members of another social group as unreasonably violent toward me and members of my social group, or violent for no justifiable reason, then my willingness to be concerned about members of that group often diminishes. This is especially the case if I take unreasonable violence to be evidence of malice toward members of my social group, or consider myself to be innocent of any causal responsibility for the violence. Given the connection between caring and motivation, when my care is diminished, my corresponding motivation to try to empathize with and respect the moral demands of others will be similarly reduced.

REMEMBRANCE AND RESPECT FOR MORAL AGENCY

The argument from the previous section suggested that the narrative understanding of social groups influences the exercise of the three central

---

[23] Ross, *Cultural Contestation*, p. 15.

capacities of moral agents and, consequently, respect for the moral agency of others being realized in interaction. This implies that in certain contexts the cultivation of respect for moral agency depends on changing the narrative understanding of political communities and of social groups within political communities. In particular, a more inclusive definition of membership in the political community may need to be developed and the view of members of certain groups countered. In this section I consider the role that a truth commission may play in promoting such changes. That is, I focus on how truth commissions may contribute to the process of redrawing the boundaries of membership in the political community and challenge the stereotypes that have undermined the capacities of moral agents and subsequently respect for moral agency in the past.

Truth commissions document and record patterns of human rights abuses and atrocities over a specified time period within a society. Thus, truth commissions are one way that a society can acknowledge and remember the past. Such acknowledgement and remembrance has an expressive function. Remembering requires work and effort. This is especially true when what one wants to remember are abuses or wrongdoing that have been officially denied and about which little is publicly known. Who and what we remember tells us on whose behalf we are motivated to put in the work of remembering. Given the connection between motivation and caring, who and what we remember expresses who and what we care about.

Remembering is also a way in which a community expresses or communicates its self-understanding.[24] The collective memory of a community, reflected in its narrative understanding of its history, conveys how it conceptualizes membership in its group and whom it views as part of the community. Conversely, the exclusion of certain individuals from the collective memory of a group or community conveys the fact that such individuals are not considered part of the group or their experiences part of the experiences of the group. In these ways, who and what are not remembered can tell us who is marginalized within a community.

There is an additional way in which remembering expresses who a community takes itself to be. As noted above, certain events or experiences can take on a special, symbolic importance for a community, reflecting

[24] Bluestein, *Moral Demands of Memory*, pp. 164–5.

the values to which a community is committed and which have been displayed or failed to be displayed in its past. Thus, how the past is remembered communicates how a community evaluates and understands its central normative commitments and success in living up to those commitments.

As a forum for remembering the past, truth commissions have the expressive or communicative functions described above. The way in which a truth commission fulfills its expressive functions determines the influence it will have on the narrative understanding of a political community. In particular, how the expressive functions of a truth commission are realized affects its ability to reconstitute group identity such that respect for moral agency is fostered. I discuss below ways in which a truth commission can serve to influence the narrative understanding of a political community and the cultivation of the capacities of moral agents, and to promote political reconciliation in the process.

First, the very establishment of a truth commission represents a way for a society to communicate that the people who suffered matter. The message expressed by the establishment of a truth commission is that those who were victims of human rights abuses are significant enough to remember and to have their suffering acknowledged. Insofar as the victims of human rights abuses are drawn from or include members of a previously targeted community or marginalized social group, the communicative message about the significance of the victims can have a larger resonance, signaling that the communities from which the victims come are significant enough to remember. The motivation to establish a truth commission and document and acknowledge past abuses demonstrates a care and concern about those who were met with indifference in the past and counters denial that their suffering mattered.

Second, a truth commission communicates and testifies to the fact that victims are part of the political community, and that they have the authority to demand better treatment than they have received in the past. The very act of inclusion of victims from members of historically marginalized communities asserts their standing as part of the history of a community that is under investigation. In addition, truth commissions are premised on the fact that the past being investigated is past *wrongdoing*, which should not have occurred and will not occur in the future. Thus, by openly rejecting the justifiability or permissibility of the abuses inflicted on victims, a truth commission communicates the authority of those who were victims to demand and to receive better treatment and counters interpretive denial.

Further, the operation of a truth commission can, under certain conditions, call into question a community's self-understanding, both in terms of the values to which it is committed and the success it has had in fulfilling those values and commitments in the past. The necessity of establishing a truth commission is a product of the failure of a political community to have acknowledged or fully known the extent of the wrongdoing and abuse of the recent past. The proceedings of a truth commission and the final report it produces present a community with its record of systematic and widespread wrongdoing. In place of denials of responsibility for wrongdoing and rationalizations for wrongdoing that was known, a society is confronted with the systematic, typically officially sanctioned violence and abuse that occurred. Insofar as this report is accepted within a community and its findings become culturally established, it effectively closes off certain kinds of rationalizations and denials of the past. For example, hearings of the South African TRC and the Final Report subsequently produced made it clear to the public as a whole that apartheid was a system that could only have been maintained with violence.

Finally, the testimony of victims illustrates the very real human costs and, through the narrative victims provide of the circumstances in which such abuse occurred, demonstrate the legitimate grievances of social groups within communities targeted for violence.[25] The particular stories of victims can also serve to counter stereotypes implicitly invoked to rationalize injustice, such as that everyone in a particular social group was part of the violent oppositional campaign or that a social group was by nature violent and unreasonable. By countering stereotypes, members of the larger political community are able to see and understand why victims feel resentment, anger, and indignation. The emotional and psychological barriers to understanding individuals from antagonistic social groups can be countered in this way. A truth commission can open the door to and facilitate the exercise of empathy with others in a way that will make members of a political community more susceptible to the emotional address of their fellows in the future.[26]

---

[25] Jonathan Allen makes a similar point about truth commissions in his "Balancing Justice and Social Utility," 330. Allen argues that the TRC also strengthened citizens' sensitivity to injustice. In his view, this is crucial for maintaining just institutions and was undermined during apartheid. The TRC strengthened this sense by providing "information about moral evils and about the breakdown of the sense of injustice."

[26] This argument resonates with that put forth by Nir Eisikovits in "Rethinking the Legitimacy of Truth Commissions: 'I am the Enemy You Killed, My Friend,'" *Metaphilosophy*, 37(3–4) (2006), 489–514. Eisikovits discusses the importance of cultivating sympathy to promote reconciliation. According to him, sympathy facilitates reconciliation in a number of ways. It can counter moral

These ways of cultivating the recognition of the normative authority of all individuals within a political community, expressing a care and concern for those previously shown indifference, and cultivation of empathy can offer members of a political community in transition some grounds for hope that moral agency will be respected in the future. This in turn can influence the hope that members of a community have about the possibility of cultivating political relationships characterized by mutual respect for the rule of law, reasonable trust, and extensive relational as well as basic capabilities. Insofar as the understanding of a community's history of unjustified human rights abuses becomes culturally established, people may become more willing to believe that their fellows will be committed to a system of human rights and rule by law. In general, once the community as a whole is perceived to be in agreement that the past was intolerable and will not be returned to, then there is a better chance that they will trust that others have an interest in moving forward together to a better, democratic, and reciprocal system. A truth commission can thus contribute to the creation of an environment conducive to hope in the possibility of political trust.

THREE CONCERNS

To conclude, I would like to address three possible concerns that could arise about the analysis given thus far. One concern stems from an ambiguity in my analysis. In the discussion of the previous section, I highlight the fact that the function of a truth commission is to document patterns of human rights abuses in the recent past and so remember the past. However, this form of remembrance is compatible with documented information not becoming part of the narrative understanding, or collective memory, of a political community. As the philosopher Jeffrey Bluestein notes: "A particular historical account of events in a group's past may be clearly favored by the balance of evidence and may be widely accepted as true at least by those who are qualified to make this determination. Yet, that account may have little significance or value for the members of that group ... History can provide causal

blindness, or "the propensity to look through people, to act as if what we do has no specific impact on specific human beings" (498), because it fundamentally involves seeing people in detail and understanding their actions and reactions. However, he sees sympathy as facilitating reconciliation, whereas my argument makes the achievement of empathy a constitutive achievement of reconciliation.

explanations of past events and of their relations to the present, but this is quite compatible with a group's not *caring* about its history, caring about it enough and in such a way that those who belong to it seek to actively transmit what they know of the past to their posterity and accept the past as a significant resource for the present."[27] For truth commissions to promote reconciliation by cultivating the capacities of moral agents and redefining the narrative understanding of a political community, the past they document must become part of the collective memory of a political community. However, according to the first concern, I have given no reason to think that the historical record produced by a truth commission and the testimony it gathers will serve as anything other than a one-time event and, ultimately, token acknowledgement that will have no grip on members of a political community, either conceptually (in terms of how they conceptualize themselves) or motivationally.

A second, related concern stems from the discussion in the second section on how the narrative understanding of groups can undermine the capacities to care about, empathize with, or acknowledge the normative authority of members of certain groups. The narrative understanding that led to indifference toward, an inability to empathize with, and failure to acknowledge the normative authority of certain individuals or groups is still present at the time that a truth commission operates. This calls into question whether the expressive function of the truth commission will be realized in the ways that I suggested in the previous section. Why should we expect that the larger political community will care to listen to or know about the suffering of victims? Why should we think that the narratives of victims will be ones that the larger population will be motivated or able to empathize with? Why should we think that the experiences of victims will be experiences about which a population cares and is moved to consider how such experiences challenge the received narrative understanding of history?

In response, I want to grant the validity of these underlying concerns. There is no guarantee that particular truth commissions will play the expressive roles described in the previous section. Recognition of this fact highlights the importance of understanding the social and political conditions that influence the impact of a truth commission on a political society. In my view, there are three conditions in particular that may

[27] Bluestein, *Moral Demands of Memory*, p. 203.

influence the degree to which a truth commission changes the narrative understanding of a political community and cultivates the capacities of moral agents. The conditions below are designed to ensure that truth commissions can serve as an experience and source of new images that can invite new or revised ways of understanding the past and fellow members of society.[28]

First, the perceived legitimacy of the commission plays an important role in determining the impact it will have on the larger society. Insofar as a commission is widely viewed as legitimate, there is *prima facie* reason to think that members of a political community will not reflexively dismiss the proceedings or discount its findings. Perceptions of legitimacy in turn could be dependent on a number of factors: how representative a commission is of sub-groups within a general population, how it was established, and who is willing to participate in its hearings. The broader the base of the participants and commissioners, the more difficult it becomes to levy charges of bias and the more likely its proceedings and findings are to be seen as authoritative. In addition, the more inclusive a commission is in its composition and participants, the more its practice reinforces the central message that a truth commission should be conveying, regarding the more inclusive understanding of membership in the political community that should be cultivated and endorsed.

A second condition that can influence the impact of a commission is the degree to which the hearings and final report are made publicly accessible. A minimum condition for the testimony and findings of a truth commission to influence the collective memory and self-understanding of a community is that they be heard. The more extensive and widespread the public emphasis on the workings of a truth commission, the more difficult it will be for a community to avoid and eschew its work, and the more likely it is that a commission will become part of the larger public discussion and a subject of ongoing debate.

The public and accessible character of a truth commission can also contribute to the giving of a public and prominent role to victims and their testimonies. This is critical for ensuring that truth commissions are able to counter the stereotyping that undermined the capacity to care and empathize in the past. The testimony of victims of the abuse that they suffered, told in their own voice and framed in their own terms, is often

---

[28] Ross, *Cultural Contestation*, pp. 46–7.

more powerful than third-person narratives of violence or even official reports with compilations of patterns of abuse and wrongdoing. Victims humanize the victims of violence and the costs of violence. They concretize and personalize the abstract understanding of the recent past, and the violence that was constitutive of it. The power of personal testimony and images of individuals is attested to by the power that photographic images can have, where the reality of warfare and repressive rule and its concomitant human costs come to the fore.

Individual testimony can have a more powerful impact on a community than even the final report a commission produces. It is more likely to force a community to ask itself: what have we allowed? Who have we been or become to make the infliction of such suffering possible? Thus, testimony of victims, I am suggesting, can motivate a reflective space or moment within a community, precisely of a kind that can lead to the rethinking within a political community of its history, its success in achieving ideals with which it identifies, as well as the ideals themselves. Further, the stories of victims serve to challenge stereotypical views that may be widely held regarding the motivations and character of marginalized and stereotyped individuals. What can emerge from the testimony of victims is a more complicated story about the motivations, actions, and experiences of individuals throughout the conflict, some of whom may have sympathized with an armed opposition movement, for example, while others did not. In addition, the justifiability of resentment, anger, and other reactive attitudes, which may have been dismissed as irrational, can come to the fore as a society is forced to confront the character and extent of the way individuals suffered.

However, it is precisely this pivotal role that the testimony of a truth commission plays that may lead to a third and final concern that I want to consider. Successful truth commissions place a significant burden on victims and other testifiers to be truthful, fair-minded, and relevant when detailing human rights abuses. This is a burden that many testifiers may have difficulty meeting in practice. Truthful testimony can be incredibly painful for victims, and being charitable with respect to the motives of perpetrators is difficult. However, unless the burden for testifiers is regularly fulfilled, truth commissions can descend into a public forum for settling old scores and for airing grudges, prejudices, and incidents tangentially related to the mandate of the commission. Instead of leading to critical self-examination among perpetrators and members of the larger political community, truth commissions may instead become a forum for recriminations and revenge, further entrenching denial and divisions.[29]

In response, I want first to grant that testimony, especially testimony in public hearings, must be truthful, fair-minded, and relevant if it is to have the powerful impact on a community and contribute to political reconciliation in the ways I discussed above. The question the objection raises is: to what degree are truth commissions able to constrain the character of public testimony given as part of their hearings? The ability of a truth commission to influence the character of testimony so as to ensure it is truthful, relevant, and fair-minded depends on several factors. One is the powers delegated and resources devoted to a truth commission. Of special concern is whether the powers of a commission are sufficient to enable it to identify false claims and allegations, for example, in interviews conducted prior to a public testimony from a particular survivor or family member of a victim, or the publication of the final report of a commission.[30] Powers of subpoena, search and seizure, and witness protection enhance the ability of a commission to corroborate or dispute particular claims. Resources affect the ability of a commission to exercise the powers granted. In particular, the qualifications, training, and the size of the truth commission staff as well as the budget and time frame for the commission's work impact the extent to which a commission can exercise its powers. Finally, the availability of evidence determines how well a commission can sort out false claims. In this context, access to official data that could corroborate claims articulated in interviews with commissioners is critical. Effective access depends on the extent of official records kept during a period of conflict and repressive rule, and whether such records have been suppressed or destroyed, or instead made available to a commission.

Corroboration of claims is one way in which a commission may be able to ferret out truthful from untruthful testimony. However, for many commissions the primary challenge is not to identify false allegations and to weed out those individuals motivated by private

---

[29] I am grateful to a reviewer for pressing this concern.

[30] In South Africa, for example, TRC commissioners determined who was invited to testify in public hearings. For a discussion of these constraints see Audrey R. Chapman and Patrick Ball, "The Truth of Truth Commissions: Comparative Lessons from Haiti, South Africa, and Guatemala," *Human Rights Quarterly*, 23(1) (2001), 1–43; Joanna R. Quinn and Mark Freeman, "Lessons Learned: Practical Lessons Gleaned from Inside the Truth Commission of Guatemala and South Africa," *Human Rights Quarterly*, 25(4) (2003), 1117–49.

retaliation or revenge; rather, it is to encourage participation. One of
the main challenges for truth commissions is to create a safe space for
survivors and the family members of victims who participate. Fear of
retaliation for testifying and uncertainty about whether their account
will be met with the same indifference or hostility as in the past often
undermine the willingness of victims and their family members to
participate in truth commissions. Thus the ability of a commission
to protect victims and support them during their testimony, public or
otherwise, is often critical in determining the extent to which they
can learn about the past. Such protection and support can be demonstrated in a number of ways, including through the establishment of a
witness protection program, the provision of psychological counseling
before and following testifying, and the gathering of testimony in an
objective manner, as opposed to the adversarial manner characteristic
of criminal trials.[31]

The abilities of a truth commission to encourage participation and to
corroborate claims do not by themselves determine whether public testimony by actual victims and their family members will be relevant and
fair-minded. Optimism that this testimony will have these characteristics
depends in part on why victims and family members are motivated to
testify in the first place. Examining this question, I suggest below, leads to
qualified optimism about the ability of testifiers to fulfill the burdens of
fair-mindedness and relevance.

There is a deep need for many victims and family members to
understand and make sense of what happened to them and why,
to have their suffering acknowledged, and, consequently, to be able
to express their grief and anger. South African clinical psychologist
Brandon Hamber has conducted the most extensive work on the
psychological needs of testifiers and the consequences of testifying
before a truth commission.[32] As Hamber notes, and as I emphasized

[31] In this last respect, a truth commission may provide less protection to the accused. In a regular
courtroom the truthfulness of claims is evaluated in part through the adversarial cross-examination
of witnesses. However, especially given that a truth commission does not itself prosecute anyone
and that an adversarial system might alienate victims from participating, a non-adversarial format
of testimony gathering is reasonable. In addition, should information gathered in a truth
commission be used later to prosecute someone, the prosecution process itself would use
adversarial cross-examination. This latter process might, of course, be hard on the victims.
However, the victims would be better off for having their points of view validated in the truth
commission process, even if the criminal process is unable to convict. I am grateful to Linda Radzik
for drawing this point to my attention.

[32] Hamber himself notes that little work has been done on the psychological consequences for victims
of testifying in truth commissions. See Brandon Hamber, "Do Sleeping Dogs Lie? The

in Chapter 3, there is often a culture of silence surrounding human rights abuses within societies in conflict and under repressive rule. The official story of alleged abuses (either that they did not occur or were not perpetrated by the government) is enforced and not openly challenged or discussed for fear of repercussions.[33] The cognitive ramifications of human rights abuses and the subsequent silence can be severe, as individuals struggle to understand why they have suffered and how they can still believe that the world is meaningful.[34] This silence further renders victims, survivors, and their family members unable to articulate their legitimate anger and rage, and often creates a sense of being misunderstood and socially isolated. In Hamber's words, "Survivors and the victims for whom they grieve both inhabit a liminal space, which is both part of society but removed from society; it could be called an experience of 'the living dead.' This space is characterised by uncertainty and doubt."[35]

Truth commissions offer a forum that can address the deep psychological needs of victims. A truth commission provides an opportunity for victims to try to make some sense of their experiences and to construct a coherent account of them. Participation also affords an opportunity to have their suffering acknowledged, as a counterpoint to the denial and subsequent social exclusion they experienced in the past. In the words of Priscilla Hayner, "Truth commissions seem to satisfy – or at least *begin* to satisfy – a clear need of some victims to tell their stories and to be listened to ... the simple act of recognizing a person's traumatic experience could be extremely important to their psychological healing."[36] Given the deep psychological need of many victims, there is reason to think that the testimony offered will be relevant in

Psychological Implications of the Truth and Reconciliation Commission in South Africa," paper presented at the Centre for the Study of Violence and Reconciliation, seminar no. 5 (1995), 1–12.

[33] Brandon Hamber, "The Burdens of Truth: An Evaluation of the Psychological Support Services and Initiatives Undertaken by the South African Truth and Reconciliation Commission," *American Imago*, 55(1) (1998), 9–28.

[34] Brandon Hamber and Richard A. Wilson, "Symbolic Closure through Memory, Reparation and Revenge in Post-conflict Societies," 2002, http://digitalcommons.uconn.edu/hri_papers/5. Accessed April 22, 2009. For an extensive discussion of post-traumatic stress disorder and its implications for the breakdown of the rule of law, see Colleen Murphy, "Political Reconciliation, the Rule of Law, and Post-traumatic Stress Disorder," in Nancy Nyquist Potter (ed.), *Trauma, Truth, and Reconciliation: Healing Damaged Relationships* (Oxford University Press, 2006), pp. 83–110.

[35] Hamber and Wilson, "Symbolic Closure," 5.

[36] Hayner, *Unspeakable Truths*. Hayner cites Chilean psychologist Elizabeth Lira in making this point.

the sense that it communicates the wrong that was experienced and the impact of that wrong on the victim. It is the abuse suffered that leads to the need to tell one's story in the first place.

With respect to the burden of fair-mindedness, it is important to recognize that an impartial perspective need not be an unemotional perspective; rather, it must be free from bias and not driven by self-interest. An impartial perspective on the atrocities that are committed during a conflict can lead to outrage and indignation. Such emotions express legitimate and justifiable judgments regarding the unjustifiability of the abuses that occurred. The testimony by victims and their family members in truth commissions is often emotional as well, including the expression of rage, resentment, and grief as a testifier attempts to make sense of what has happened to her or to her family members.[37] However, such expressions are analogous to the indignation that third-party impartial observers might express, and also articulate legitimate judgments that what happened was wrong and unjustified.

Finally, though it may be difficult for victims to be charitable with respect to the motives of perpetrators of abuse, the conduct of a truth commission itself may affect this ability. In particular, it is important that a truth commission conveys the complexity of a conflict, a history, and a repressive regime, including the fact that the categories of perpetrator, victim, bystander, and collaborator often overlap and apply to the same people or social groups. Insofar as a truth commission is able to gather testimony from diverse groups, including victims and perpetrators, this testimony will enrich a community's understanding of the complicated and wide-ranging toll that a conflict or repressive regime had, and it is likely to further encourage fair-mindedness among those who testify.

[37] Hamber and Wilson, "Symbolic Closure."

CHAPTER 6

International criminal trials

INTRODUCTION

This chapter focuses on the role of the international community, and of international criminal trials specifically,[1] in the promotion of political reconciliation within transitional societies. An inquiry into the role of international criminal trials in promoting political reconciliation may seem unpromising for two reasons. For one thing, the operations of some hybrid and international criminal tribunals are hampered by insufficient financial resources, a lack of international personnel familiar with local cultures and languages, hostility to international personnel in certain transitional contexts, and rejection of the legitimacy of such tribunals. Such limitations call into question the ability of international trials to prosecute and successfully convict perpetrators and counter impunity. For those who see impunity as an obstacle to reconciliation, the limitations with international criminal tribunals strengthen skepticism about the ability of such trials to promote reconciliation.

One objective of this chapter is to temper such skepticism. My thesis is that international criminal trials can contribute to political reconciliation by fostering the social conditions necessary for law's efficacy. This chapter builds on Chapter 1, in which I argue that the cultivation of mutual respect for the rule of law is a constitutive part of the process of political reconciliation.[2] The

An earlier version of this chapter was presented at the IVR World Congress in Kraków, Poland as part of a panel on "International Criminal Trials." I am very grateful to Larry May for inviting me to participate in that panel and for the helpful feedback I received. I would also like to thank Kathleen Murphy, Susanne Sreedhar, Nancy Lawrence, Cyndy Brown, and Paolo Gardoni for their valuable comments on previous drafts.

[1] In this chapter international criminal trials are understood broadly to include ad hoc international tribunals, and the permanent International Criminal Court, as well as hybrid tribunals operating in domestic contexts.

[2] See also my "Lon Fuller and the Moral Value of the Rule of Law," *Law and Philosophy*, 24(3) (2005), 239–62; "Political Reconciliation, the Rule of Law, and Post-traumatic Stress Disorder"; "Political Reconciliation, the Rule of Law, and Genocide," *The European Legacy*, 12(7) (2007), 853–65.

(re-)establishment of mutual respect for the rule of law is an important part of the process of repair because relationships structured by law realize three important moral values: agency, reciprocity, and justice. As I discussed in Chapter 1, the absence or erosion of the rule of law damages relationships by undermining these values and by cultivating distrust, resentment, and a sense of betrayal among citizens.

My chapter departs in two respects from prominent themes in contemporary discussions of international criminal trials and political reconciliation. First, I focus on the character of the international criminal trials process, rather than defending or challenging the contributions of international criminal trials to justice, deterrence, or ending the historic impunity enjoyed by perpetrators of human rights abuses.[3] Second, since my interest lies in the conduct of criminal trials rather than their outcome, I do not address the question of the compatibility between criminal trials, retributive justice, and reconciliation.[4] Instead, I emphasize what I take to be subtler, more easily overlooked contributions of international criminal tribunals to political reconciliation.[5]

The first of the four sections in this chapter explains the social conditions on which law's efficacy depends, drawing on the insights of the legal philosopher Lon Fuller. The second highlights the absence of these

---

[3] For a discussion of general justifications of international criminal trials, see Naomi Roht-Arriaza, *Impunity and Human Rights: International Law Practice* (New York: Oxford University Press, 1995); Jaime Malamud-Goti, "Transitional Governments in the Breach: Why Punish State Criminals?" *Human Rights Quarterly*, 12(1) (1990), 1–16; Martha Minow, *Between Vengeance and Forgiveness: Facing History after Genocide and Mass Violence* (Boston: Beacon Press, 1998); Neil Kritz, *Transitional Justice: How Emerging Democracies Reckon with Former Regimes* (Washington, DC: United States Institute of Peace Press, 1995); M. Cherif Bassiouni, "Searching for Peace and Achieving Justice,". *Law and Contemporary Problems*, 59(4) (1996), 9–28; Aryeh Neier, *War Crimes: Brutality, Genocide, Terror, and the Struggle for Justice* (New York: Crown Publisher, 1998). Nancy Combs questions whether international criminal trials, as currently structured, are effective in ending the legacy of impunity in her *Guilty Pleas in International Criminal Law* (Stanford University Press, 2007).

[4] For a discussion of this relationship, see Ruti Teitel, "Bringing the Messiah through Law," in Carla Hesse and Robert Post (eds.), *Human Rights in Political Transitions: Gettysburg to Bosnia* (New York: Zone Books, 1999), pp. 177–93.

[5] Analyses that focus on other potential contributions of trials to reconciliation include Larry May, *Genocide: A Normative Account* (Cambridge University Press, 2010); Mark Osiel, *Mass Atrocity, Collective Memory, and the Law* (City: Transaction Publishers, 1999); Michel Feher, "Terms of Reconciliation," in Carla Hesse and Robert Post (eds.), *Human Rights in Political Transitions: Gettysburg to Bosnia* (New York: Zone Books, 1999), pp. 325–39; Julie Mertus, "Only a War Crimes Tribunal: Triumph of the International Community, Pain of the Survivors," in Belinda Cooper (ed.), *War Crimes: The Legacy of Nuremberg* (New York: TV Books, 1999). Challenges to these accounts of the contributions of trials to political reconciliation include Teitel, "Bringing the Messiah through Law"; and Laurel Fletcher and Harvey Weinstein, "Violence and Social Repair: Rethinking the Contribution of Justice to Reconciliation," *Human Rights Quarterly*, 24 (2002), 573–639.

conditions in societies in conflict or under repressive rule. The third shows how international criminal trials can promote reconciliation by cultivating the social conditions on which law depends. I also discuss the circumstances that must be in place for these contributions to be realized in practice. The fourth considers three objections to my analysis.

SOCIAL CONDITIONS OF LAW

My focus in this section is the social and moral conditions required for a system of legal rules to regulate the behavior of citizens and officials in practice. My aim is expository and constructive, namely, to articulate Fuller's argument for the necessity of four conditions.[6] These conditions are ongoing cooperative interaction between citizens and officials, systematic congruence between law and informal social practices, legal decency and good judgment, and faith in law. The first condition, ongoing cooperative interaction, is the most fundamental. The second, third, and fourth conditions facilitate ongoing cooperative interaction and ensure that it is of the kind necessary for law to function as it should.

Typically, in stable social contexts the presence of each of these four social conditions is assumed or taken for granted. However, as I discuss in greater detail in the next section, these conditions are characteristically undermined or absent during periods of repressive rule or civil conflict. Appreciating the role of these social conditions in cultivating or maintaining a system of legal rules that regulate the behavior of citizens and officials in practice is thus critical for understanding what processes of reconciliation must address if political relationships in transitional societies are to be repaired.

Law refers to "the enterprise of subjecting human conduct to the governance of rules."[7] To understand the social conditions required for law to be effective, it is important first to discuss the central task of law. Law's primary function is, in the words of Fuller, to maintain "a sound and stable framework (or baselines) for self-directed action and interaction."[8] There are three senses in which the action and interaction structured by law are self-directed.[9] First, law influences behavior by

---

[6] Fuller never systematically argued for these general conditions, though references to them occur throughout his writings. My reconstruction of Fuller's argument draws on his work and on Gerald Postema's discussion of Fuller on implicit law. See Postema, "Implicit Law"; Fuller, *Morality of Law*, Fuller, *Anatomy of the Law*, Fuller, "Human Interaction and the Law."

[7] On this point see Fuller, *Morality of Law*, p. 130.   [8] Ibid., p. 210.

[9] See Postema, "Implicit Law," for a complete discussion of these first two conditions.

providing reasons for choosing specific courses of action, rather than psychologically manipulating or altering the social conditions for action. Agents choose whether to act on these reasons. Second, legal rules specify general norms, which agents follow by interpreting and applying them to their situation. Action governed by law is self-directed because citizens discover in a general rule a reason for acting in a specific way. Finally, the framework of law enables citizens to pursue their goals and plans. Individuals pursue their goals in a social context where they interact with others. To pursue their goals successfully, individuals must be able to formulate reliable and stable mutual expectations of how others will behave. Such expectations enable individuals to anticipate how others will respond to different actions.

The ability of law to provide general and shared baselines for interaction depends on ongoing cooperative interaction between citizens and officials.[10] The norms of law must be common, public norms if they are to provide shared baselines. Cultivating shared, public understandings requires officials and citizens to consider how others are likely to interpret and determine the practical import of general norms. Citizens must consider how officials are likely to understand this practical import in order to be confident that their interpretation of which actions are prohibited or permitted coincides with the interpretation of officials and other citizens. Similarly, officials must consider how citizens are likely to understand legal rules when determining the practical import of general legal norms. The substantive aims of law are undermined if the interpretation of the law by officials does not roughly coincide with the understanding of citizens. When citizens and officials can be confident that they share the same understanding, the ability of citizens to successfully pursue their goals and lead self-directed lives is enhanced; they are in a very real sense able to determine what kind of treatment their actions are likely to receive. When there is no congruence, officials dictate the meaning of law instead of facilitating self-directed interaction.

The required ongoing cooperative effort also entails a willingness on the part of officials and citizens to comply with such rules and, as such, be governed by law. Citizens generally must fulfill the expectation of officials and fellow citizens that the law will influence their deliberations and determine which actions they choose. Officials must judge and respond to the conduct of citizens in accordance with declared rules.[11] Implicit in

---

[10] See Fuller, "Human Interaction and the Law," pp. 234–5, and *Morality of Law*, pp. 206–20.
[11] Fuller, *Anatomy of the Law*, p. 9.

governance by law is the commitment of the government to the citizen that law in fact specifies the standard of conduct that citizens are expected to obey and to which they will be held.

If and when there is an absence of a willingness to comply with law, then the efforts of citizens and officials become futile. As Fuller writes, "A gross failure in the realization of either of these anticipations – of government toward citizen and of citizen toward government – can have the result that the most carefully drafted code will fail to become a functioning system of law."[12] Equally significantly, the incentive or willingness of citizens and officials to comply with the law is responsive to the actions of others. To the extent that others refuse to restrict their actions, the corresponding willingness of others will decline. As Fuller writes, "If the citizen knew in advance that in dealing with him government would pay no attention to its own declared rules, he would have little incentive to abide by them. The publication of rules carries with it the 'social meaning' that the rulemaker will himself abide by his own rules."[13]

The second social condition is systematic congruence between informal practices and the law, which facilitates the ability of citizens and officials to understand how others will interpret and apply general rules. Individuals determine the practical import of a general legal norm, what it requires in specific situations, by imagining acting on it. This imaginative exercise draws on knowledge of one's social context and practices.[14] As an illustration of this, consider Fuller's example of a statute that makes it a "misdemeanor to bring any 'vehicle' within the park area."[15] Determining which objects are permitted or prohibited by this statute, and thus the statute's practical import, depends on knowing the social function played by parks as an institution. This social function may differ in various social contexts, leading to correspondingly different understandings of what constitutes a vehicle for the purposes of the statute. What is permissible to bring to a park will differ if a park functions as a place of quiet versus as a place for social gathering and "enjoyment."

When a norm has no connection with social practices, it can become more difficult to determine its practical import and to be confident that one's interpretation will be congruent with the interpretation of other citizens and lawmaking and law-enforcing officials. A likely result is that

---

[12] Fuller, "Human Interaction and the Law," p. 255.   [13] Fuller, *Morality of Law*, p. 217.

[14] It becomes clear from the social context, Fuller writes, that, for example, a ten-ton truck is excluded but a baby carriage is not, though both fall under the dictionary definition of "that in or on which a person or thing is or may be carried" (*Anatomy of the Law*, p. 58).

[15] Ibid., p. 58.

individuals will become "dependent on what officials and formal institutions do," rather than on their own understanding.[16] In addition, laws disconnected from a given social context are more likely to seem unreasonable or arbitrary, which may lead to outright evasion of the law.[17]

Third, the efficacy of law depends on legal decency and good judgment among lawmaking and law-enforcing officials. Maintaining law is a practical art[18] that "depends upon repeated acts of human judgment at every level of the system."[19] The required legal decency consists of an understanding of and appreciation for the distinctive way that officials govern when they govern by law.[20] When they govern by law, officials are responsible for providing and maintaining shared baselines for interaction. This is fundamentally different from using political power to eliminate enemies or rivals, or viewing legal power as a tool to control citizens and other officials. Legal decency also includes a respect for the implicit limitations on official action that law entails. For law to successfully provide baselines for interaction that citizens have a genuine opportunity to follow, legal rules must take a specific form. The requirements of the rule of law specify the form rules should take and these must be systematically respected in order for legal rules to be able to govern the conduct of citizens and officials in practice. The lawmaking and law-enforcing process should be constrained by these requirements.

The eight requirements of the rule of law discussed in Chapter 1, which include clarity, promulgation, prospectivity, and congruence between official action and the law, capture the implicit expectations made within contexts where officials govern by law. Fuller writes, for example, "Every exercise of lawmaking function is accompanied by certain tacit assumptions, or implicit expectations, about the kind of product that will emerge from the legislator's efforts and the form he will give to the product ... there is implicit in the very notion of a law the assumption that its contents will, in some manner or other, be made accessible to the citizen so that he will have some chance to know what it says and be able to obey it."[21] Law cannot provide shared baselines for interaction if the baselines themselves are kept secret and remain unknown to citizens.[22]

---

[16] Postema, "Implicit Law," 265.
[17] Kenneth Winston makes this point when introducing Fuller's essay "Human Interaction and the Law." See p. 231 of his *Principles of Social Order*.
[18] See Fuller, *Morality of Law*, p. 91.   [19] Fuller, *Anatomy of the Law*, p. 39.
[20] Ibid., p. 65.   [21] Ibid., p. 60.
[22] Similarly, declared rules that are systematically unclear or vague will not be able to provide the relevant guidance for citizens and officials. This problem with vagueness is why it makes sense,

The eighth desideratum requires that there be congruence between official action and the law. Fuller discusses various procedural mechanisms, such as the right to representation by counsel, the right to cross-examine witnesses, the right to appeal a decision, and the right to *habeas corpus*, that are designed to maintain such congruence. He also lists factors like "bribery, prejudice, indifference, stupidity, and the drive toward personal power" that can destroy or impair congruence by undermining legal decency.[23]

Good judgment as well as decency by officials is required because there is no simple formula that lawmakers can follow to maintain a system of rules that respect the requirements of the rule of law, and that effectively govern the behavior of citizens and officials in practice.[24] For example, adherence to the requirements may at times undermine legality, and violations of requirements of the rule of law promote the purpose of law. To illustrate the former point, Fuller writes, "Suppose the absurd situation of a government that has only one law in the books: 'Do right and avoid evil.' In this case a rule is general, but general in a way that thoroughly undermines legality."[25] On the other hand, in certain situations retrospective legislation may be appropriate and not inimical to the rule of law. Fuller illustrates this point by drawing on an example of a statute in New Hampshire that required the performer of a marriage to fill out a form within five days of the marriage ceremony. The state printing press burned down after the legislature adjourned, leaving no legal way to repeal or postpone the date that the statute became effective. A retroactive statute provided a way of validating performed marriages until the legislature resumed session, which would otherwise have been invalid.

Recognition of the fact that certain instances may permit the violation of the requirements of the rule of law opens the door to potential corruption and abuse. Decency and good judgment are required to understand when and why it is appropriate to violate the requirements of the rule of law. The use of retroactive legislation can be deeply problematic and inimical to the rule of law, as Hitler's use of retroactive legislation following the Night of the Long Knives vividly demonstrates. In 1934, after deciding that certain "dissident" members of the Nazi Party posed a threat and needed to be eliminated, Hitler went to Munich where he and his followers shot and killed seventy individuals deemed

---

Fuller writes, to consider due process guarantees as being violated when a law is so vague that it is not clear what law it prohibits or permits. Fuller, *Morality of Law*, p. 102.
[23] Ibid., p. 81.
[24] Fuller's most extended discussion of this condition occurs in *Anatomy of the Law*, pp. 13–39.
[25] Fuller, "Human Interaction and the Law," 256.

threatening. Afterward, Hitler demanded that legislation be passed stating that "he had acted as 'the supreme judicial power of the German people.' The fact that he had not lawfully been appointed to any such office, and that no trial had ever been held of the condemned men – these 'irregularities of form' were promptly rectified by a statute retrospectively converting the shootings into lawful executions."[26]

The fourth social condition is faith in the law among citizens. Fuller writes, "Normally, and by and large, the citizen must of necessity accept on faith that his government is playing the game of law fairly," by, for example, formulating clear, general rules that are actually respected and enforced in practice.[27] Fuller never explicitly explains why such faith is necessary. Presumably, faith is required in part because a chronic suspicion of government officials and continual checking up on government actions would lead to paralysis at the individual or societal level, instead of self-directed action and interaction. Similarly, the willingness of citizens to follow the requirements, and thus the ability of law to provide an effective framework for interaction, depends on citizens having a certain degree of faith in legal procedures. Such faith is not inviolable, nor does Fuller claim that citizens should maintain their faith in the law regardless of revelations of how government officials are acting in practice. As he notes, "Precisely because this faith plays so important a role in the functioning of a legal system, a single dramatic disappointment of it, or a less conspicuous but persistent disregard for legality over a whole branch of law, can undermine the moral foundations of a legal order, both for those subject to it and for those who administer it."[28] Indeed, the clear abuse of or indifference to the requirements can undermine the faith of citizens and lead to a subsequent erosion of the willingness among citizens or officials to maintain this kind of social order. The faith required is not identical to blind obedience or no oversight on the part of citizens. Thus Fuller's recognition of the importance of faith does not imply that citizens are expected or required to disregard or be indifferent to what government officials are doing.

THE ABSENCE OF SOCIAL AND MORAL CONDITIONS IN TRANSITIONAL CONTEXTS

In societies in conflict or under repressive rule, declared legal rules frequently do not govern the behavior of officials and citizens in practice, and the social conditions required for law to be effective are absent or

---

[26] Ibid., p. 64.   [27] Fuller, "Human Interaction and the Law," p. 255.   [28] Ibid.

undermined.[29] In Chapter 1 I discussed historical examples of the system-atic violation of the requirements of the rule of law by officials within societies during periods of civil conflict or repressive rule. In this section I illustrate the absence of the four social conditions described in the previous section, using concrete, historical examples.[30] The absence of such conditions is significant because it negatively impacts the prospects for reconciliation, understood as the (re-)building of a mutual commit-ment among citizens and officials to respect the rule of law. It is in fostering the social conditions for the efficacy of law, I suggest in the next section, that international criminal trials can contribute to reconciliation.

Let us first consider Argentina. The legal scholar and politician Carlos Nino, who was actively involved in the transition to democracy and the efforts to deal with the legacy of human rights abuses, eloquently captures the absence of the cooperative interaction at the heart of law in his native Argentina in his discussion of anomie, "a disregard for social norms, including the law."[31] In Nino's view, anomie contributed to the conduct of the military junta from 1976 to 1983. Nino traces anomie to the colonial period "when local officials frequently proclaimed: 'Here the law is respected, but not obeyed.'"[32] Other examples of official anomie include the recurrent use of the coup d'état and "unconstitutional mechanisms" to first acquire and then increase political power. Courts facilitated anomie by recognizing the legitimacy of coups d'état rather than checking the illegal and extralegal exercise of political power. In Nino's words, "Argen-tine judges have developed the doctrine of de facto laws to legitimate laws enacted by the military governments."[33] A robust black market, extensive tax evasion, and smuggling and bribery illustrate the systematic disregard for law by citizens. Consequently, "everyone would be better off if the laws were obeyed, but no single individual is motivated to do so."[34]

This absence of ongoing cooperative effort was coupled with an erosion of legal decency and judgment, vividly displayed in the systematic, unoffi-cial disappearing of citizens discussed in Chapter 1.[35] Government officials

---

[29] For a detailed description of the absence of these conditions prior to a transition away from conflict and repressive rule, see Paul van Zyl, "Justice Without Punishment"; Paul van Zyl, "Dilemmas of Transitional Justice: The Case of South Africa's Truth and Reconciliation Commission," *Journal of International Affairs*, 52(2) (1999), 647–67; Roht-Arriaza, "State Responsibility"; TRC, *Truth and Reconciliation Commission of South Africa Report*, vol. 4.

[30] These examples serve illustrative purposes. I recognize that the extent of the impairment of the functioning of the law as well as the depth and pervasiveness of the erosion or absence of the four social conditions varies in different transitional contexts.

[31] Carlos Nino, *Radical Evil on Trial* (New Haven, CT: Yale University Press, 1996), pp. 47–8.

[32] Ibid.   [33] Ibid.   [34] Ibid.   [35] Disappearing also displays a lack of more general decency.

in transitional societies also often lack the judgment and competence required to maintain a system of law. The legal scholar Paul van Zyl writes that newly established governments "inherit ... criminal justice systems that are practically inoperative."[36] Even when committed to the rule of law, officials may lack the knowledge of what respect for due process entails or may construct a legal system in which appropriate due process guarantees are not included. As van Zyl writes, "In certain countries, criminal justice systems were created in a climate of oppression and human rights abuses. Law enforcement personnel were trained and authorized to employ methods of evidence-gathering, prosecuting and adjudicating that would be impermissible in a constitutional democracy."[37] In South Africa after apartheid, the police were unprepared to deal with crime using more difficult but legitimate methods of gathering evidence. This lack of preparation is confirmed by the "collapse in the capacity of the police to investigate and arrest, attorneys general to prosecute, judges to convict and correctional facilities to imprison ... The South African police have an extremely small number of poorly trained detectives. In certain jurisdictions more than a third of prosecutorial posts are empty and cannot be filled."[38] The retraining of the police may thus be necessary in transitional contexts.

Given the absence of the cooperative effort required to maintain law, incongruence between informal practices and declared rules, and the erosion of decency and judgment among officials, it is not surprising that citizens living in societies emerging from a period of repressive rule or civil conflict often have little faith in law. Even in contexts where the erosion of the social conditions required for law is not as dramatic or pervasive as in the contexts described above, the faith of citizens in law can be undermined nonetheless. Consider Northern Ireland. Historically, there has been deep distrust among the predominantly Catholic nationalists of the Royal Ulster Constabulary (RUC), the police force in Northern Ireland from 1922 to 2001.[39] Reforming the police force was one of the primary commitments of the UK in the most recent peace agreement, and remains an important condition for the long-term success of that agreement. Evidence of the distrust includes the historically low level of participation of Catholics in the police force. At the time of the Northern Ireland

---

[36] Van Zyl, "Justice Without Punishment," p. 44.   [37] Ibid.
[38] Van Zyl, "Dilemmas of Transitional Justice."
[39] The RUC was assimilated in 2001 into the newly constituted Police Service of Northern Ireland.

Agreement, cultural Catholics composed 43 percent of the population, but only 7.5 percent of the RUC personnel.[40] Other indications include fear of the RUC, hostility toward their presence, and a refusal to cooperate in police investigations.[41]

Sources of the distrust of and lack of faith in the police among the largely Catholic, nationalist population include unlawful state-sanctioned killing by police, and collusion between the police and paramilitary organizations.[42] Such events, but equally importantly the non-representative composition of the police, contributed to the perception of partiality. In the words of the political scientists John McGarry and Brendan O'Leary, experts on Northern Ireland, "A police service composed primarily of recruits from the dominant ethnic or national group will not be seen as impartial by members of excluded groups, irrespective of the behaviour of police officers. Such a service is also unlikely to be impartial in practice, as its officers are more likely to reflect the values of their own community of origin, and not those of others."[43] Increasing a representative police force will "increase nationalist confidence that the police service(s) represent(s) everybody. It will erode the partisan unionist culture."

THE CONTRIBUTIONS OF INTERNATIONAL CRIMINAL TRIALS

Transitional societies aspire to foster political reconciliation, or to repair damaged political relationships. An important component of this process is (re-)building a system of shared legal rules to regulate the behavior of citizens and officials in practice. The general lesson from the Fullerian analysis in the first section of this chapter is that the cultivation of law depends not simply on drafting and ratifying a constitution that specifies protected rights. In addition, the social conditions of law need to be cultivated. The characteristic absence of these conditions in transitional

---

[40] John McGarry and Brendan O'Leary, *Policing Northern Ireland: Proposals for a New Start* (Belfast: Blackstaff Press, 1999).

[41] Ibid.

[42] John McGarry and Brendan O'Leary, "Stabilising Northern Ireland's Agreement," *The Political Quarterly* (2004), 213–25, at 217. See also Fionnuala Ni Aolain, *The Politics of Force: Conflict Management and State Violence in Northern Ireland* (Belfast: Blackstaff Press, 2000).

[43] McGarry and O'Leary, *Policing Northern Ireland*. Other important studies of the police in Northern Ireland include John Brewer, Adrian Guelke, and Ian Hume, *The Police, Public Order, and the State: Policing in Great Britain, Northern Ireland, the Irish Republic, the United States, Israel, South Africa, China* (New York: St. Martin's Press, 1988), p. 12; John Brewer, *Inside the RUC: Routine Policing in a Divided Society* (Oxford University Press, 1991), p. 250.

contexts constitutes an obstacle to the (re-)building and repairing of social relationships predicated on mutual respect for and shaped by the law in practice. Thus processes of reconciliation should address, at least in part, and attempt to promote the cooperative interaction, decency, good judgment, and faith in the law that enables self-directed interaction to flourish.[44]

Understanding how to cultivate each of these social conditions of law requires both theoretical and empirical knowledge.[45] Theoretical analysis of the function and defining characteristics of social processes (e.g., criminal trials, truth commissions, reparations) can shed light on connections between such processes and the goals of and preconditions for reconciliation. Empirical studies can then provide important information about the circumstances that are conducive to or inimical for the achievement of the function of social processes like law. Such information can provide guidance in terms of whether, for example, international criminal trials are likely to realize their potential contribution to reconciliation in specific transitional contexts.

In this section, I first offer a theoretical argument to support the claim that international criminal trials contribute to reconciliation by cultivating legal decency and good judgment among officials and encouraging faith in law among citizens. I then explore some of the empirical conditions that can influence whether these contributions are, in fact, realized. My empirical discussion is largely speculative. Further empirical research is required to confirm or disconfirm the considerations I advance or point to overlooked considerations that might be relevant. After considering and responding to a series of objections, I end this section by highlighting the limits of the contributions to reconciliation that international criminal trials can make.

The starting premise of my theoretical argument is an empirical observation: the international community is extensively involved in the legal processes of transitional societies, especially during their transitional period from conflict or repressive rule to peace and democracy. Ad hoc international criminal tribunals, like the International Criminal Tribunal for the former Yugoslavia (ICTY) and International Criminal Tribunal for Rwanda (ICTR), as well as the permanent International Criminal Court (ICC), represent one dimension of this involvement. These tribunals

---

[44] These conditions capture only part of the obstacles because the repair that reconciliation entails is broader than the restoration of mutual respect for the rule of law.

[45] I am grateful to Leslie Francis for helping to clarify this point for me.

cover serious violations of international humanitarian law, including violations of the Geneva Conventions, laws of war, genocide, and crimes against humanity in a specific area during a specific period of time.[46] Such tribunals are the product of international cooperation and interaction. Separate United Nations Security Council resolutions created the ICTY and ICTR, and the ICC is based on a treaty signed by 104 countries. Trial proceedings draw on both civil and common law systems, and the staff of such tribunals is drawn from around the globe.[47] The collection of evidence, detention of the accused, and funding of such tribunals depends on cooperation and contributions from the international community.[48]

Hybrid tribunals have also been established in contexts including Sierra Leone, Timor-Leste, Kosovo, Bosnia, and Cambodia.[49] Such courts are hybrid in the sense that judges and prosecutors include both national and international representatives, and the rules regulating such courts include national and international regulations. They operate in the location where the crimes occurred.[50] The operating budget for such hybrid tribunals is influenced by the scale of voluntary contributions from international donors.[51]

Complementing such formal involvement is the work of non-governmental organizations (NGOs). William Schabas has documented the influential role of the United States Institute of Peace, Priscilla Hayner, and Paul van Zyl in determining the relationship between the court and the Truth and Reconciliation Commission in Sierra Leone.[52] The ICTJ advises countries on whether to confront the legacy of human rights abuses through criminal trials and/or truth commissions, and the appropriate relationship to establish between different programs (i.e., the Truth and Reconciliation Commission and Special Court in Sierra Leone);

---

[46] http://69.94.11.53/default.htm. Accessed September 9, 2007.
[47] As of February 2007, the staff of the ICTY had members representing eighty-one countries; the ICTR has eighty-five nationalities represented in the staff.
[48] www.un.org/icty/glance-e/index.htm. Accessed September 9, 2007. The relationship between these international tribunals and national courts is defined differently. Though both national courts and the ICTY have concurrent jurisdiction over such violations, the ICTY can "claim primacy" if it is in the interests of international justice. The ICC, on the other hand, represents a "court of last resort," that is, it only pursues cases if not investigated or prosecuted in a genuine way by a national court.
[49] ICTJ, www.ictj.org/en/index.html. Accessed December 4, 2008.
[50] ICTY, www.un.org/icty/glance-e/index.htm. Accessed December 4, 2008.
[51] William Schabas, "A Synergistic Relationship: The Sierra Leone Truth and Reconciliation Commission and the Special Court for Sierra Leone," *Criminal Law Forum*, 15 (2004), 3–54.
[52] Ibid., 25. Hayner and van Zyl both work at the ICTJ.

trains and assists prosecution efforts in both domestic and hybrid tribunals; files *amicus curiae* briefs in domestic tribunals; monitors domestic criminal justice proceedings; publishes studies on the study of hybrid tribunals; and holds conferences on domestic prosecutions with international representatives involved in such efforts to create a network of advisors and offer a forum for exchanging investigation strategies.[53] It currently works in such capacities in over twenty-five countries around the world, including Burundi, the Democratic Republic of the Congo, Ghana, Kenya, Liberia, Sierra Leone, South Africa, Uganda, Argentina, Colombia, Guatemala, Mexico, Nicaragua, Panama, Peru, Afghanistan, Cambodia, Sri Lanka, Algeria, and Iraq.

This intense level of involvement in the legal processes of transitional societies by the international community differs significantly from the role that the international community plays in the legal processes of non-transitional societies. This deep level of involvement suggests that the international community is positioned to affect the norms, practices, and patterns of interaction within transitional societies in a much more profound manner than in non-transitional contexts. That is, the operations of the ICTY and the newly formed ICC, for example, have more immediate and direct ramifications on the social and legal processes of the former Yugoslavia and Uganda than they do on those of France.

International criminal trials can influence prospects for reconciliation in transitional contexts, I want to suggest, by playing an educative role. International proceedings can thus offer a stark contrast to the practices and procedures of the past in transitional contexts. International criminal trials are structured to respect the constraints of due process and adhere to internationally recognized standards. In the words of the ICTY, "The Rules of Procedure and Evidence guarantee that ICTY proceedings adhere to internationally recognised principles of fair trial ... important elements include the presumption of innocence, the right to be tried without undue delay, the right to examine adverse witnesses and the right of appeal. Procedural provisions for the protection of witnesses, identities and the actual assistance provided before, during and after the proceedings by the Victims and Witnesses Section within the Registry ensure that witnesses can testify freely and safely."[54] To the extent that such procedures are followed, international criminal trials provide a model for how criminal proceedings should be conducted. The procedures and safeguards

---

[53] www.ictj.org/en/tj/781.html. Accessed September 7, 2007.
[54] ICTY, www.un.org/icty/glance-e/index.htm. Accessed December 4, 2008.

characteristic of the structure of international criminal trials prioritize and take seriously the view of all persons, including criminals, as self-directed agents whose actions determine the official response to them. As discussed in the previous section, the lawmaking and law-enforcement officials within societies under repressive rule or emerging from civil conflict are characteristically corrupt, incompetent, and ineffective.

To illustrate some of the ways in which properly conducted international criminal trials can provide a sharply contrasting model for how the criminal justice process proceeds, consider first the presumption of innocence until proven guilty. Taking this presumption seriously implies the requirement that it be demonstrated, to a sufficiently justifiable degree, that the alleged perpetrator was indeed responsible for specific crimes. It implies the refusal to suspect or assume guilt simply because the perpetrator belongs to a suspect group or category. This is in contrast to practices in areas of conflict, where being Catholic in Northern Ireland or African in South Africa sometimes eroded the seriousness with which the presumption of innocence was maintained. The presumption of innocence is especially important to respect in transitional contexts. A shift in power often occurs in conjunction with a transition.[55] To the extent that previously powerful groups, who may have assumed the guilt of individuals who were members of a suspect group, are not themselves subject to the same practice by the international community or newly empowered groups working with the international community, this demonstrates in practice that the holding or losing of power should not and need not be responsible for or determine the outcomes of criminal trials.

Another important component of international criminal trials is the treatment of alleged perpetrators during the period leading up to a trial and during the course of pretrial interrogation and evidence-gathering phases. In international criminal trials, suspects are not to be held in inhumane conditions, tortured into confessions, or suffer cruel and unusual punishment. Taking seriously these basic protections, even with respect to those suspected or convicted of failing to show the same respect toward others in the past, sets an important precedent that contrasts sharply with practices of the past. Respecting constraints against torturing suspects into confession or holding suspects in inhumane conditions signals an acknowledgement of the dignity that stems in part from the agency of all individuals. The conduct of prosecutors and law enforcement

---

[55] This is not to suggest that those who previously held power no longer hold power after a transition. How dramatically the power dynamic shifts differs between societies.

officials throughout the legal process, specifically with respect to the gathering and sharing of evidence, is critical. In contrast to the practices described by van Zyl, official conduct should be performed in a forthright manner, not manipulated.

Finally, a legal system depends on the cooperation of citizens, who are often important sources of information and can serve as witnesses who play a critical role in the successful conviction of perpetrators of crime. In situations of conflict, cooperating with law enforcement officials may be dangerous, leading to serious bodily harm and rarely resulting in the elimination of the original threat. Thus it is critical that the witnesses who do cooperate in such trials be provided with adequate and serious protection, and this commitment is reflected in the provisions established by tribunals like the ICTY.

There are two primary respects in which the model provided by the process of international criminal trials can be educative in a way that is conducive toward reconciliation. First, such trials can cultivate decency and better judgment among lawmaking and law-enforcement officials in transitional contexts. They do so by highlighting the absence of legal decency and good judgment among government officials during periods of conflict or repressive rule, when diminished significance was attached to proving the guilt of criminals and recognizing their humanity throughout the criminal process. In addition, by working with local officials, representatives of the international community can communicate training, knowledge, and understanding regarding how and in what way their practices must change in order for law to function as it should and to regulate conduct in practice.

The second way in which the educative role of international criminal tribunals can facilitate political reconciliation is by restoring confidence and faith in law among ordinary citizens. Seeing respect given to the constraints of due process and prohibitions against certain types of treatment can promote conditions conducive to faith in the legal system by reducing the risks involved in participation. Knowing that arrest does not entail torture, that conviction does not entail death, and that cooperation does not risk death reduces the incentive of individuals to opt out of or do everything to avoid contact with the law enforcement system. Seeing norms of international law enforced, and seeing officials held accountable for failing to respect the constraints that law imposed can restore confidence in the fact that law will be enforced and declared rules will provide an accurate picture of what the actual practice of law enforcement officials will be.

OBJECTIONS

Those acquainted with the actual operations of hybrid and international criminal tribunals like the ICTY may be skeptical about whether such trials can contribute to reconciliation in the way I suggest. They may point to the failure of such tribunals to respect the due process guarantees in practice, stemming, for example, from resource constraints both financially and in terms of personnel trained in the language of witnesses and alleged perpetrators. In response, I would note that this objection does not call into question the validity of my analysis. The proposed contributions of criminal trials are based on the assumption that criminal proceedings with an international dimension operate as they should, where the specific normative understanding of how criminal trials should function is framed by the fundamental commitment of law to pursue justice and respect the agency of perpetrators and victims alike. Highlighting the degree to which international criminal tribunals fail to operate the way they should draws attention to the importance of reforming international criminal trials and the necessity of the international community providing sufficient funding so that the contributions I have discussed can be realized in practice.

This response may not alleviate the concerns about whether international criminal trials will contribute to reconciliation, even if trials are reformed to respect due process guarantees in practice. There are two potential sources of lingering doubt. International personnel are not always welcome in transitional contexts, nor are international or hybrid trials necessarily viewed as legitimate. One source of uncertainty about whether such trials will provide an educative moment stems from the recognition of these conditions.

In response, I want to recognize the validity of this underlying concern. That the international community is deeply involved in transitional contexts does not guarantee that its involvement will always be beneficial. In practice, the international community may change norms or patterns of interaction within transitional societies for the worse rather than for the better.[56] Interaction with members of the international community may entrench rather than alleviate the perception of the partiality of law.

Important empirical work needs to be done in order to refine our understanding of the conditions that are likely to facilitate the realization of the potential educative role of international criminal tribunals in practice. The objection draws attention to the critical importance of international

---

[56] I am grateful to Laurel Fletcher for drawing my attention to this point.

criminal courts being viewed as legitimate. Viewing representatives of the international community as legitimate is more likely to encourage acknowledgement and understanding of the failures of past law-enforcement and lawmaking practices among domestic officials.

Whether trials are viewed as legitimate is likely to depend on whether specific conditions are in place. I want to suggest some circumstances that, in my view, are influential in this regard. How and which cases are selected for prosecution will affect the image of the impartiality of the international community. Especially in deeply divided societies where atrocities were committed by members of both sides of a conflict, solely singling out representatives of one community for prosecution is likely to erode the perception of impartiality among the targeted community. Second, local law enforcement officials are more likely to view international representatives as legitimate if the practice of the international community is consistent with its rhetoric (and is thus, for example, impartial).[57] Partiality and corruption by international officials will only serve to entrench, and potentially legitimate, the practices too often found within transitional contexts.

A different source of skepticism about whether criminal trials will facilitate reconciliation stems from concern about the consequences of enhancing due process guarantees. Of particular concern may be the consequence that more guilty individuals go free. According to this objection, it is most important to see that criminals responsible for egregious wrongdoing are punished. Without punishment, victims will not have the opportunity to express their resentment and hatred, and have the benefit of seeing justice done. Absent this opportunity, the willingness of victims to engage with the new society, or with the members of the community from which perpetrators came in cases of divided conflict, will diminish. In addition, allowing guilty individuals to go free may represent a pattern that is disturbingly similar to the past. If the standards are too high, then it appears that the legacy of impunity, far from being successfully countered, will in fact be continued through international criminal trials.

In response, a note of caution is in order. Commitment to the rule of law entails that responsibility for specific wrongdoing be proven, and not

---

[57] For a discussion of the significance of perceptions of legitimacy, see Laurel E. Fletcher and Harvey M. Weinstein, "A World unto Itself? The Application of International Justice in the Former Yugoslavia," in Eric Stover and Harvey Weinstein (eds.), *The Former Yugoslavia, My Neighbor, My Enemy: Justice and Community in the Aftermath of Mass Atrocities* (Cambridge University Press, 2004), pp. 29–48.

merely assumed. If one eases the presumption of innocence that respect for the rule of law requires in cases where respecting this presumption might lead to acquittal, one risks replicating behavior characteristically displayed during civil conflict and by repressive regimes. Nor will an appeal to the importance of countering the legacy of impunity be sufficient to justify a cavalier attitude toward this presumption. Repressive regimes normally disregard due process considerations not merely to instill terror, but also to counter an alleged or real threat to an important value or to the continued existence of their society.

At the same time, the objection raises an important point. If no alleged perpetrators are ever successfully prosecuted, then perpetrators have little reason to fear or anticipate punishment. Nor do members of transitional societies have reason to think human rights will be respected, regardless of whether they are respected by law. Thus, if it turns out that few, if any, convictions can be achieved by adhering to stringent standards of due process, given, for example, current financial and personnel resource constraints, careful consideration may need to be given to whether it is possible to ease specific standards so as to make convictions possible but in a way that avoids the appearance or reality of replicating problematic patterns displayed during conflict or by repressive regimes.

There is one final objection to consider. Transitional societies often have extremely limited resources to devote to the pursuit of reconciliation, as well as more general societal reconstruction. Similarly, the international community has limited resources to devote to the various needs faced by societies emerging from a period of repressive rule or civil conflict. Societies and the international community may face the choice of investing in education and health care, or investing to ensure due process guarantees are more robustly protected. Given these tough choices, so the objection goes, it is unjustifiable to demand that further resources be placed to protect due process more strongly when other ways of promoting reconciliation are more cost-effective, and needs other than reconciliation are equally pressing.

In response, I first want to recognize that this objection points to the limits of the contributions international criminal tribunals can make to political reconciliation. It is critical to recognize the contributions, as well as the limits. First, respect for the rule of law constitutes one important, but not the only, dimension of repair that relationships in transitional contexts require. Second, international criminal trials address some but not all of the social conditions required for law to be effective, and thus for the dimension of reconciliation on which I have focused in this chapter to be achieved. For example, international criminal trials do not address the broader reform of social practices required for congruence between laws protecting rights and social practices to be realized and the law to thus be effective. For example, in contexts like South Africa racism is deep and pervades all social institutions. Such racism needs to be addressed if the laws specifying the equality of all citizens are to be viewed as reasonable and the concrete implications of such laws knowable by both citizens and officials. International criminal trials are ill suited to effect the change in information that social practices require to successfully combat racism.[58]

Given these limits, and the other pressing demands in transitional contexts that the objection rightly highlights, it may sometimes be unjustifiable to devote resources to strengthening due process guarantees. However, this needs to be demonstrated and cannot simply be assumed. In my view, much more careful analysis is required before we can conclude that this contribution is too costly. Such analysis requires, at a minimum, weighing the relative importance of the competing interests or values that might be pursued and assessing the likelihood that each competing value could be realized, should resources be devoted to its pursuit. How to determine and balance relative weights and likelihoods are complicated tasks, the resolution of which is beyond the scope of this chapter.[59] I hope that this chapter has succeeded in showing that this erosion or incomplete realization of due process guarantees will involve a significant cost, not only in terms of justice but also in terms of reconciliation. It is a cost that we should be extremely cautious about accepting.

[58] Although such trials may have some limited impact through expressing condemnation of specific crimes.

[59] For a discussion on these questions, see Colleen Murphy and Paolo Gardoni, "Determining Public Policy and Resource Allocation Priorities for Mitigating Natural Hazards: A Capabilities-based Approach," *Science and Engineering Ethics*, 13(4) (2007), 489–504; and Colleen Murphy and Paolo Gardoni, "The Acceptability and the Tolerability of Societal Risks: A Capabilities-based Approach," *Science and Engineering Ethics*, 14(1) (2008), 77–92.

Conclusion

I began this book with a discussion of three central questions about political reconciliation, sparked by the establishment of the TRC in South Africa, for which a conception of reconciliation should provide theoretical resources for addressing and resolving. The first concerns the source of the normative significance of political reconciliation. The second centers on the criteria that should be used to evaluate the effectiveness and moral justifiability of processes of political reconciliation. The third is the grounds for the claim that political reconciliation is critical for successful democratization. I also articulated a series of desiderata for an adequate conception. A conception of political reconciliation, I argued, should be able to capture the institutional and interpersonal dimensions of the problems that afflict political interaction during periods of civil conflict and repressive rule. It should respond to the urgent and pressing practical need for a normative theory of political reconciliation by specifying the particular characteristics of damaged and rebuilt political relationships in detail. Finally, a conception of reconciliation should have a certain unity; when capturing the complex dimensions of damage to political relationships, a conception should not simply combine disparate moral concerns in an ad hoc manner. Rather, it should provide a coherent picture of the multifaceted ways in which political relationships suffer during periods of conflict and repression. By way of conclusion, I first return to these central questions about political reconciliation, review the answers my analysis suggests, and explain why my analysis fulfills the desiderata of an adequate account. I then highlight some of the broader implications of my analysis for contemporary discussions and debates about political reconciliation and transitional justice.

Over the course of this book, I have argued that at its most general level the goal of processes of political reconciliation is to cultivate political relationships premised on reciprocity and respect for moral agency. Such cultivation is necessary because civil conflict and repressive rule damage political relationships by undermining the conditions under which political relationships can express these two values. Each of the chapters in Part I considered a specific dimension of the damage to political relationships that stems from civil conflict and repressive rule, and the corresponding respects in which political relationships are in need of repair.

The first dimension of damage that I considered is a product of the erosion of a system of legal rules to govern behavior that are knowable, able to be followed, and enforced in practice. Such a system plays an important role in defining political relationships by clarifying the expectations that citizens and officials should hold for each other. Law facilitates self-directed action and interaction by maintaining a framework for interaction premised on reliable and stable mutual expectations of how others will behave. The absence or erosion of the ongoing cooperative effort required by citizens and officials in order for law to govern behavior, detailed in Chapters 1 and 6, contributes to a political climate of instability and fear in which citizens cannot turn to declared rules or rely on their interpretation of them to develop stable expectations about what the official treatment or response to their actions is likely to be. In such an environment it is difficult for citizens to know about, let alone contest, systematic injustice and oppression.

The second dimension of damage I discussed concerns the attitude that citizens and officials characteristically adopt toward each other during civil conflict and repressive rule, namely distrust. Distrust is marked by pessimism about the competence and lack of ill will of citizens and officials, as well as the absence of an anticipation that those trusted will prove reliable. Often distrust is reasonable during civil conflict and repressive rule and trust is unwarranted. It is not reasonable to assume that fellow citizens and officials understand and are willing to follow norms for social and political interaction and to respect the boundaries or constraints on permissible interaction, nor is it reasonable to anticipate that they will be motivated by the demands and expectations that we place on them. Equally importantly, periods of conflict and repressive rule are marked by a refusal to acknowledge the capability of (certain groups of) citizens to exercise the responsibilities associated with citizenship, often based on a denial of their agency. The absence of trust or conditions that make trust reasonable damages political relationships by undermining the possibility of expressing respect and a commitment to reciprocity through the attitudes we take toward fellow citizens and officials. Trust, when reasonable, represents an important way of expressing these values in political relationships. Such trust reflects an acknowledgement of the agency of fellow citizens and officials and their decency, coupled with a reciprocal willingness to prove reliable when trust is placed in us in the same way that we hope others will prove.

The final dimension of damage I took into account centered on the ways in which civil conflict and repressive rule diminish the genuine opportunity of individuals to achieve central relational goods, such as being respected, being recognized as a member of a political community, and participating in the social, economic, and political life of a community. Violence, economic repression, and the construction of identities during periods of civil conflict and repressive rule reduce the personal and external resources as well as social and institutional conditions required for individuals to enjoy these capabilities, which are constitutive of membership in a political community.

A virtue of my analysis is that it satisfies the requirements of complexity and unity in a theory of political reconciliation. It is complex in the sense that it draws attention to different kinds of damage to political relationships, both institutional and interpersonal, about which we may speak. It is unified in two respects. First, there is a shared moral concern for reciprocal agency underpinning the different normative frameworks I discuss. Thus, while distinct in the dimensions of interaction on which they concentrate, there is a unifying theoretical core to the concerns and forms of damage that I consider. Second, and relatedly, there are important practical connections among the different kinds of damage to political relationships I consider. For example, political relationships premised on the rule of law, reasonable political trust, and relational capabilities depend on similar social and political conditions; all three dimensions of political relationships are affected by the degree to which there is a commitment to respect for agency and hope. Furthermore, one kind of damage can lead directly or indirectly to a different kind of damage. To illustrate, the erosion of the rule of law undermines the reasonableness of citizens trusting officials; citizens have little justification for being optimistic about the competence of officials and their willingness to prove trust-reliable when the expectation that officials will govern on the basis of declared rules is consistently flouted. Alternatively, the diminishment of the genuine opportunity of individuals to be recognized as members of the community can undermine the rule of law insofar as the absence of such recognition diminishes the willingness of citizens to respect and abide by rules structuring political interaction.

The specificity of my conception satisfies the urgent need for a normative theory of political reconciliation, in part by providing the requisite theoretical resources for clarifying what should count as success for public policies designed to promote political reconciliation and why such success is important to achieve. Consider first the view my conception offers with respect to what is at stake in rebuilding political relationships, that is, the value of promoting political reconciliation. In my view, one important source of the value of the pursuit of political reconciliation is instrumental in nature. Conceptualizing political reconciliation as a process of cultivating reciprocal agency in political relations helps us to appreciate the fundamental role that the pursuit of political reconciliation plays in the process of democratization. Political reconciliation involves promoting political relationships premised on equal respect for individuals and their agency; a commitment to the reciprocal sharing of the benefits and burdens of social cooperation; and an institutional structure that is based on the rule of law and political, economic, and social institutions structured so that all citizens have a genuine opportunity to participate in them. Such relationships are fundamentally democratic political relationships. Democracy is a form of governance premised on equal respect and concern for individuals and relationships based on these values.[1] Thus we can explain the conviction that political reconciliation is necessary for democratization once we notice that the promotion of political reconciliation is partly constitutive of such democratization.

The value of pursuing political reconciliation, however, is not only instrumental. Political reconciliation has non-instrumental value as well. Each of the ways in which relationships can go wrong and become damaged during civil conflict and repressive rule, represented by the frameworks of the rule of law, political trust, and relational capabilities, is wrong or damaging precisely because it undermines or violates the moral values of reciprocity and respect for agency. These values underpin and unify the various dimensions of the process of rebuilding political relations. The moral significance of the transformation of political relations stems from what the process of cultivating the rule of law, reasonable political trust, and relational capabilities represents, namely a way of cultivating agency and reciprocity in interactions among citizens and officials.

In terms of public policy evaluation, the conception of reconciliation I developed in the previous chapters provides a general framework for identifying in particular contexts whether, and in what way, efforts to

---

[1] On this point see Ronald Dworkin, *Freedom's Law: The Moral Reading of the American Constitution* (Cambridge, MA: Harvard University Press, 1996).

rebuild political relationships have been successful. In my account, the goal of processes of reconciliation is to cultivate mutual respect for the rule of law, the conditions that make trust reasonable, and central relational capabilities. As I discussed in detail in Chapter 4, policies for promoting political reconciliation can be effective by promoting these characteristics of political relationships directly or by fostering the particular social and moral conditions on which relationships premised on reciprocal agency depend. The general goal of the pursuit of reconciliation includes multiple diverse objectives; thus policies and processes may successfully address some but not all of the dimensions of political interaction in need of repair. Processes may have implications for political trust, but not for the rule of law. Alternatively, a process may enhance capabilities but in ways that do not affect the promotion of trust and the rule of law. Thus my framework helps us pinpoint precisely where the success of particular policies lies.

By way of illustration I discussed the contribution of truth commissions and international criminal tribunals to political reconciliation, identifying the particular dimensions of political relationships that each kind of process is well suited to address. In regard to international criminal trials I argued that punishment and political reconciliation are not necessarily incompatible; indeed, criminal prosecution in the international context can contribute positively to the development of the conditions required for law to function as it should. However, I also claimed that political reconciliation does not require or depend on punishment as a response to wrongdoing. Under certain conditions, processes like truth commissions can also have an important impact on the transformation of political relationships by challenging stereotypes, promoting a more inclusive understanding of membership in a political community, and, in the process, fostering the capacities of moral agents to care about, empathize with, and respond to the second-personal reasons of others.

Throughout my discussion of processes of political reconciliation I emphasized the importance of paying attention to the particular dynamics within a given context when deciding how to promote political reconciliation and evaluating the effectiveness of processes adopted. While numerous societies emerging from periods of conflict or repressive rule face the challenge of reconciliation, the particular character of this challenge differs because of variations in the way in which relationships were damaged. The particular history and character of relations in specific transitional contexts will determine the specific needs that a process of reconciliation must address. It thus serves as a caution against general prescriptions for the path that the pursuit of political reconciliation should take in transitional contexts; rather, it implies that policies for political reconciliation must be particularized to the case in question and be formulated on the basis of an understanding of the particular history and character of the damage to political relationships.

The conception of reconciliation developed in this book has broad implications for the framing of discussions about the promotion of political reconciliation and transitional justice. I want to highlight some of these broader implications and, in particular, consider how this conception challenges the way many discussions of political reconciliation and transitional justice within the literature are framed.

Consider first the discourse about political reconciliation. Discussions of the promotion of political reconciliation largely focus on official, legal responses to wrongdoing such as truth commissions or criminal trials. They also characteristically emphasize the importance of fostering what I would take to be the initial conditions required for peaceful interaction to be possible and political relationships to be rebuilt, such as hope or sympathy. Consequently, discussions implicitly suggest that if a truth commission or set of criminal trials is established, political reconciliation has been achieved. By contrast, my analysis explicitly points out that the work of rebuilding political relationships is largely just beginning when processes like truth commissions and criminal trials end. Rebuilding political relationships in the aftermath of civil conflict and repressive rule is enormously complicated and difficult, given the comprehensive and often extraordinary changes demanded of political relationships in transitional contexts. Few transitional societies will be able to achieve the required changes in political relationships immediately, or even in a short-term period, following a transition to democratic governance; it is very likely that the process of reconciliation will occur over an extended period of time. In some contexts the achievement of more than minimal reconciliation may not be possible. Thus, as a corrective to current discussions, my analysis suggests that discourse about political reconciliation be framed more explicitly in terms of degrees of achievement and the promotion of specific kinds of repair, remaining ever mindful of the damage that remains to be addressed and of the long road to rebuilding political relationships that characteristically remains ahead.

My analysis also highlights the need to look beyond responding to violations of human rights, important though that is, in considering what might count as potential processes of reconciliation. While truth commissions or criminal trials may play a useful role in fostering some of the social or moral conditions for the successful cultivation of respect for the rule of law, political trust, and relational capabilities, their contributions are still quite limited. Indeed, there is little reason to think that political reconciliation will be achieved solely through institutional responses to wrongdoing. Responding to human rights abuses through official mechanisms like truth commissions and criminal trials will not be sufficient to enhance individuals' capabilities of participating in the social, political, and economic life of the community. Such processes do not improve the external resources needed for such participation or constitute the reform of discriminatory laws and informal practices that may have previously precluded the participation of some. Truth commissions and criminal trials do not address the social and economic inequalities that are a product of economic oppression, and that can prevent certain groups within transitional societies from having the minimally sufficient external resources needed to achieve basic functionings. Nor will political reconciliation be achieved through public policy alone. Governments, for example, are not best suited to combat stereotypes that undermine respect toward members of certain groups and prevent the competence of certain groups from being acknowledged.

Furthermore, my analysis of political reconciliation provides resources for linking recent critiques of transitional justice theory and practice more explicitly with the goal of political reconciliation, and for demonstrating that theorists should respond to the identified limitations differently than they are currently doing. In the literature on transitional justice the emphasis on law is increasingly subject to critique. One general criticism is motivated by a concern that current transitional practices are insufficiently democratic.[2] Legal institutions and processes of legal reform have largely been designed and run by state officials, with input or guidance coming primarily from the international community. In practice, the substantial participation of a local community in determining the shape of its transition is often missing. This is reflected in the exclusion of local communities from having a meaningful say in the decision-making processes regarding how the legacy of wrongdoing will be addressed (e.g., via truth commissions and/or criminal trials) and what the contours of established processes will be (e.g., the goals of truth commissions or particular kinds of wrongdoing that will be considered).

---

[2] This criticism is offered by Lundy and McGovern in "Whose Justice?"

Two problems have been identified with the undemocratic character of transitional justice practices. First, excluding or constraining members of transitional communities from meaningful participation in the processes of societal reform and transformation is taken to be intrinsically troubling. Without such participation, it has been argued, transitional processes risk traumatizing victims of human rights abuses a second time. The same population that was excluded from meaningful political and social participation during periods of conflict and repression are excluded a second time from meaningful participation in the process of rebuilding their community and establishing a new political regime. This occurs when victims are prevented or discouraged from offering the kind of testimony they would like to make in truth commissions if such testimony conflicts with the overall objectives of truth commissions established by a national government or the international community. Excluding the local community from meaningful participation in transitional processes has disturbing consequences. It removes incentives for transitional justice efforts to be accountable to the communities they are designed to serve and transform, and risks becoming ineffective or even outright resisted as local communities fail to be transformed by processes that seem remote and disconnected from their concerns and practices. As Kieran McEvoy writes, transitional justice processes "may fail to take sufficient account of local customs and practical knowledge and to engage properly with community and civil society structures. Such failures, often justified in the name of efficiency ... may in turn lead to incompetence or maladministration and encourage grass-roots resistance to such state-led initiatives."[3]

Another general criticism is that the almost exclusive emphasis on law and the pursuit of legal justice has resulted in the failure of transitional justice theory and practice to address fundamental causes of conflict and structural sources of injustice.[4] Legal justice emphasizes the punishment of individual perpetrators for individual crimes. This focuses effort on responding to human rights abuses that were a product of conflict, but were not themselves the immediate sources of conflict. Equally significantly, an emphasis on law risks encouraging the misperception that human rights abuses will not occur if liberal norms of accountability are promoted.

---

[3] McEvoy, "Beyond Legalism," 424.
[4] See Lundy and McGovern in "Whose Justice?" for an articulation of this criticism.

In light of these problems, critics have suggested modifying transitional justice theory and practice so that the law's role is more limited. For example, legal processes and legal institutions structured by the state and influenced by the international community should function alongside local, non-legal processes.[5] Scholarship on transitional justice should focus on resources from disciplines outside of law so that critical questions about the effectiveness and justifiability of transitional processes can be evaluated and debated. Criminology, McEvoy argues, recognizes the limits of the ability of the state and its legal institutions to address crime, even in stable political contexts, and rejects the idea that the state should have exclusive control over the pursuit of justice. It focuses attention on the small number of crimes actually prosecuted, even in stable democratic contexts, and emphasizes the work on policing and intelligence, for example, by organizations that are privately organized within states (e.g., private security firms) or are based outside of a particular state context (e.g., the US involvement in intelligence and policing in Latin America). Similarly, it highlights the increasingly prominent role of civil society organizations in restorative justice processes. It thus creates a conceptual space for thinking through the capacity of other programs to promote justice, and the importance of devoting resources to support such initiatives.

My conception of political reconciliation suggests a number of modifications to these contemporary discussions of transitional justice. First, current discussions overlook a reconciliation-related reason to be concerned about the democratic deficit in transitional justice theory and practice, and about addressing structural sources of injustice and causes of conflict. As I discussed in Chapter 4, a concern for reciprocal agency in political relationships requires a larger role for public dialogue and participation in determining the course that the pursuit of political reconciliation will take in a particular political context. To the extent that is feasible, I argued, democratic processes should guide decision making regarding which sources of damage to political relationships will be prioritized and addressed by government policy. In this way members of a political community become the collective authors of the path to reconciliation that is taken within their society and become collectively responsible for its outcomes. Addressing social and economic inequalities and rights violations is necessary for achieving political reconciliation, insofar as such inequalities and rights violations damage political relationships by undermining the relational capabilities.

---

[5] McEvoy, "Beyond Legalism," 428.

Second, my analysis highlights that it is a mistake to link the democratic deficit with an emphasis on law, as critics currently do. If we view law as fundamentally a practice whose purpose is the subjection of conduct to governance by rules, we can recognize that there are reasons *internal to law*, and a commitment to law, for promoting greater participation of local communities in legal processes of transitional justice, including efforts at legal reform and legal responses to wrongdoing. What the normative framework of the rule of law draws attention to is the fact that law *intrinsically* depends on the cooperation and involvement of citizens. Cooperative interaction among citizens and officials, attention to the local meanings, social practices, and norms is necessary for a system of legal rules to actually govern the conduct of citizens and officials; only such a system counts as a legal system. This perspective on law implies that insofar as officials are pursuing legal reform and the establishment of a legal system without taking into consideration the members of the communities that the norms of law are intended to regulate, their efforts at legal reform are fundamentally self-defeating. For one thing, the substantive aims of law are undermined if officials' interpretation of the law does not roughly coincide with the understanding of citizens. The norms of law must be common, public norms if they are to provide shared baselines for interaction. However, as I discussed in Chapter 6, cultivating shared, public understandings of the meaning of legal rules requires officials and citizens to consider how others are likely to interpret and determine the practical import of general norms. Citizens must consider how officials are likely to understand this practical import in order to be confident that their interpretation of which actions are prohibited or permitted coincides with the interpretation of officials and other citizens. Similarly, officials must consider how citizens are likely to understand legal rules when determining the practical import of general legal norms.

In addition, the ability of citizens and officials to understand how others will interpret and apply general rules depends on systematic congruence between informal practices and the law. Individuals determine the practical import of a general legal norm, what it requires in specific situations, by imagining acting on it. This imaginative exercise draws on knowledge of one's social context and practices. When a norm has no connection with social practices it can become more difficult to determine its practical import and to be confident that one's interpretation will be congruent with the interpretation of other citizens and lawmaking and law-enforcing officials. A likely result is that individuals will become unable to formulate their own understanding of the meaning of legal norms. In addition, laws disconnected from a given social context are more likely to seem unreasonable or arbitrary, which may lead to outright evasion of the law.

Third, my analysis demonstrates that critics are mistaken in thinking that legal responses to wrongdoing have no impact on structural injustice. My discussion of the rule of law in Chapter 1 helps us recognize the indirect contribution of legal processes that respond to wrongdoing to addressing structural causes of conflict and institutional sources of damage to political relationships. By strengthening the practice of governing conduct on the basis of rules, legal responses to wrongdoing contribute to the cultivation of a form of social order that is premised on the respect for individual agency and that constrains the substantive injustice pursued by officials in practice. One of the important factors that contributes to or facilitates the systematic violation of human rights stems from the erosion of the rule of law. The erosion of the rule of law undermines the environment of stable and consistent expectations that law creates, and generates an environment conducive to the pursuit of structural and systematic injustice. In addition, the erosion of the rule of law during periods of civil conflict and repressive rule can itself constitute a form of structural injustice, given that the overall framework of law is such that it enables citizens to pursue their goals and plans and be appropriately held responsible for their actions.

I have drawn attention to some of the ways in which my conception of political reconciliation challenges assumptions underlying debates within the literature on transitional justice. However, I also want to recognize that the literature on transitional justice correctly draws attention to the fact that the pursuit of political reconciliation is not the only significant moral imperative in transitional contexts, nor is its pursuit compatible with all of the goals that transitional societies often have. Transitions following periods of civil conflict and repressive rule thus involve genuine dilemmas and hard choices. Transitional societies face the question of how to reconcile extraordinary, temporary responses to wrongdoing, like truth commissions, with core principles of the rule of law and with the assumption in "normal conditions" that it is not justifiable to grant amnesty to perpetrators of gross human rights abuses. When debating the permissibility of establishing truth commissions that grant amnesty to such perpetrators, or granting amnesty in general, in transitional contexts authors often emphasize the "extraordinary" character of transitional contexts in order to justify the claim that responding to wrongdoing in such contexts is different from responding in ordinary political contexts.[6] Such arguments raise important theoretical questions about whether the demands of justice are context-dependent, the way in which context influences the content and justification of the demands of justice, and what the content of justice's demands are in transitional contexts. They also generate questions about the weight that should be given to political reconciliation as a moral imperative within transitions, and the basis on which different dimensions of relationships in need of repair should be prioritized.

One general contribution of this book to these ongoing debates about transitional justice, and the place of political reconciliation within transitional justice, is to clarify what is at stake in the pursuit and achievement of political reconciliation. The analysis of political reconciliation I have advanced provides us with a compelling and comprehensive account of its normative significance. It thus deepens our understanding of the import of one of the objectives implicated in choices about how to confront past wrongdoing and rebuild transitional communities. This understanding is necessary to be able to decide in an informed manner how to balance competing and conflicting objectives and values in transitional contexts. However, recognition of the value of political reconciliation is not sufficient. To resolve the moral dilemmas of transitional justice in an informed manner, it is also necessary to know the import of competing objectives and values, and to determine the basis for deciding which among alternative important objectives should be pursued, tasks that are beyond the scope of this book.

I want to close my book by recognizing one additional limit of my account. A sobering and recurring theme throughout the chapters of this book is that human beings have the capacity to inflict horrific suffering on each other. When analyzing political reconciliation, it is imperative to remain cognizant of the fact that theoretical analysis cannot fully convey

---

[6] Transitional societies, it has been claimed, must deal with far more grave and systematic wrongdoing, not simply isolated cases of wrongdoing that institutional legal mechanisms are designed to address in ordinary contexts. Legal responses to wrongdoing must not only respect the core values of the rule of law such as stability, but must also contribute to the societal transformation of what constitutes wrongdoing. The demands of retributive justice are not the only moral consideration in transitional contexts; equally salient is consolidating a transition to peace and democracy. See Ruti Teitel, *Transitional Justice* (New York: Oxford University Press, 2000); Ruti Teitel, "Transitional Justice Genealogy," *Harvard Human Rights Journal*, 16 (2004), 69–94; Naomi Roht-Arriaza and Javier Mariezcurrena (eds.), *Transitional Justice in the Twenty-First Century: Beyond Truth versus Justice* (Cambridge University Press, 2006); Bronwyn Anne Leebaw, "The Irreconcilable Goals of Transitional Justice," *Human Rights Quarterly*, 30 (2008), 95–118.

through words the torment, anguish, and pain that actions and institutions that damage people and relationships leave in their wake. It is important to acknowledge the necessary limits inherent in any theoretical analysis of a subject like political reconciliation, no matter how compelling and comprehensive that analysis may be. Even more importantly, it is critical to recognize that theory cannot address such suffering and damage. Philosophical analysis of the kind I have engaged in here can play an important role in informing and shaping how people think about certain issues, such as that of rebuilding political relationships in the wake of enormous human suffering. However, it can never be a substitute for action. Indeed, at its best philosophy serves as a call for action, in this case to end and address the widespread and deep suffering affecting human beings and damaging interaction in many contexts around the world today, and to ultimately prevent similar suffering from being inflicted on humanity in the future.

Bibliography

Allen, Jonathan, "Balancing Justice and Social Utility: Political Theory and the Idea of a Truth and Reconciliation Commission," *University of Toronto Law Journal*, 49 (1999), 315–53.

Argentine National Commission on the Disappeared, *Nunca Mas: The Report of the Argentine National Commission on the Disappeared*, English edition (New York: Farrar Straus Giroux, 1986).

Arneson, Richard, "Liberalism, Distributive Subjectivism, and Equal Opportunity for Welfare," *Philosophy and Public Affairs*, 19 (1990), 158–94.

Baier, Annette, "Demoralization, Trust, and the Virtues," in Chesire Calhoun (ed.), *Setting the Moral Compass: Essays by Women Philosophers* (New York: Oxford University Press, 2004), pp. 176–90.

"Trust and Antitrust," *Ethics*, 96(2) (1986), 231–60.

Baker, John, "Trust and Rationality," *Pacific Philosophical Quarterly*, 68 (1996), 1–13.

Bassiouni, M. Cherif, "Searching for Peace and Achieving Justice," *Law and Contemporary Problems*, 59(4) (1996), 9–28.

Becker, Lawrence C., "Trust as Noncognitive Security About Motives," *Ethics*, 107(1) (1996), 43–61.

Benson, Paul, "Free Agency and Self-Worth," *The Journal of Philosophy*, 91(12) (1994), 650–68.

Blustein, Jeffrey, *The Moral Demands of Memory* (New York: Cambridge University Press, 2008).

Brewer, John, *Inside the RUC: Routine Policing in a Divided Society* (Oxford University Press, 1991).

Brewer, John, Guelke, Adrian, and Hume, Ian, *The Police, Public Order, and the State: Policing in Great Britain, Northern Ireland, the Irish Republic, the United States, Israel, South Africa, China* (New York: St. Martin's Press, 1988).

Brown, DeNeen L., "The Brutal Truth: A Filmmaker Confronts the Rapists of the Congo and Finds No Remorse," *Washington Post*, April 8, 2008, www.washingtonpost.com/wpdyn/content/article/2008/04/07/AR2008040702782.html.

Buchanan, Allen, *Secession: The Morality of Political Divorce from Fort Sumter to Lithuania to Quebec* (Boulder: Westview Press, 1991).

Cave, Damien, "In Iraq, It's Hard to Trust Anyone in Uniform," *New York Times*, August 3, 2006, www.nytimes.com/2006/08/03/world/middleeast/03uniforms.html.

Chapman, Audrey R., and Ball, Patrick, "The Truth of Truth Commissions: Comparative Lessons from Haiti, South Africa, and Guatemala," *Human Rights Quarterly*, 23(1) (2001), 1–43.

Cohen, G. A., "Where the Action Is: On the Site of Distributive Justice," *Philosophy and Public Affairs*, 26 (1997), 3–30.

Cohen, Stanley, *States of Denial: Knowing About Atrocities and Suffering* (Cambridge: Polity Press, 2001).

Coleman, James S., *Foundations of Social Theory* (Cambridge, MA: Harvard University Press, 1990).

Combs, Nancy, *Guilty Pleas in International Criminal Law* (Stanford University Press, 2007).

Cook, Karen S., Hardin, Russell, and Levi, Margaret, *Cooperation Without Trust?* (New York: Russell Sage Foundation Publications, 2007).

Cudd, Ann E., *Analyzing Oppression* (New York: Oxford University Press, 2006).

Dasgupta, Partha, "Trust as a Commodity," in Diego Gambetta (ed.), *Trust: Making and Breaking Cooperative Relations* (Oxford: Basil Blackwell, 1988), pp. 49–71.

de Klerk, B. J., "Nelson Mandela and Desmond Tutu: Living Icons of Reconciliation," *The Ecumenical Review* (October 2003), http://findarticles.com/p/articles/mi_m2065/is_4_55/ai_111979985/pg_3?tag=artBody;col1.

de Sousa, Ronald, *The Rationality of Emotion* (Cambridge, MA: MIT Press, 1987).

Doxtader, Erik, "Reconciliation – A Rhetorical Conception," *Quarterly Journal of Speech*, 89 (2003), 267–92.

Dunn, John, "Trust and Political Agency," in Diego Gambetta (ed.), *Trust: Making and Breaking Cooperative Relations* (Oxford: Basil Blackwell, 1988), pp. 73–93.

Dworkin, Ronald, *Freedom's Law: The Moral Reading of the American Constitution* (Cambridge, MA: Harvard University Press, 1996).

Dwyer, Susan, "Reconciliation for Realists," *Ethics & International Affairs*, 13 (1999), 81–98.

Dyzenhaus, David, *Judging the Judges, Judging Ourselves* (Oxford: Hart Publishing, 1998).

"Survey Article: The South African TRC," *Journal of Political Philosophy*, 8(4) (2000), 470–96.

Editorial, "The War Amputees of Sierra Leone," *CMAJ* (*Canadian Medical Association Journal*), 162(13) (2000), www.cmaj.ca/cgi/content/full/162/13/1797?ck=nck.

Eisikovits, Nir, "Rethinking the Legitimacy of Truth Commissions: 'I am the Enemy You Killed, My Friend,'" *Metaphilosophy*, 37(3–4) (2006), 489–514.

Feher, Michel, "Terms of Reconciliation," in Carla Hesse and Robert Post (eds.), *Human Rights in Political Transitions: Gettysburg to Bosnia* (New York: Zone Books, 1999), pp. 325–39.

Feitlowitz, Marguerite, *A Lexicon of Terror: Argentina and the Legacies of Torture* (Oxford University Press, 1998).

Fletcher, Laurel, and Weinstein, Harvey, "Violence and Social Repair: Rethinking the Contribution of Justice to Reconciliation," *Human Rights Quarterly*, 24 (2002), 573–639.

"A World unto Itself? The Application of International Justice in the Former Yugoslavia," in Eric Stover and Harvey Weinstein (eds.), *The Former Yugoslavia, My Neighbor, My Enemy: Justice and Community in the Aftermath of Mass Atrocities* (Cambridge University Press, 2004), pp. 29–48.

Fox-Decent, Evan, "Is the Rule of Law Really Indifferent to Human Rights?" *Law and Philosophy*, 27 (2008), 533–81.

Fruhling, Hugo, "Stages of Repression and Legal Strategy for the Defense of Human Rights in Chile: 1973–1980," trans. Frederick Woodbridge, Jr., *Human Rights Quarterly*, 5(4) (1983), 510–33.

Fukuyama, Francis, *Trust* (New York: Basic Books, 1995).

Fuller, Lon, *Anatomy of the Law* (Westport: Greenwood Press Publishers, 1968).

"Human Interaction and the Law," in Kenneth Winston (ed.), *The Principles of Social Order: Selected Essays of Lon F. Fuller* (rev. ed.) (Portland: Hart Publishing, 2001), pp. 231–66.

The Morality of Law (rev. ed.) (New Haven, CT: Yale University Press, 1969).

Gambetta, Diego (ed.), *Trust: Making and Breaking Cooperative Relations* (Oxford: Basil Blackwell, 1988).

Gershoni, Yekutiel, "From War Without End and an End to a War: The Prolonged Wars in Liberia and Sierra Leone," *African Studies Review*, 40 (3) (1997), 55–76.

Ghobarah, Hazem Adam, Huth, Paul, and Russett, Bruce, "Civil Wars Kill and Maim People – Long after the Shooting Stops," *The American Political Science Review*, 97(2) (May 2003), 189–202.

Gibson, James, *Overcoming Apartheid: Can Truth Reconcile a Divided Nation?* (New York: Russell Sage Foundation, 2004).

Godobo-Madikizela, Pumla, *A Human Being Died That Night* (Boston: Houghton Mifflin Co., 2003).

Govier, Trudy, "Self-Trust, Autonomy, and Self-Esteem," *Hypatia*, 8 (1993), 99–120.

Social Trust and Human Communities (Montreal and Kingston: McGill-Queen's University Press, 1997).

Govier, Trudy, and Verwoerd, Wilhelm, "Trust and the Problem of National Reconciliation," *Philosophy of the Social Sciences*, 32(2) (2002), 178–205.

Gutmann, Amy (ed.), *Multiculturalism* (Princeton University Press, 1994).

Gutmann, Amy, and Thompson, Dennis, "The Moral Foundations of Truth Commissions," in Robert I. Rotberg and Dennis Thompson (eds.), *Truth v.*

Justice: The Morality of Truth Commissions (Princeton University Press, 2000), pp. 22–44.

Hamber, Brandon, "The Burdens of Truth: An Evaluation of the Psychological Support Services and Initiatives Undertaken by the South African Truth and Reconciliation Commission," *American Imago*, 55(1) (1998), 9–28.

"Do Sleeping Dogs Lie? The Psychological Implications of the Truth and Reconciliation Commission in South Africa," paper presented at the Centre for the Study of Violence and Reconciliation, seminar no. 5 (1995), 1–12.

Hamber, Brandon, and Wilson, Richard A., "Symbolic Closure through Memory, Reparation and Revenge in Post-conflict Societies," 2002, http://digitalcommons.uconn.edu/hri_papers/5.

Hardin, Russell, "The Street-Level Epistemology of Trust," *Politics & Society*, 21 (4) (1993), 505–29.

Trust and Trustworthiness (New York: Russell Sage Foundation, 2002).

"Trustworthiness," *Ethics*, 107(1) (1996), 26–42.

(ed.), *Distrust* (New York: Russell Sage Foundation Publications, 2009).

Hardwig, John, "The Role of Trust in Knowledge," *The Journal of Philosophy*, 88 (12) (1991), 693–708.

Hayner, Priscilla, "Same Species, Different Animal: How South Africa Compares to Truth Commissions Worldwide," in Charles Villa-Vicencio and Wilhelm Verwoerd (eds.), *Looking Back, Reaching Forward: Reflections on the Truth and Reconciliation Commission of South Africa* (University of Cape Town Press, 2000), pp. 32–41.

Unspeakable Truths: Confronting State Terror and Atrocity (New York: Routledge, 2001).

Hieronymi, Pamela, "Articulating an Uncompromising Forgiveness," *Philosophy and Phenomenological Research*, 62(3) (2001), 529–55.

"The Reasons of Trust," *Australasian Journal of Philosophy*, 86(2) (2008), 213–36.

Holton, Richard, "Deciding to Trust, Coming to Believe," *Australasian Journal of Philosophy*, 72 (1994), 63–76.

Hughes, Paul M., "Moral Atrocity and Political Reconciliation: A Preliminary Analysis," *International Journal of Applied Philosophy*, 15(1) (2001), 123–35.

"What Is Involved in Forgiving?" *Philosophia*, 25 (1997), 33–49.

Human Rights Watch, "Coercion and Intimidation of Child Soldiers to Participate in Violence" (April 2008), http://hrw.org/backgrounder/2008/crd0408/8.htm.

"Getting Away with Murder, Mutilation and Rape," *A Human Rights Watch Report*, 11(3)(A) (June 1999).

"Sowing Terror: Atrocities Against Civilians in Sierra Leone," *A Human Rights Watch Report*, 10(3)(A) (July 1998), http://hrw.org/reports/2004/sierraleone0904/1.htm#_Toc81830567.

Internal Displacement Monitoring Centre, *Internal Displacement: Global Overview of Trends and Developments in 2007*, www.unhcr.org/refworld/publisher,IDMC,THEMREPORT,48074b842,0.html.

Jones, Karen, "Second-hand Moral Knowledge," *The Journal of Philosophy*, 96(2) (1999), 55–78.

"Trust as an Affective Attitude," *Ethics*, 107 (1996), 4–25.

Korsgaard, Christine M., *Creating the Kingdom of Ends* (Cambridge University Press, 1996).

Kritz, Neil, *Transitional Justice: How Emerging Democracies Reckon with Former Regimes* (Washington, DC: United States Institute of Peace Press, 1995).

Krog, Antjie, *Country of My Skull: Guilt, Sorrow, and the Limits of Forgiveness in the New South Africa* (New York: Three Rivers Press, 1998).

Kymlicka, Will, *Multicultural Citizenship* (Oxford University Press, 1995).

(ed.), *The Rights of Minority Cultures* (Oxford University Press, 1995).

Lacey, Marc, "Across Globe, Empty Bellies Bring Rising Anger," *New York Times*, December 4, 2008, www.nytimes.com/2008/04/18/world/americas/18food.html.

Lagerspetz, Olli, *Trust: The Tacit Demand* (Dordrecht, the Netherlands: Kluwer Academic Publishers, 1998).

Leebaw, Bronwyn Anne, "The Irreconcilable Goals of Transitional Justice," *Human Rights Quarterly*, 30 (2008), 95–118.

Linz, Juan, *Totalitarian and Authoritarian Regimes* (Boulder, CO: Lynne Rienner Publishers, 2000).

Llewellyn, Jennifer, and House, Robert, "Institutions for Restorative Justice: The South African Truth and Reconciliation Commission," *University of Toronto Law Journal*, 49 (1999), 355–88.

Luban, David, "Natural Law as Professional Ethics: A Reading of Fuller," *Social Philosophy and Policy*, 18(1) (2001), 176–205.

Luhmann, Nicklas, "Familiarity, Confidence, Trust: Problems and Alternatives," in Diego Gambetta (ed.), *Trust: Making and Breaking Cooperative Relations* (Oxford: Basil Blackwell, 1988), pp. 94–107.

Trust and Power (Toronto: Wiley Press, 1979).

Lundy, Patricia, and McGovern, Mark, "Whose Justice? Rethinking Transitional Justice from the Bottom Up," *Journal of Law and Society*, 35(2) (2008), 265–92.

MacCormick, Neil, "Rhetoric and the Rule of Law," in David Dyzenhaus (ed.), *Recrafting the Rule of Law: The Limits of Legal Order* (Oxford: Hart Publishing, 1999), pp. 163–78.

Malamud-Goti, Jaime, "Transitional Governments in the Breach: Why Punish State Criminals?" *Human Rights Quarterly*, 12(1) (1990), 1–16.

May, Larry, *Genocide: A Normative Account* (Cambridge University Press, 2010).

McEvoy, Kieran, "Beyond Legalism: Towards a Thicker Understanding of Transitional Justice," *Journal of Law and Society*, 24(4) (2007), 411–40.

McGarry, John, and O'Leary, Brendan, *Explaining Northern Ireland: Broken Images* (Oxford: Wiley-Blackwell, 1995).

Policing Northern Ireland: Proposals for a New Start (Belfast: Blackstaff Press, 1999).

"Stabilising Northern Ireland's Agreement," *The Political Quarterly* (2004), 213–25.

McGeer, Victoria, "Trust, Hope, and Empowerment," *Australasian Journal of Philosophy*, 86(2) (2008), 237–54.

Mertus, Julie, "Only a War Crimes Tribunal: Triumph of the International Community, Pain of the Survivors," in Belinda Cooper (ed.), *War Crimes: The Legacy of Nuremberg* (New York: TV Books, 1999).

Minow, Martha, *Between Vengeance and Forgiveness: Facing History after Genocide and Mass Violence* (Boston: Beacon Press, 1998).

Moellendorf, Darrell, "Reconciliation as a Political Value," *Journal of Social Philosophy*, 38(2) (2007), 205–21.

Murphy, Colleen, "Lon Fuller and the Moral Value of the Rule of Law," *Law and Philosophy*, 24 (2005), 239–62.

"Political Reconciliation, the Rule of Law, and Genocide," *The European Legacy*, 12(7) (2007), 853–65.

"Political Reconciliation, the Rule of Law, and Post-traumatic Stress Disorder," in Nancy Nyquist Potter (ed.), *Trauma, Truth, and Reconciliation: Healing Damaged Relationships* (Oxford University Press, 2006), pp. 83–110.

Murphy, Colleen, and Gardoni, Paolo, "The Acceptability and the Tolerability of Societal Risks: A Capabilities-based Approach," *Science and Engineering Ethics*, 14(1) (2008), 77–92.

"Assessing Capability Instead of Achieved Functionings in Risk Analysis," *Journal of Risk Research*, 13(2) (2010), 137–47.

"Determining Public Policy and Resource Allocation Priorities for Mitigating Natural Hazards: A Capabilities-based Approach," *Science and Engineering Ethics*, 13(4) (2007), 489–504.

Murphy, Jeffrie and Hampton, Jean, *Forgiveness and Mercy* (Cambridge University Press, 1998).

Murray, C. J. L., King, G., Lopez, D., Tomijima, N., Krug, E.G, "Armed Conflict as a Public Health Problem," *British Journal of Medicine*, 324 (2002), 346–9.

Nadler, Jennifer, "Hart, Fuller, and the Connection Between Law and Justice," *Law and Philosophy*, 27 (2007), 1–34.

Neier, Aryeh, *War Crimes: Brutality, Genocide, Terror, and the Struggle for Justice* (New York: Crown Publisher, 1998).

Ni Aolain, Fionnuala, *The Politics of Force: Conflict Management and State Violence in Northern Ireland* (Belfast: Blackstaff Press, 2000).

Nino, Carlos, *Radical Evil on Trial* (New Haven, CT: Yale University Press, 1996).

Nussbaum, Martha, "Adaptive Preferences and Women's Options," *Economics and Philosophy*, 17 (2001), 67–88.

"Aristotle, Politics, and Human Capabilities: A Response to Antony, Arneson, Charlesworth, and Mulgan," *Ethics*, 111(1) (2000a), 102–40.

Women and Human Development: The Capabilities Approach (Cambridge University Press, 2000b).

O'Donnell, E. E., *Northern Irish Stereotypes* (Dublin: College of Industrial Relations, 1977).

O'Leary, Brendan, and McGarry, John, *The Politics of Antagonism: Understanding Northern Ireland*, 2nd ed. (London: Athlone Press, 1996).

Osiel, Mark, *Mass Atrocity, Collective Memory, and the Law* (Piscataway, NJ: Transaction Publishers, 1999).

Oxfam, "Africa's Missing Billions: International Arms Flows and the Cost of Conflict," October 2007, www.oxfam.org.uk/resources/policy/conflict_disasters/bp107_africasmissingbillions.html.

Pettit, Philip, "The Cunning of Trust," *Philosophy and Public Affairs*, 24(3) (1995), 202–25.

Phillips, James, "What Is Needed for Reconciliation in Iraq," June 28, 2006, www.heritage.org/research/iraq/wm1139.cfm.

Philpott, Daniel, "Introduction," in Daniel Philpott (ed.), *The Politics of Past Evil: Religion, Reconciliation, and the Dilemmas of Transitional Justice* (Notre Dame, IN: University of Notre Dame Press, 2006), pp. 1–9.

Postema, Gerald J., "Implicit Law," *Law and Philosophy*, 13 (1994), 361–87.

Putnam, Robert D., Leonardi, Robert, and Nanetti, Raffaella Y., *Making Democracy Work: Civic Traditions in Modern Italy* (Princeton University Press, 1994).

Quinn, Joanna R., and Freeman, Mark, "Lessons Learned: Practical Lessons Gleaned from Inside the Truth Commission of Guatemala and South Africa," *Human Rights Quarterly*, 25(4) (2003), 1117–49.

Radzik, Linda, *Making Amends: Atonement in Morality, Law and Politics* (Oxford University Press, 2009).

Rawls, John, *A Theory of Justice* (Cambridge, MA: Harvard University Press, 1971).

Raz, Joseph, *Authority of Law* (Oxford: Clarendon Press, 1979).

Richards, Norman, "Forgiveness," *Ethics*, 99(1) (1988), 77–97.

Roberts, Robert C., "What an Emotion Is: A Sketch," *The Philosophical Review*, 97(2) (1988), 183–95.

Robeyns, Ingrid, "The Capability Approach: A Theoretical Survey," *Journal of Human Development*, 6(1) (2005), 93–114.

Roemer, John E., *Theories of Distributive Justice* (Cambridge, MA: Harvard University Press, 1996).

Roht-Arriaza, Naomi, *Impunity and Human Rights: International Law Practice* (New York: Oxford University Press, 1995).

"State Responsibility to Investigate and Prosecute Grave Human Rights Violations in International Law," *California Law Review*, 78 (1990), 449–51.

Roht-Arriaza, Naomi, and Mariezcurrena, Javier (eds.), *Transitional Justice in the Twenty-First Century: Beyond Truth versus Justice* (Cambridge University Press, 2006).

Rondeaux, Candace, "Musharraf Exits, but Uncertainty Remains," *Washington Post*, August 19, 2008, www.washingtonpost.com/wpdyn/content/article/2008/08/18/AR2008081800418.html.

Rorty, Amelie (ed.), *Explaining Emotions* (Los Angeles: University of California Press, 1976).

Ross, Marc Howard, *Cultural Contestation in Ethnic Conflict* (New York: Cambridge University Press, 2007).

Rotberg, Robert I., and Thompson, Dennis (eds.), *Truth v. Justice: The Morality of Truth Commissions* (Princeton University Press, 2000).

Roth, John, "Useless Experience: Its Significance for Reconciliation after Auschwitz," in David Patterson and John K. Roth (eds.), *After-Words: Post Holocaust Struggles with Forgiveness, Reconciliation, Justice* (Seattle: University of Washington Press, 2004), pp. 85–99.

Save the Children, "Armed Conflict Creating Crisis in Education for 43 Million Children, New Save the Children Report Finds," September 12, 2006, www.savethechildren.org/newsroom/2006/armed-conflict-creating-crisis-in-education.html.

Schaap, Andrew, *Political Reconciliation* (New York: Routledge, 2005).

Schabas, William, "A Synergistic Relationship: The Sierra Leone Truth and Reconciliation Commission and the Special Court for Sierra Leone," *Criminal Law Forum*, 15 (2004), 3–54.

Sen, Amartya, "Capability and Well-Being," in Martha Nussbaum and Amartya Sen (eds.), *The Quality of Life* (Oxford: Clarendon Press, 1993) pp. 30–53.

   Commodities and Capabilities (Oxford University Press, 1999a).

   "Development as Capabilities Expansion," *Journal of Development Planning*, 19 (1989), 41–58.

   Development as Freedom (New York: Anchor Books, 1999b).

   "Elements of a Theory of Human Rights," *Philosophy and Public Affairs*, 32(4) (2004), 315–56.

   "Freedom of Choice: Concept and Content," *European Economic Review*, 32 (2–3) (1988), 269–94.

   Inequality Reexamined (Cambridge, MA: Harvard University Press, 1992).

   Rationality and Freedom (Cambridge, MA: Harvard University Press, 2004).

Shoemaker, David, "Moral Address, Moral Responsibility, and the Boundaries of the Moral Community," *Ethics*, 118 (2007), 70–108.

Steele, David A., "Reconciliation Strategies in Iraq," *United States Institute of Peace Special Report*, 213 (October 2008), www.usip.org/pubs/specialreports/sr213.pdf.

Tamir, Yael, *Liberal Nationalism* (Princeton University Press, 1993).

Taslioulas, John, "Punishment and Reptentence," *Philosophy*, 81 (2006), 279–322.

Teitel, Ruti, "Bringing the Messiah Through Law," in Carla Hesse and Robert Post (eds.), *Human Rights in Political Transitions: Gettysburg to Bosnia* (New York: Zone Books, 1999), pp. 177–93.

   Transitional Justice (New York: Oxford University Press, 2000).

   "Transitional Justice Genealogy," *Harvard Human Rights Journal*, 16 (2003), 69–94.

Thompson, Leonard, *A History of South Africa* (New Haven, CT: Yale University Press, 2000).

Truth and Reconciliation Commission of South Africa, *Truth and Reconciliation Commission of South Africa Report*, 5 vols. (London: Macmillan Publishers, 1999).

Ugalde, Antonio, Selva-Sutter, Ernesto, Casatillo, Carolina, Paz, Carolina, and Canas, Sergio, "The Health Costs of War: Can They be Measured? Lessons from El Salvador," *BJM*, 321(7254) (2000), 169–72.

United Nations High Commissioner for Refugees, "2007 Global Trends: Refugees, Asylum-seekers, Returnees, Internally Displaced and Stateless Persons" (June 2008), www.unhcr.org/statistics/STATISTICS/4852366f2.pdf.

van Zyl, Paul, "Dilemmas of Transitional Justice: The Case of South Africa's Truth and Reconciliation Commission," *Journal of International Affairs*, 52 (2) (1999), 647–67.

"Justice Without Punishment: Guaranteeing Human Rights in Transitional Societies," in Charles Villa-Vicencio and Wilhelm Verwoerd (eds.), *Looking Back, Reaching Forward: Reflections on the Truth and Reconciliation Commission of South Africa* (University of Cape Town Press, 2000), pp. 42–57.

Villa-Vicencio, Charles, and Verwoerd, Wilhelm, (eds.), *Looking Back, Reaching Forward: Reflections on the Truth and Reconciliation Commission of South Africa* (University of Cape Town Press, 2000).

Waldron, Jeremy, "Hart and the Principles of Legality," in Matthew H. Cramer, Claire Grant, Ben Colburn, and Antony Hatzistavrou (eds.), *The Legacy of H.L.A. Hart* (Oxford University Press, 2008), pp. 67–83.

"Why Law – Efficacy, Freedom or Fidelity?" *Law and Philosophy*, 13 (1994), 259–84.

Walker, Margaret Urban, *Moral Repair: Reconstructing Moral Relations After Wrongdoing* (Cambridge University Press, 2006).

Webb, M. O., "The Epistemology of Trust and the Politics of Suspicion," *Pacific Philosophical Quarterly*, 73 (1992), 390–440.

Weinstock, Daniel, "Building Trust in Divided Societies," *The Journal of Political Philosophy*, 7(3) (1999), 287–307.

Wolff, Jonathan, and de-Shalit, Avner, *Disadvantage* (Oxford University Press, 2007).

Index

abduction, 46, 104. *See also* disappearing
Afghanistan, 2, 180
African National Congress (ANC), 3, 60
agency, 30, 54, 65, 66, 68, 78, 83, 86, 105, 113,
    117, 118, 126, 127, 132, 133, 134, 139, 159,
    168, 183, 188, 190. *See also* civil conflict,
    and agency; moral agents; officials,
    agency of; political relationships, and
    agency; repressive rule, and agency; rule
    of law, and agency
    exercise of, 29, 113, 126, 128, 135, 138
    individual, 30, 31, 34, 42, 47, 62, 132, 139, 181,
        190, 197
    of others, 132, 136, 145–6
    reciprocal, 28, 37, 189, 190, 191, 195
    recognition of, 81, 82, 84
    respect for, 28, 29, 33, 41, 42, 53, 55, 61, 62, 63,
        66, 67, 69, 70, 83, 99, 119, 131–2, 141, 142,
        145, 146, 148, 150, 156, 157, 187, 189
Algeria, 180
Allen, Jonathan, 158
al-Maliki, Nouri, 2
amnesty, 4, 6, 38, 144, 197
amputation, 12, 103, 104, 106
anger, 10, 21, 48, 158, 162, 164
anomie, 175
apartheid, 2–3, 58, 59, 60, 61, 103, 109, 110–14,
    144, 148, 149–50, 158, 176
    legal system, 58, 59, 61
Argentina, 45, 46, 47, 49, 52, 61, 103, 128, 144,
    175, 180
atrocities, 5, 42, 61, 129, 145, 156, 166, 184
authority, 56, 67, 78, 79, 81, 86, 134, 146, 153,
    154, 157
    excesses of, 61
    normative, 146, 150, 159, 160
    political, 56

Baier, Annette, 76
Bluestein, Jeffrey, 159
Bosnia, 103, 179

Buchanan, Allen, 8–9
Burundi, 180

Cambodia, 46, 179, 180
capabilities, 27, 28–9, 31, 32, 37, 95, 98–103, 104–5,
    106, 107–8, 110–12, 114, 115, 118, 119, 123,
    124, 129, 132, 133, 134, 139, 140, 142, 191.
    See also civil conflict, and capabilities;
    political relationships, and capabilities;
    repressive rule, and capabilities
    basic, 29, 32, 95, 104, 106, 108, 109, 110, 113,
        118–19, 127, 130–1, 136, 138, 140, 142, 159
    definition of, 28, 98
    diminishment of, 31, 102, 108, 109, 118, 119, 131,
        132, 136, 145
    framework of, 99, 100, 102
    group, 117
    individual, 28, 96, 99, 100, 114, 138, 189, 193
    relational, 29, 31, 33, 100, 102, 137, 159, 189,
        190, 193, 195
    value of, 98–9
Chile, 103, 144
citizenship, 18, 81, 114, 132, 135, 154, 188
civil conflict, 1–4, 6, 9, 12, 15, 16, 19, 21, 26–7, 30,
    31, 34–6, 37, 58, 62–3, 66, 69–70, 91, 94,
    102, 103, 106, 109, 110, 114, 115, 118, 123,
    127, 128, 141, 145, 148, 151, 162, 163, 165,
    166, 169, 174–5, 176, 178, 181, 182, 184–5,
    187, 189, 190, 192. *See also* violence, in
    civil conflict
    aftermath of, 8, 11, 17, 22, 26, 27, 35, 187,
        192, 197
    and agency, 132, 145, 146, 148, 150
    and capabilities, 95, 100, 102
    causes of, 195, 197
    contexts of, 12, 14, 84, 90, 93, 102, 114, 115, 118,
        131, 150
    and damage to political relationships, 11, 15,
        19, 23, 25, 28, 37, 41, 70, 71, 84, 94, 95,
        100, 118, 123, 128, 133, 137, 145, 187, 190
    and distrust, 16, 188

civil conflict (cont.)
  ethnic, 114, 151
  features of, 35, 107
  interactions in, 26, 102, 133, 188
  prevention of, 13
  and rule of law, 29, 30, 42, 53, 62, 66, 131, 197
Cohen, Stanley, 128–9
Colombia, 180
community, 6, 78, 79, 81, 94, 109, 114, 129, 138,
    152, 156, 159
  international, 57, 62, 167, 178, 179, 180, 181,
      182, 183, 184, 185, 193, 194, 195
  membership in, 105, 107, 112, 115, 119, 138, 139,
      145, 152, 154, 156, 157, 161, 184, 189
  moral, 146, 150
  participation in, 32, 36, 100, 101, 105, 107, 108,
      110, 111–12, 114, 117, 119, 132, 140, 193
  political, 18, 20, 21, 22, 31–2, 35, 78, 79, 82, 95,
      100–1, 114–15, 118, 119, 127, 132, 133, 136,
      140, 145, 154, 155, 156, 157–8, 159–61, 162,
      189, 191, 195
  sense of, 21, 30
  and truth commissions, 161, 162, 166
competence, 31, 73, 75, 77, 78, 79, 80, 81, 82–3,
    86, 92, 93, 117, 132, 133, 139, 176, 188, 189,
    193. *See also* incompetence; officials,
    competence of
congruence, 43, 44, 47, 48, 52, 67, 68, 131, 134,
    135, 169, 170, 171, 172, 186, 196
corruption, 78, 84, 91, 93, 136, 173
  moral, 30, 31
  official, 86, 184
coups d'état, 16, 175
cultural enactment, 152
cultural expression, 114, 153

death squads, 46, 60, 61
decency, 31, 33, 82, 133, 173, 176, 178, 182, 189
  basic, 81, 82, 83, 92, 93, 132
  legal, 134, 135, 169, 172, 173, 175, 178, 182
Democratic Republic of the Congo, 103, 180
democratization, 1, 6, 8, 9, 13, 33, 187, 190.
    See also political reconciliation, and
    democratization
denial, 59, 61, 128, 129, 130, 158, 163, 165.
    See also officials, and denial;
    wrongdoing, denial of
  implicatory, 128, 130
  interpretive, 128, 157
  legal, 107
  literal, 128
  official, 52, 90, 129, 130
Department of Bantu Administration and
    Development, 112
de-Shalit, Avner, 96, 98, 119, 138, 140

disappearing, 12, 46, 47, 48, 91, 175.
    See also abduction
discrimination, 35, 51, 57, 79, 117, 138
  employment, 110, 111
  wage, 110, 111, 137
distrust, 16, 30, 32, 48, 71, 72, 75, 79, 84, 86, 94,
    117, 131, 132, 135, 141, 168, 176, 188.
    See also civil conflict, and distrust; trust
  reasonableness of, 84, 85, 93, 136
Dyzenhaus, David, 57, 58, 59, 61

education, 109, 138
Eisikovits, Nir, 158
El Salvador, 46, 109, 144
emotional address, 147, 155, 159
empathy, 155, 158, 158
employment, 97, 98, 105, 106, 110, 111,
    117, 137, 140. *See also* discrimination,
    employment
equality, 18, 31, 65, 101, 109, 186
  in political relationships, 101, 102
Ethiopia, 46
ethnic cleansing, 103, 107
execution, 12, 68, 174
expectations, 22, 24, 28, 30, 31, 43, 44
  normative, 8, 57–16, 57–16, 72.
    See also political relationships, normative
    expectations in
exploitation, 72, 80, 84, 85

fair play, 82, 84
fair-mindedness, 162, 163, 164, 166
Feitlowitz, Marguerite, 45
forgiveness, 5, 6, 8, 9–10, 11, 12–13, 14, 17
Fox-Decent, Evan, 63
Fruhling, Hugo, 16
Fuller, Lon, 41–5, 46, 48–50, 52, 54–5, 60, 63–5,
    67–9, 134, 168, 169, 171, 172–4
functionings, 94, 95–8, 99, 101, 104, 107, 108, 119,
    138, 139–40, 193

Gardoni, Paolo, 97
Geneva Conventions, 179
genocide, 15, 103. *See also* ethnic cleansing
Ghana, 144, 180
Gibson, James, 141
Godobo-Madikizela, Pumla, 60
goods, 36, 73, 80, 87, 90, 189
goodwill, 74, 78, 87, 93. *See also* ill will
Guatemala, 46, 144, 180

Haiti, 144
Hamber, Brandon, 164
Hampton, Jean, 141
hatred, 10, 21, 79, 149, 184

Hayner, Priscilla, 165, 179
health care, 12, 109, 113, 185
Hegel, G. W. F., 59
hope, 32, 125–7, 130, 139, 159, 189, 192.
    See also optimism
human rights, 1, 16, 51, 159, 185
    abuses, 1, 2, 3, 4, 6, 11, 12, 21, 129, 144, 149, 150,
        156, 157, 159, 162, 165, 168, 175, 176, 179,
        193, 194, 197
    violations, 4, 6, 192, 197
Human Rights Watch, 104
Hume, David, 59
humiliation, 21, 101, 105, 112, 113, 117, 139, 152

identity, 35, 36, 114, 116, 136, 153
    group, 28, 31, 102, 114, 115, 118, 133, 145, 150, 151,
        153, 155, 157
    moral, 59, 60
    social, 35, 115
ill will, 76, 79, 86, 91, 135. *See also* goodwill
    lack of, 30, 74, 78, 79–80, 84, 85–7, 89, 90, 91,
        92, 93, 132, 133, 135, 136, 137, 188
impartiality, 78, 184
incompetence, 79, 86, 90. *See also* competence
    political, 86, 87
innocence, presumption of, 58, 180, 181, 185
institutions, 15, 17, 18, 19, 20, 24, 78, 172, 199
    cultural, 118
    economic, 28, 34, 96, 110, 190
    legal, 16–17, 28, 96, 107, 111, 118, 191, 195
    political, 16–17, 28, 34, 96, 190
    role of, 18, 100
    social, 34, 186, 190
Interim Constitution (South African), 3
International Center for Transitional Justice, 7,
    72, 179
International Criminal Court (ICC), 167, 178
International Criminal Tribunal for Rwanda
    (ICTR), 178
International Criminal Tribunal for the former
    Yugoslavia (ICTY), 178
Iraq, 1, 86, 180

Jones, Karen, 73–7
judges, 43, 58
justice, 36, 58, 65, 99, 101, 102, 119, 145, 168,
    180, 183, 184, 186, 195
    criminal, 6, 176, 180, 181
    demands of, 31, 99, 198
    legal, 194
    retributive, 5, 124, 168
    social, 34, 36
    systems, 149, 176
    transitional, 2, 5, 6, 7, 22, 24, 70, 124, 145,
        187, 192, 194, 195, 196, 197

Kenya, 180
Klerk, F. W. de, 3
Kock, Eugene de, 60
Kosovo, 179
Krog, Antjie, 148, 150

law. *See also* lawmakers
    common, 58, 59, 61, 179
    efficacy of, 167, 168, 172, 186
    enforcement of, 44, 47, 48, 50, 52, 79, 108, 131,
        171–2, 176, 181, 182, 184, 188
    faith in, 33, 48, 127, 134, 169, 174, 176, 178, 182
    international, 47, 179, 182
    judicial systems, 6, 16, 48
    obedience to, 44, 45, 49, 63–4, 119, 133, 171, 175
    purpose of, 47, 54, 65, 66, 67, 69, 169, 173
    social conditions for, 167, 168, 169, 170, 174,
        175, 176, 177, 178, 185
    written, 44, 47, 48
lawmakers, 41, 43–4, 48, 50, 65, 173
Liberia, 104, 180
Linz, Juan, 56

MacCormick, Neil, 57
Mandela, Nelson, 3, 5
marginalization, 102, 107, 112, 118, 136, 153
McEvoy, Kieran, 189, 195
McGarry, John, 58, 116, 177
media, 4, 16
Mexico, 180
Moellendorf, Darrel, 17, 18
moral agents, 81, 145–8, 149–51, 153, 154, 155, 156,
    157, 160, 161, 191
moral concern, 14, 23, 25, 42, 49, 72, 84, 85, 93,
    94, 97, 118, 131, 189
moral reasons, second-personal, 146, 150, 153
moral value, 8, 14, 25, 37, 41, 42, 49, 51, 53, 55, 72,
    73, 77, 80, 81, 83–4, 142, 168, 190
    non-instrumental, 42, 53, 62, 73, 80, 84, 85, 92, 98
morality, 53, 90, 91
    of law, 65, 66
murder, 46, 47, 48, 104
Musharraf, Pervez, 2

Nadler, Jennifer, 63–7, 68, 69
narratives, 59, 114, 151, 152, 153, 155, 156, 157, 158,
    159–60, 161, 162
Nazi Germany, 51
Nicaragua, 180
Nino, Carlos, 175
non-governmental organizations (NGOs), 2, 179
norms, 31, 78, 79, 82, 138, 170, 180, 183, 194, 196
    economic, 82
    institutional, 100
    international, 62

norms (cont.)
  legal, 82, 170, 182, 196, 197
  political, 82, 132, 188
  social, 19, 28, 81, 82, 96, 106, 108, 115, 129, 132,
    175, 188
North America, 112. *See also* United States
Northern Ireland, 2, 14, 58, 103, 115, 116, 151, 152,
    154, 176, 177, 181
  Catholics, 115, 116, 151, 153, 154, 176–7, 181
  Protestants, 115, 116, 151, 153, 154
Nussbaum, Martha, 95, 99, 102, 112

O'Leary, Brendan, 58, 116
officials, 25, 29–31, 41, 42, 44, 46, 47–8, 54, 69,
    75, 78–80, 81, 82, 83, 84, 86, 87, 90, 93,
    112, 131, 133, 135, 137, 138, 142, 149, 150,
    169–73, 174, 175, 176, 177, 178, 182, 184,
    186, 188, 193, 196
  agency of, 67, 81, 83
  competence of, 30, 75–82, 85–6, 89, 92, 132,
    135, 196
  and denial, 128–30
  and enforcement of law, 43, 45, 48, 52, 53, 137
  expectations of, 30, 77, 83, 86, 87, 88–9, 90, 91,
    132, 170, 188, 189
  government, 16, 29, 30, 44, 45, 47, 48, 50, 53,
    55, 57, 60, 64, 67, 80, 174, 175, 182
  lack of ill will, 82
  law enforcement, 29, 47, 48, 131, 171–2, 181,
    182, 184, 196
  legal, 33, 47, 134, 135
  power of, 54, 82
  public, 72, 86
  and relationship with citizens, 14, 15, 17, 19,
    24, 25, 28, 30, 42, 44, 46, 48, 49, 54, 55,
    61, 62, 65, 67, 69, 73, 77, 84, 86, 124, 130,
    134–5, 137, 169, 170, 188, 190, 196
  and rule of law, 54, 55, 58, 63–4, 67, 133, 135,
    175, 176
  security, 48, 86
  trusted, 79–84, 89–90, 136, 138, 189
oppression, 3, 11, 12, 20, 23, 59, 176, 188
  economic, 31, 102, 110, 112, 113, 114, 118, 136,
    143, 193
optimism, 30, 73, 75, 77, 79–80, 85, 125, 126, 132,
    164. *See also* hope
ostracization, 31, 101, 107

Panama, 180
peacemaking, 1, 2
perpetrators, 4, 5, 9, 12, 13, 21, 25, 105, 129, 141,
    144, 162, 166, 167, 168, 181, 182, 183, 184,
    185, 194, 197
Peru, 144, 180
Pettit, Phillip, 87, 88, 90, 91, 92
Philippines, the, 144

philosophy, 26, 72, 199
  moral, 2
  political, 2
Pinochet, Augusto, 16, 103
policy making, 24, 123, 143
political reconciliation
  analysis of, 7, 9, 23, 26, 27, 37, 41, 123, 188, 189,
    192, 198
  conception of, 7–8, 9, 10, 13, 20, 22, 23, 26, 27, 28,
    32–3, 34, 37, 38, 69, 100, 187, 189, 191, 195
  debates about, 6, 8, 24, 38, 187
  and democratization, 1, 6, 9, 13, 33, 187, 190
  as a political value, 18
political relationships. *See also* civil conflict, and
    damage to political relationships;
    equality, in political relationships;
    reciprocity, in political relationships;
    repressive rule, and damage to political
    relationships
  and agency, 29, 53, 195
  and capabilities, 95, 101, 103
  character of, 22, 24, 27, 41, 63, 94, 139, 189, 191
  conception of, 22, 23, 27
  in conflict and repression, 188
  damage to, 10, 11, 12, 14, 15, 19, 23, 25, 26, 26,
    29, 34, 36, 37, 41, 49, 53, 62–3, 70, 71,
    100, 118, 137, 187, 188, 189, 192, 195
  fragility of, 20–2, 24, 25
  normative expectations in, 16, 72
  rebuilding of, 1, 8–10, 13, 15, 16, 19, 20, 21,
    24–5, 28, 32, 34, 35, 37, 38, 41, 71, 93, 94,
    100, 118, 123, 124, 125, 128, 129, 130, 137,
    140, 141–2, 177, 187, 188, 192, 199
  and reciprocity, 28, 29, 70, 72
  and rule of law, 41, 42, 47, 48, 49, 55, 62, 142,
    159, 189
  in transitional contexts, 7, 9, 26, 33, 71, 169, 192
  and trust, 17, 71–2, 77, 78, 80–1, 84–5, 87, 88,
    93, 187
political science, 72
politicians, 1, 3, 48, 71
poverty, 31, 51, 95, 100, 102, 110, 112, 149
Promotion of National Unity and
    Reconciliation Act, 4
punishment, 5, 37, 64, 141, 181, 184, 185, 187, 194

racism, 3, 62, 186
rape, 12, 27, 103, 104–5, 106, 107
Raz, Joseph, 49–55, 62
reciprocity, 29, 30, 31, 33, 41, 42, 44, 48, 49, 53, 55,
    62–70, 80, 83, 84, 89, 92, 99, 133, 134, 142,
    168, 187. *See also* political relationships,
    and reciprocity
  absence of, 48
  commitment to, 29, 66, 70, 72, 73, 81, 83–5,
    93, 133, 134, 188

demands of, 66, 67, 68, 83, 89
  in political relationships, 28, 48, 49, 69, 70, 72
  in rule of law, 63, 65
  value of, 83, 85
reform, 78, 136, 137, 176, 183
  institutional, 19, 33
  legal, 193, 196
  social, 186
  societal, 194
regimes, 55, 61, 81, 103, 106. *See also* repressive rule
  political, 51, 194
reliance, 76, 77, 79, 81, 82, 89
repressive rule, 1, 2, 13, 16, 21, 26, 29, 34, 35, 45,
    56, 57, 62, 66, 69, 85, 91, 94, 102, 103,
    107, 110, 114, 118, 123, 128, 141, 145, 148,
    162, 163, 165, 166, 169, 174–5, 176, 181,
    182, 185, 188, 191
  aftermath of, 11, 27, 192
  and agency, 132, 145, 146, 148, 150
  and capabilities, 100, 102
  contexts of, 12, 14, 53, 90, 93, 102, 118, 131, 150
  and damage to political relationships, 15, 19,
    23, 25, 28, 37, 41, 63, 70, 71, 84, 94, 95,
    100, 118, 123, 128, 133, 137, 145, 187–8, 190
  interactions in, 19, 27, 102, 133
  and rule of law, 42, 53, 55–6, 66, 131, 197
  transition from, 2, 178, 197
  and trust, 31, 188
resentment, 5, 10, 11, 13, 14, 21, 44, 48, 79, 146,
    147, 149, 151, 153, 158, 162, 166, 168, 184
resources, 5, 9, 14, 24, 27, 28, 35, 36, 38, 59, 62,
    79, 100, 106, 113, 115, 129, 143, 146, 151,
    163, 185, 186, 193, 195
  economic, 110
  individual, 31, 32, 96, 98, 104, 107–8, 113, 117,
    127, 133, 137, 138, 189
    external, 96, 100, 102, 106, 108, 112, 113, 133,
      137, 138, 139, 189, 193
    internal, 96, 102
  monetary, 106, 113, 167
  theoretical, 8, 14, 15, 24, 27, 28, 33, 76, 123, 128,
    187, 189
Revolutionary United Front, 104
Roht-Arriaza, Naomi, 47
Ross, Marc Howard, 151, 152, 154
Rousseau, Jean-Jacques, 59
rule of law, 3, 18, 28, 29–30, 32–4, 44, 45, 48, 49,
    55–6, 57–8, 59, 60, 69, 70, 78, 86, 94, 97,
    119, 124, 129–31, 133, 134–5, 136, 137, 140,
    173, 174, 176, 177, 178, 179, 182–3, 184,
    188, 189, 190, 191, 193, 197. *See also* civil
    conflict, and rule of law; morality, of
    law; political relationships, and rule of
    law; reciprocity, in rule of law; repressive
    rule, and rule of law
  and agency, 29, 54

breakdown of, 29–30, 37, 49, 53, 62–3, 66, 71,
    95, 131, 137, 140, 141, 145, 168, 189, 197
  conditions for, 134, 135, 139
  cultivation of, 32, 198
  framework of, 30, 33, 37, 44, 45, 48, 54, 65, 69,
    70, 94, 99, 123, 142, 190, 196, 197
  government transparency, 29, 91, 136
  requirements of, 29, 30, 33, 41, 42–4, 47, 48,
    49, 50, 51–3, 53–4, 54–5, 58, 60, 61, 62–9,
    79, 127, 131, 133, 135, 137, 172, 173, 175, 197
  respect for, 29, 32, 33, 41, 42, 44, 49, 50–2,
    53–6, 57–9, 60, 61–3, 119, 124, 142, 159,
    167–8, 175, 185, 191, 193
  role of, 63, 66, 193
  value of, 42, 51–2, 55, 61
  violations of, 6, 30, 44, 45, 49, 51, 52, 53, 57–8,
    62, 131, 136

Schaap, Andrew, 20–1, 22
Schabas, William, 179
Second Carnegie Inquiry into Poverty and
    Development, 112
segregation, 51, 110, 111, 137
self-worth, 11, 105
Sen, Amartya, 95, 96, 98, 101, 102, 106
shame, 1, 19, 105, 117
Shoemaker, David, 146, 147
Sierra Leone, 2, 7, 103, 104, 144, 179
South Africa, 2–5, 6, 52, 58, 61, 103, 110, 113, 141,
    144, 148, 150, 176, 180, 181, 186, 187.
    See also apartheid; Truth and
    Reconciliation Commission
  South Africans, 60, 109, 111–13, 149, 154
Sri Lanka, 46, 144, 180
stereotypes, 115–18, 135, 136, 138, 139, 152, 156, 161,
    162, 193, 195

Thompson, Leonard, 3
Timor-Leste, 179
torture, 4, 12, 29, 45, 47, 48, 61, 62, 91, 103,
    104–5, 105–6, 128–9, 131, 182
trials, 16, 182, 184
  criminal, 32, 38, 142, 164, 167, 168, 178, 179,
    181, 183, 184, 192, 193
  international, 38, 134, 167, 169, 175, 178, 180,
    181, 182, 183, 184, 185, 191
trust, 8, 10, 13–15, 17, 29, 30, 32, 37, 48, 56, 71–7,
    79–83, 84, 86, 87, 88, 90, 92, 94, 99, 105,
    106, 119, 124, 127, 131, 132, 134, 135–6, 138,
    139, 141, 142, 159, 188, 191, 195.
    See also political relationships, and trust;
    repressive rule, and trust;
    trust-responsiveness
  absence of, 14, 71, 72, 133, 188
  default, 86, 133–4, 136
  demands of, 90

trust (cont.)
　erosion of, 17, 48
　political, 27, 28–9, 37, 71–3, 77, 78, 79–80, 81,
　　　84–5, 88, 89, 90, 92, 93, 94, 123, 124,
　　　129–31, 134, 137–8, 145, 159, 189
　reasonableness of, 30, 31, 32, 33, 37, 48, 71, 72, 85,
　　　91, 93, 94, 95, 133, 134, 136, 142, 159, 188, 191
　stabilization of, 15, 17, 18
　value of, 71–2, 80
　violation of, 14, 75, 140
trust-responsiveness, 29, 32, 76, 83, 87, 88, 92,
　　　124, 134, 136, 138. *See also* trust
　default, 77, 80, 83, 84, 85, 133, 136
　expectation of, 30, 91
　motivation of, 136
　presumption of, 87, 89
trustworthiness, 74, 89, 117
Truth and Reconciliation Commission (TRC),
　　　4, 103–4, 144, 148
truth commissions, 4, 5, 32, 38, 141–2, 144, 156–8,
　　　160–1, 162–4, 165–6, 179, 191, 193, 194.
　　　See also community, and truth
　　　commissions
　contributions of, 145, 150, 156, 162
　participation in, 164, 164
　and political reconciliation, 144, 145, 157, 178, 191
　testimony, 4, 158, 160, 161–2, 163, 164, 165, 166, 194
Tutu, Desmond, 5

Uganda, 19, 144, 180
　Lord's Resistance Army, 19
United Nations Security Council, 179
United States, 195

United States Institute of Peace, 2, 179
Uruguay, 46, 105

van Zyl, Paul, 176, 179, 182
victims, 4, 6, 11, 12–13, 14, 25, 27, 103, 104,
　　　105, 106, 107, 108, 114, 130, 144, 149–50,
　　　157, 158, 160, 161, 162, 164, 164–6, 183,
　　　184, 195
Videla, Jorge Rafael, 46
violence, 3, 12, 19, 31, 32, 86, 103, 104, 114, 116, 117,
　　　127, 136, 138, 141, 143, 149, 151, 154, 155,
　　　158, 162. *See also* amputation; rape;
　　　torture
　cessation of, 127, 137
　in civil conflict, 11, 102, 103, 107, 115, 118, 189
　impact of, 19, 103, 104–7, 108, 109, 118
　in repressive rule, 11
　sexual, 12, 103, 104
　systematic, 94, 109
　threat of, 107–8, 114

Walaza, Nomfundo, 108
Waldron, Jeremy, 54, 55–6
Walker, Margaret Urban, 14, 19, 72, 139
war, civil, 3, 103, 104, 109, 114
Weinstock, Daniel, 81
Wolff, Jonathan, 96, 98, 119, 138, 140
World Bank, 112
wrongdoing, 9, 13, 14, 19, 21, 32, 141, 143, 146, 157,
　　　158, 162, 184, 193, 197, 198
　denial of, 16, 61, 92, 156
　responses to, 2, 10, 191, 192, 193, 195, 197
　systematic, 11, 25, 158